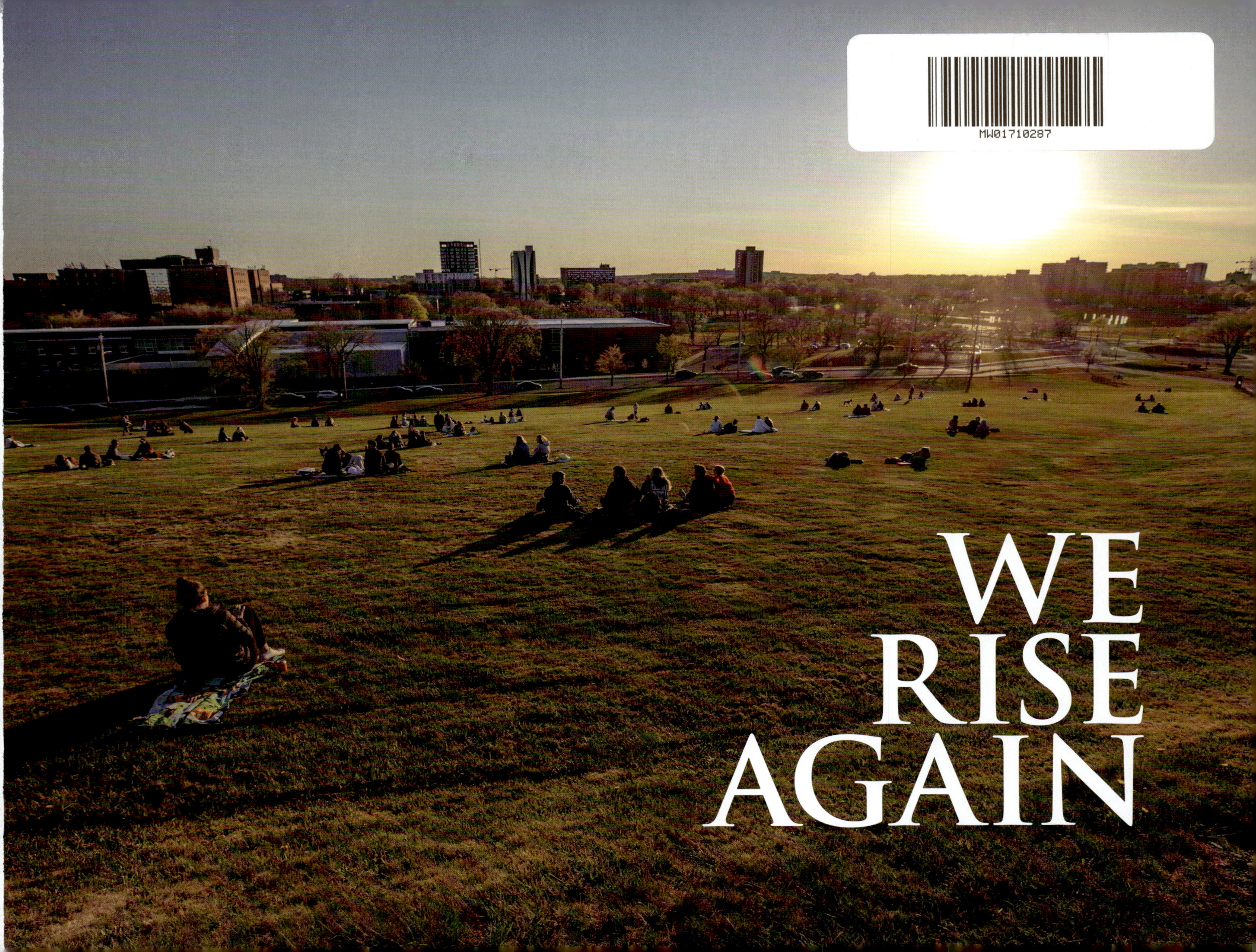

WE RISE AGAIN

MORE STORIES OF HOPE AND RESILIENCE
FROM NOVA SCOTIA DURING THE COVID-19 PANDEMIC

WE RISE AGAIN

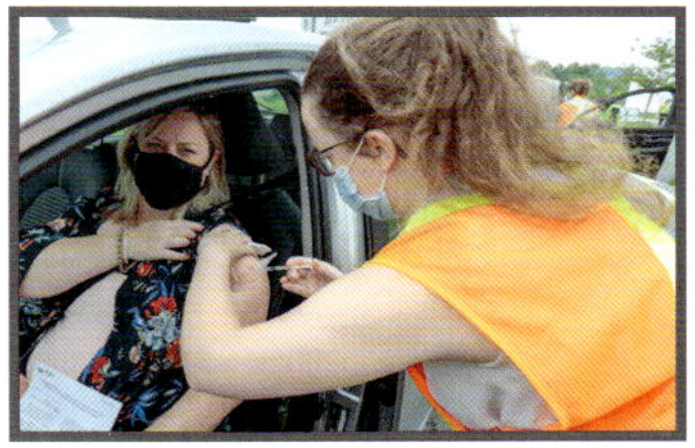
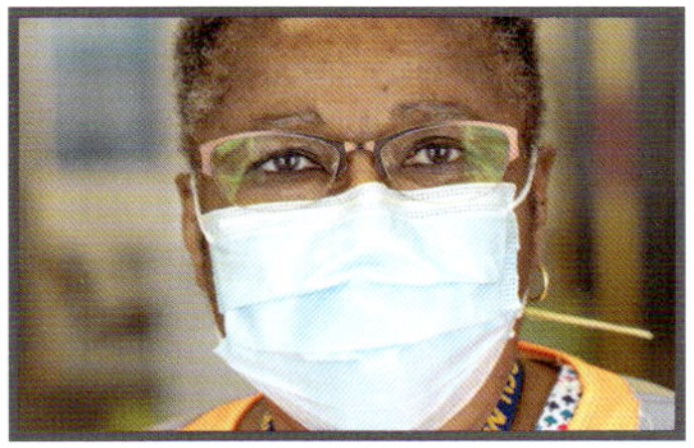
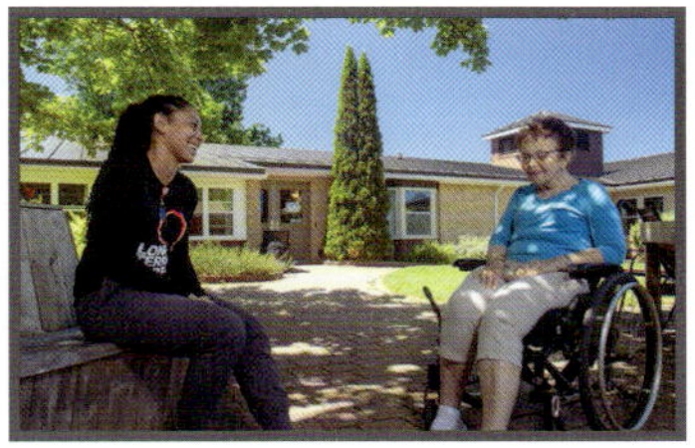
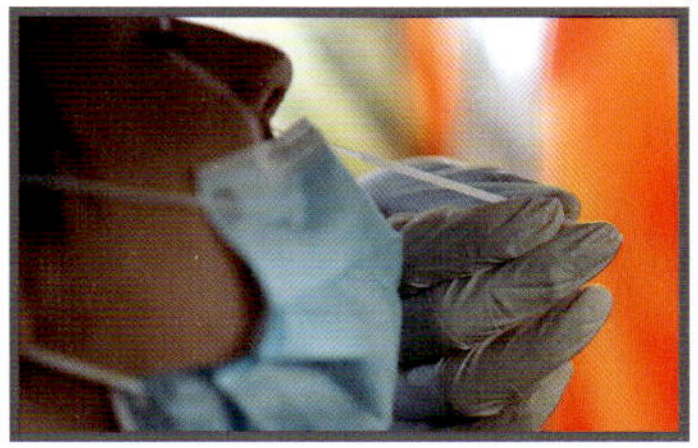

LEN WAGG &
ANGELA MOMBOURQUETTE

NIMBUS
PUBLISHING
NIMBUS.CA

Nimbus Publishing Limited
3660 Strawberry Hill Street, Halifax, NS, B3K 5A9
(902) 455-4286 nimbus.ca

Printed and bound in Canada

NB1602

Editor: Angela Mombourquette
Design: Jenn Embree

Library and Archives Canada Cataloguing in Publication

Title: We rise again : stories of hope and resilience from Nova Scotia during the second wave of the COVID-19 pandemic / Len Wagg & Angela Mombourquette.
Names: Wagg, Len, author. | Mombourquette, Angela, author.
Identifiers: Canadiana (print) 20210216514 | Canadiana (ebook) 20210216549
ISBN 9781774710227 (softcover)
ISBN 9781774710234 (EPUB)
Subjects: LCSH: COVID-19 Pandemic, 2020-—Social aspects—Nova Scotia. | LCSH: COVID-19 Pandemic, 2020-—Social aspects—Nova Scotia—Pictorial works. | LCSH: Nova Scotia—Social conditions—21st century.
Classification: LCC FC2318 .W34 2021
DDC 971.6/05—dc23

Canada Council for the Arts / Conseil des arts du Canada

Nimbus Publishing acknowledges the financial support for its publishing activities from the Government of Canada, the Canada Council for the Arts, and from the Province of Nova Scotia. We are pleased to work in partnership with the Province of Nova Scotia to develop and promote our creative industries for the benefit of all Nova Scotians.

Dedicated to those who thought of others before themselves and helped us get to the other side

TABLE OF CONTENTS

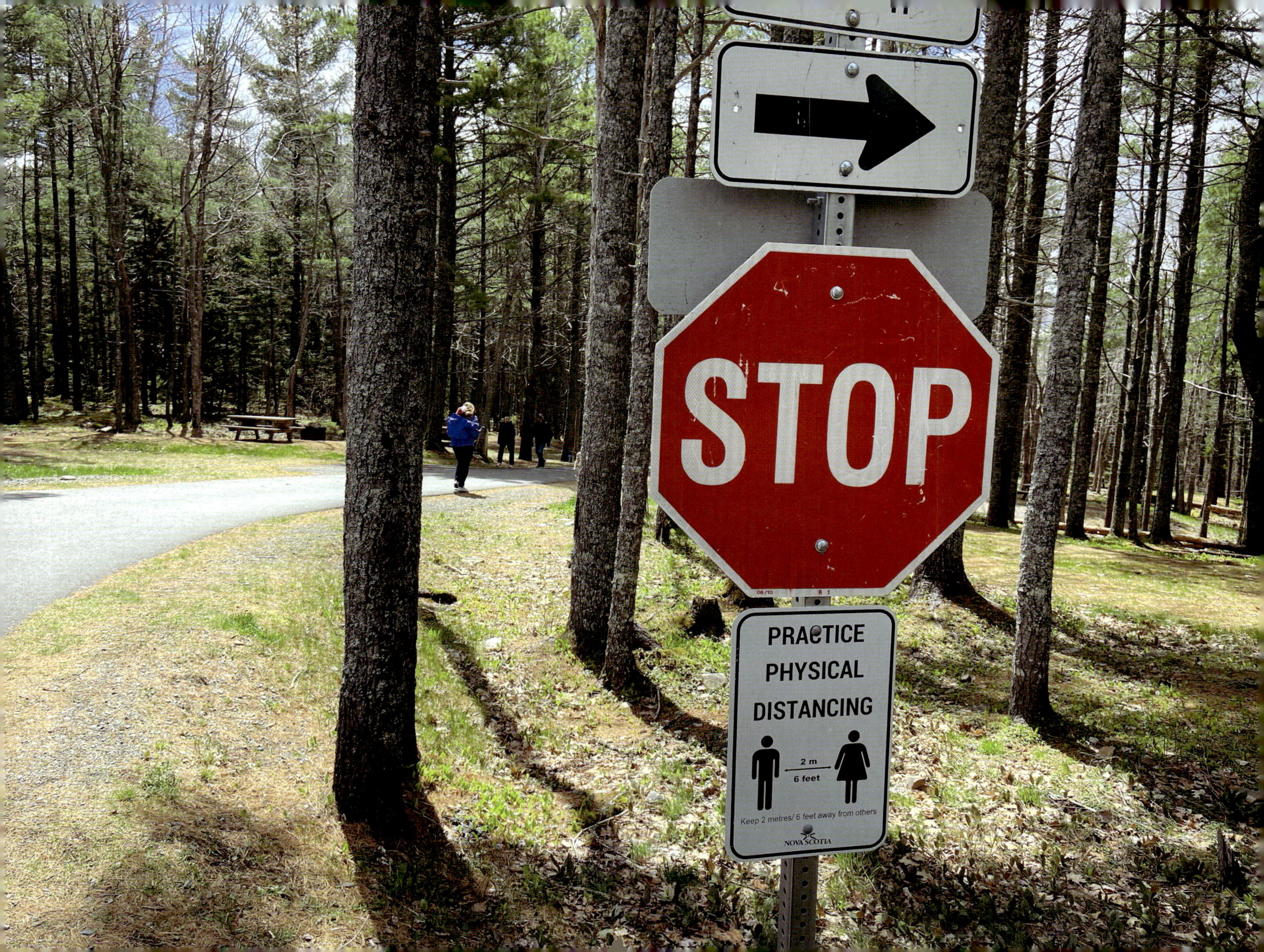
STOP
PRACTICE
PHYSICAL
DISTANCING
2 m
6 feet
Keep 2 metres/ 6 feet away from others
NOVA SCOTIA

Ultimately, the path this [pandemic] takes in the next few weeks is up to each and every Nova Scotian. Now is the time for each of us to be our best.

I was asked yesterday about the COVID storm. My response is that we can be the storm and roar back.

Lock arms, Nova Scotia, and stay strong.

DR. ROBERT STRANG,
MEDIA BRIEFING,
APRIL 25, 2021

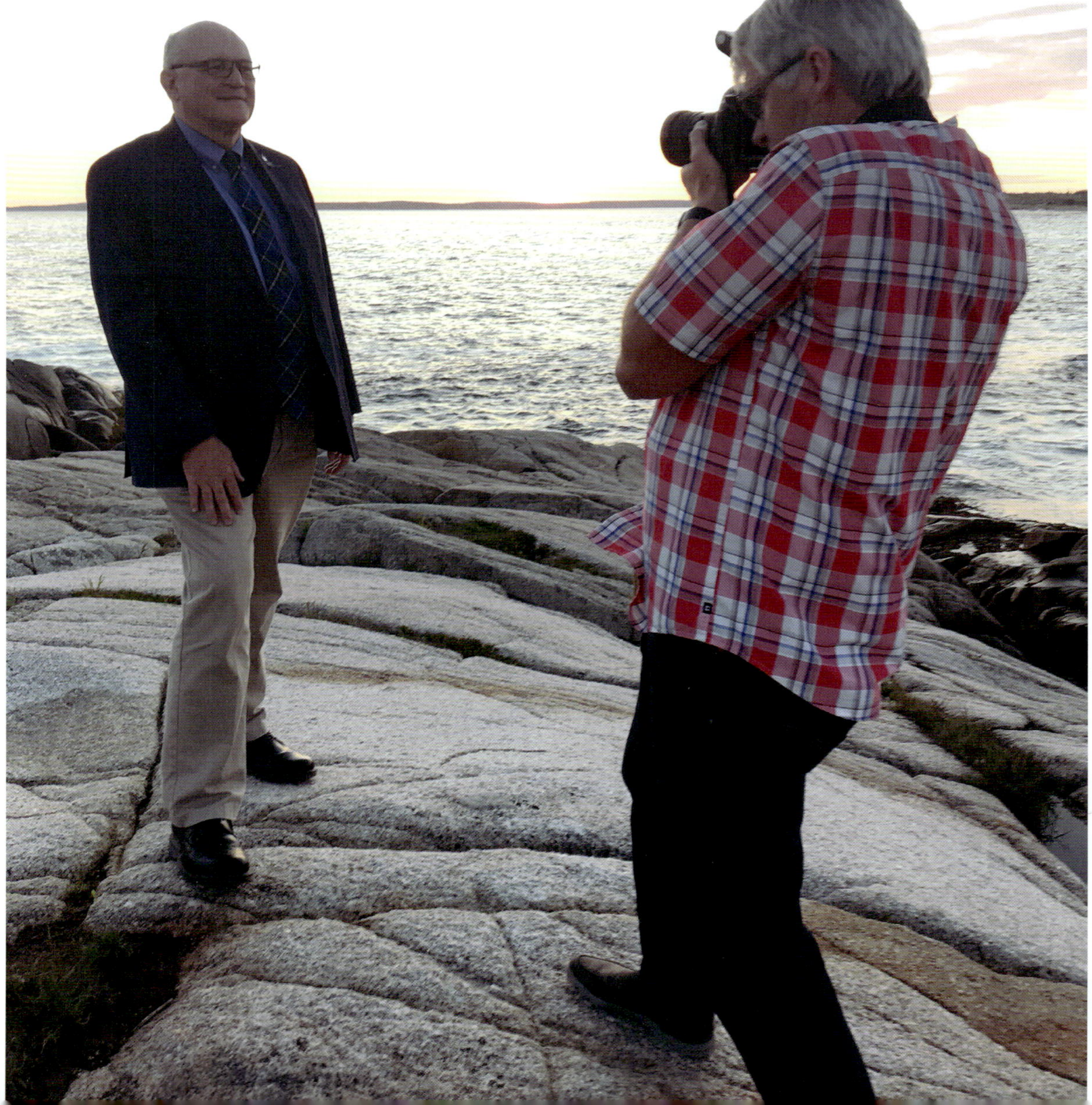

Len Wagg (right) photographs Nova Scotia's chief medical officer of health, Dr. Robert Strang, on the rocks at Peggys Cove.

FOREWORD

We are now in the fortunate position of almost being able to look back at the COVID-19 pandemic and remember our collective journey through this historic time.

It is important that we use this opportunity to be honest about the realities of living through COVID-19 in Nova Scotia. It has presented substantial challenges for many—to our social, financial, mental, and physical health.

This pandemic has often had a greater impact on those with existing challenges and fewer supports. The ways we recognize and respond to the underlying factors that put those parts of our communities at greatest risk will be the true legacy of COVID-19, and will determine how prepared we are for future pandemics or other global events.

Throughout the pandemic there have been countless moments of compassion, creativity, and innovation. For many people, their own decisiveness and sheer determination have created the path forward. Key to all this has been the caring and kindness provided by countless health-care workers and community members across Nova Scotia. It is these stories that capture the spirit and resilience that has allowed Nova Scotia to so successfully roar back at COVID-19.

Thank you to Len Wagg and Angela Mombourquette for so beautifully capturing the images and words behind these stories.

My deepest thanks to each one of these Nova Scotian heroes, and to the many more whose stories have not been recognized. Your deeds will create a lasting memory and serve as a reminder for future generations about how best to approach their challenges—together and with compassion.

Dr. Robert Strang
Chief Medical Officer of Health, Nova Scotia

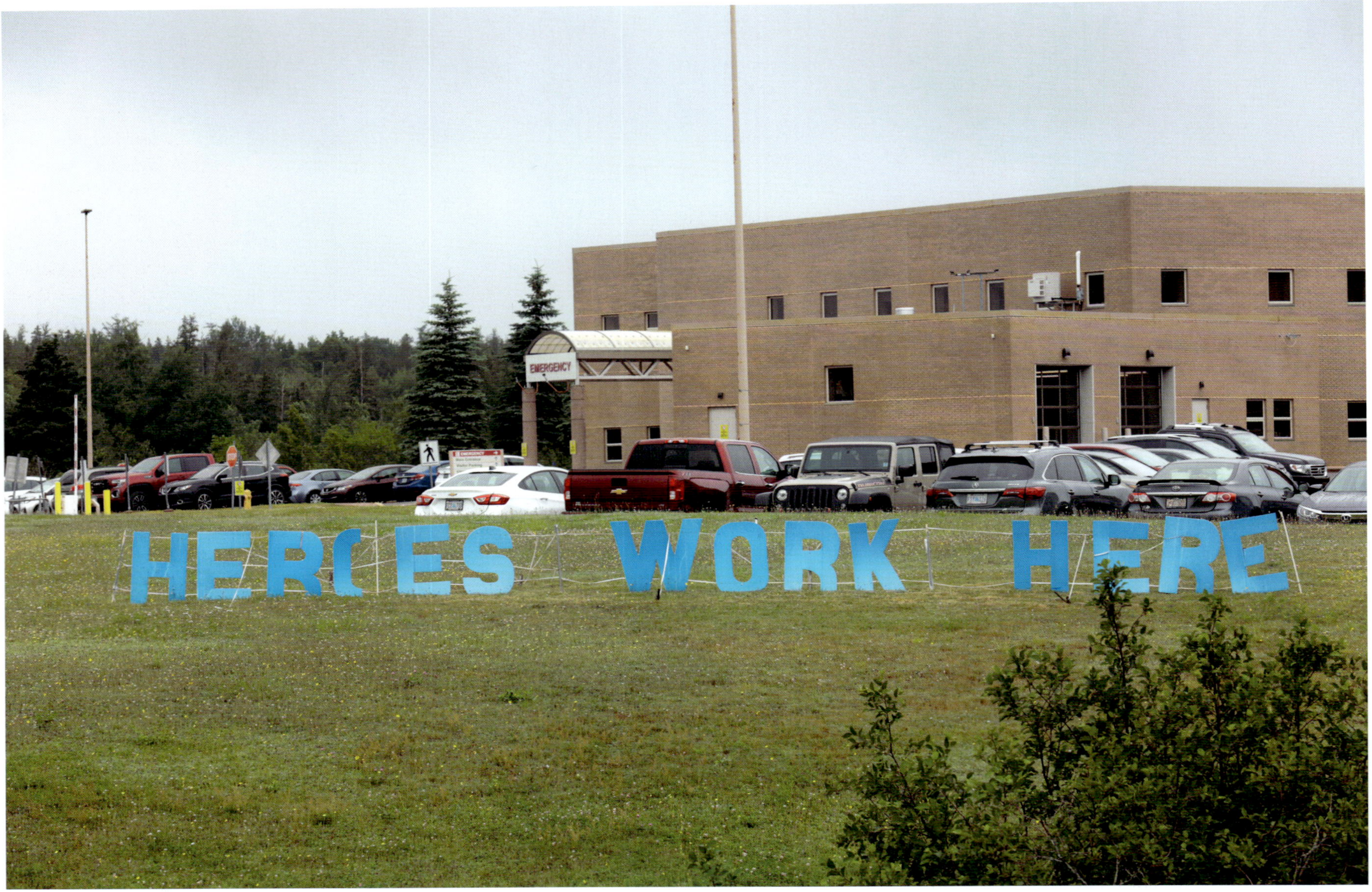

"Heroes work here." Cumberland Regional Health Care Centre, Amherst.

INTRODUCTION

Just when we thought it was over—or almost over—and that Nova Scotians had once again weathered the COVID-19 storm, we woke up in late April 2021 to the news that a cluster of coronavirus cases had led to community spread, and daily case numbers were rapidly heading in the wrong direction. Tragically, after more than six months during which not a single Nova Scotian had died after contracting COVID-19, another Nova Scotian passed away, the first in a series of such deaths.

We had entered the dreaded third wave. On April 28, as case numbers rose alarmingly, the provincial government imposed a "circuit breaker"—another lockdown restricting gathering limits, curtailing retail and restaurant services, and closing schools.

Now, we're not saying Nova Scotians are good in a crisis, but Nova Scotians *do* seem to be pretty good in a crisis.

Who would you want on your team in the middle of a pandemic? The people who put on their masks, keep their distance, and voluntarily go for asymptomatic testing when the premier and the chief medical officer ask them to—stopping outbreaks in their tracks? Or, you know—the other people?

We think we know the answer to that.

Still, 2021 has been a challenge. This book is our way of documenting the many responses Nova Scotians have had to the pandemic. In particular, it's a love letter to health-care workers—and to all those behind the scenes, in the government offices, and on the front lines—who have stepped up to the plate to make sure Nova Scotians get through the second, third, and fourth waves as safely as possible.

Getting through hasn't been easy. It's meant converting libraries, gyms, meeting rooms, and curling clubs into COVID testing sites. It's meant converting legions, hockey arenas, bingo halls, fire stations, churches, mosques, and pharmacies into vaccination clinics. Many of the places where we used to get together to have fun were repurposed for much more serious endeavours.

But we didn't let that get us down. We showed up for our vaccinations in prom dresses, wedding dresses, suits, and hats—just to bring a little humour to it all. We witnessed tears of joy and hope, both from those giving and those receiving the vaccine. At the drive-through clinics, the music often blared and the atmosphere was light-hearted and fun as the workers moved from car to car.

The vaccine was a beacon of hope that meant that soon—soon—we might be able to go back to those churches, bingo halls, and arenas, and spend time with friends and family doing the things we used to do.

And although we know the names of Nova Scotia's chief medical officer of health, Dr. Robert Strang—our granite during this storm—and Dr. Lisa Barrett, whose innovative approach to rapid testing was one of the keys to our successful navigation of the third wave, the names of other people who have been key to our success are less well known.

They include people like Charles Heinstein, who managed the microbiology lab, making the processing of massive numbers of COVID tests possible. People like Holly Gillis, who organized the public health mobile units to bring testing and vaccination directly to communities all over the province. People like Dr. Sarah McMullen who cared for COVID patients in the ICU and then contracted COVID-19 herself. And people like Richard Martell and Debbie Johnson-Powell, who provided sign-language interpretation for Deaf and hard of hearing Nova Scotians during the COVID press briefings—and who ended up with a fan-following of their own.

It's hard to get any of those folks to take credit for the important work they've done, and if there's one theme we heard over and over again as we researched this book, it was this: "I couldn't have done it without my incredible team."

In truth, we are all part of that incredible team as we continue to step up to the plate for one another.

And in our very Nova Scotian way, as vaccination becomes more widespread and testing continues apace—and life begins to return to some kind of normal—we rise again.

We always will.

Len Wagg and Angela Mombourquette

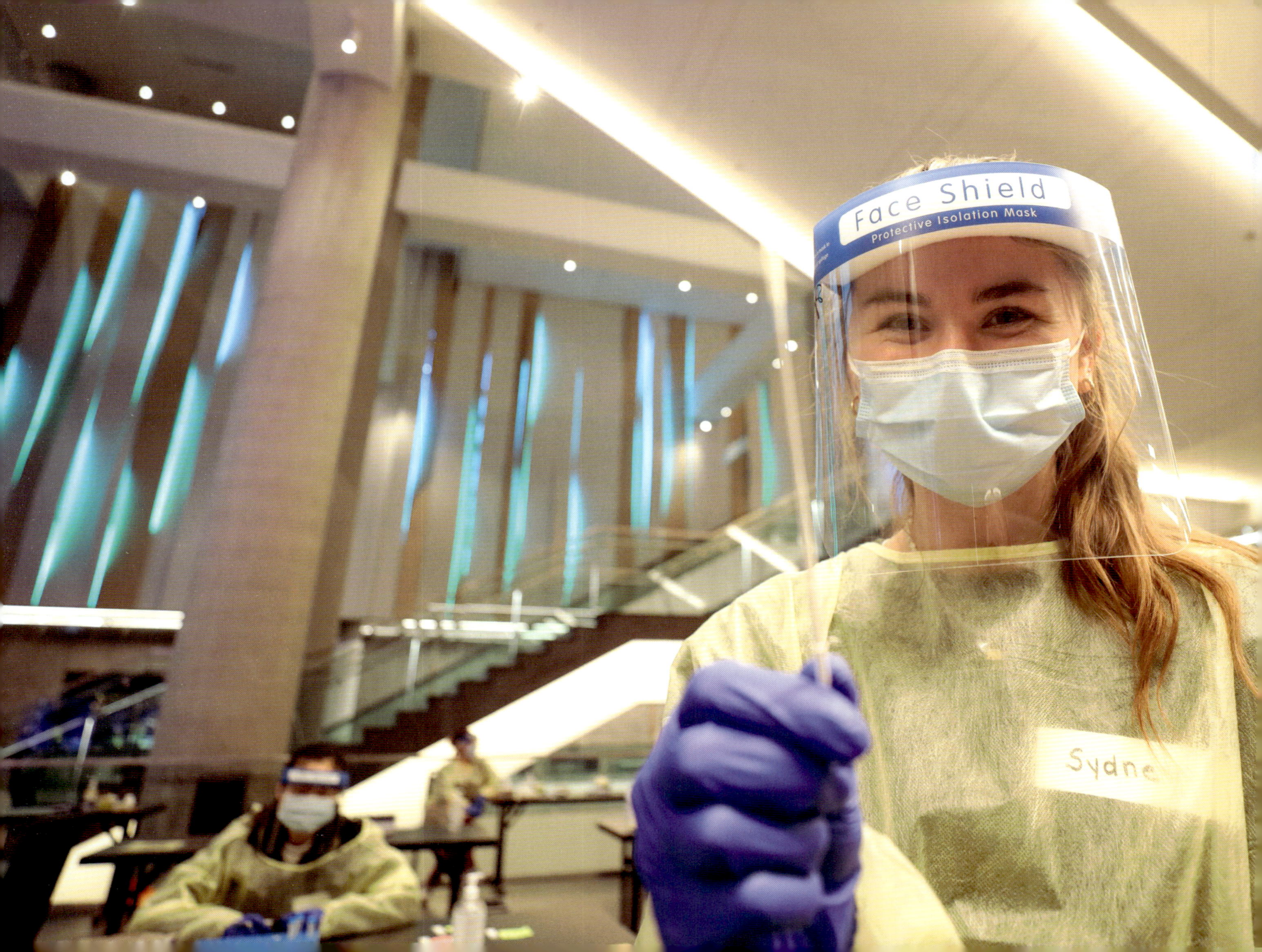
Face Shield
Protective Isolation Mask
Sydne

Part One: LEADING THE CHARGE

FACING PAGE: *Sydney Hayden of Halifax prepares to perform a COVID nasal swab on a client at the Halifax Convention Centre in March 2021.*

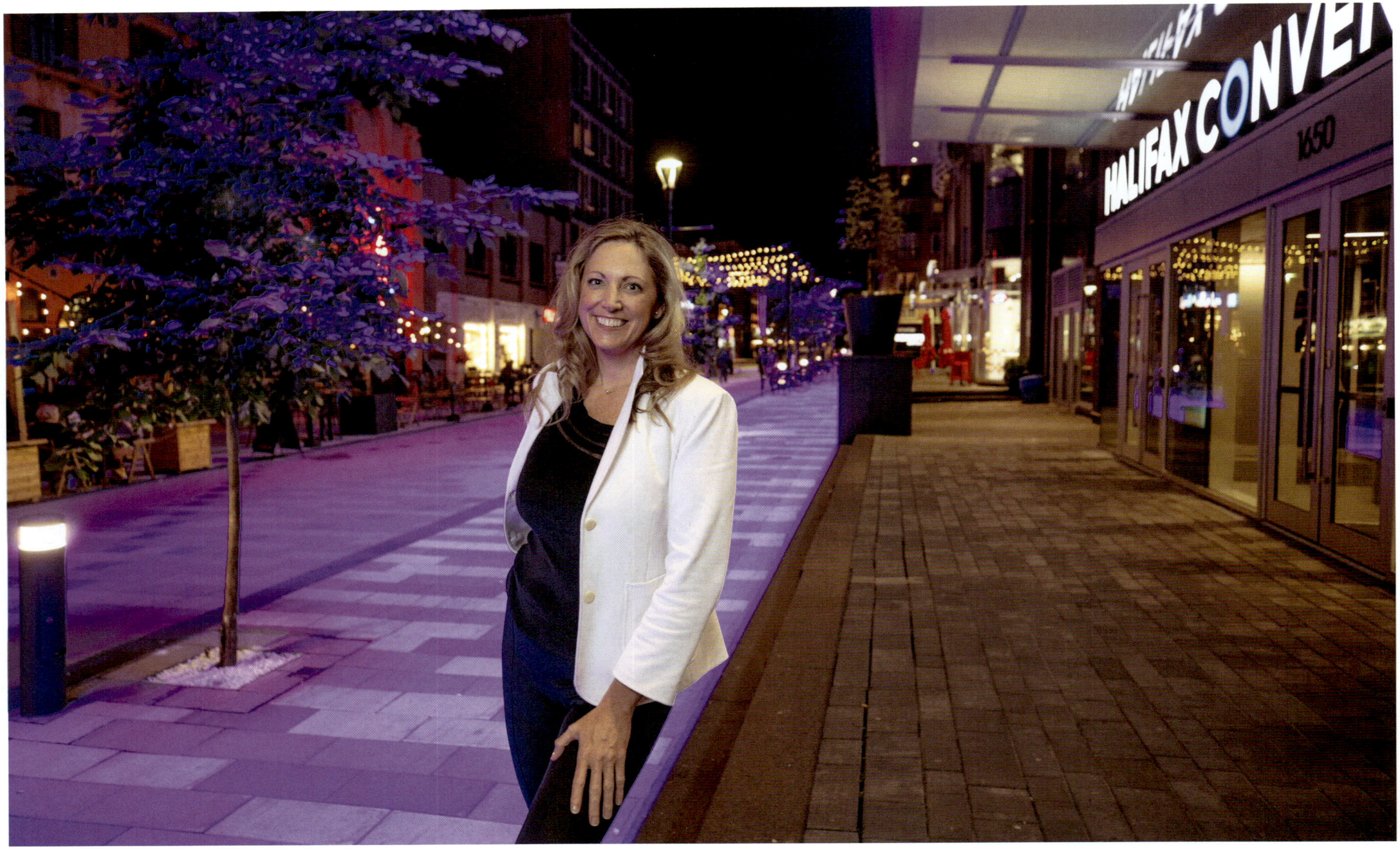

Infectious diseases specialist Dr. Lisa Barrett, shown here outside a rapid-testing site at the Halifax Convention Centre, was one of the key people behind Nova Scotia's rapid testing strategy—a strategy that has been credited with helping to tame the third wave of the pandemic in Nova Scotia.

THE RADICAL WISDOM OF RAPID TESTING: *Dr. Lisa Barrett*

If you're like many Nova Scotians, you have, through one simple act, played an essential part in helping the province as a whole to "rise above" the second and third waves of the COVID-19 pandemic—you've gotten tested, probably more than once, for the virus.

And one person in particular has been key to creating the culture telling you it's the right thing to do: Dr. Lisa Barrett, an infectious diseases doctor and researcher at Dalhousie University.

You likely recognize her face and her voice by now. As the second and third waves washed over Nova Scotia, she became a prominent personality, advocating for the necessity of widespread testing, and in particular, for rapid asymptomatic testing. It was an idea that had not gained traction in other parts of Canada, and one that was considered risky in terms of cost versus benefit. But her key concept—pop-up rapid testing sites—has become one of Nova Scotia's not-so-secret weapons in the fight against COVID-19.

As a clinician/scientist, and as someone who has no "official" role as a spokesperson for the Nova Scotia Health Authority or the government of Nova Scotia, she may seem an unlikely go-to person for media who are hungry for answers during a confusing time. But her clear, accessible communication style has made her something of a media favourite, and her message has clearly resonated with Nova Scotians.

"Most infectious disease doctors are not public-facing folks for the most part. I probably am a little more, just because of the nature of the work and the research I do," she says. "I've always been of the opinion that if you have an opportunity to say something, particularly around crisis, take the opportunity."

Her reputation for straight talk very quickly took off. "I think I've done six hundred individual bits of media in the last twelve months," she says.

That ability to communicate clearly proved particularly important when the guidance coming from various authorities and government bodies sometimes changed from one day to the next.

"I always tell people everything happens in 'pandemic standard time,' and the only constant is change," she says. "Some people think that means we don't have the right information, and that's not true; it's just that information gets interpreted differently in different situations. My goal through most of this has been to make sure people have a set of information in reasonable, understandable terms."

Implementing her strategy for rapid testing was no simple matter. (See "Grace Under Pressure: Charles Heinstein, Diagnostic Microbiology Laboratory," page 14.) But she says easy access to rapid testing has meant people won't have to spend their lives hiding behind closed doors. "You can do all the other stuff and you can get vaccinated, but vaccines aren't perfect. Masks aren't perfect, and you can't stay away from everyone forever. So rapid testing is a way to give people extra layers of protection," Barrett says. "How lucky are we to have that?"

But as vaccines are rolled out and restrictions eased, she cautions Nova Scotians against thinking of the pandemic in the past tense. "I don't think it's ever over. I think there'll be an end to the stricter things in terms of restrictions. But it's going to be graded in terms of six- to twelve-month periods. So [after] we get everyone vaccinated, then it's another six months of dealing with the next round of this and learning what the 'new' is going to look like. Then another six months to make sure what we learned in that first six months post–first vaccines is real, then another six months. So, we're talking a couple of years," she says.

Ultimately, she says, she is glad she has been at the table to help with the response. "I'm very grateful, actually, to have been a part of some of the conversations that have happened in Nova Scotia."

And as Nova Scotians do, many people have reached out to her to thank her. Barrett says she's received numerous cards and letters that have thanked her for being so calm and straightforward.

"For me, honestly, it's not just that someone thinks I do a good job—that feels great—but that people care about each other enough in a pandemic to reach out and say thank you. How amazing is that?" she asks. "That blows me away. It reminds me how amazing people are."

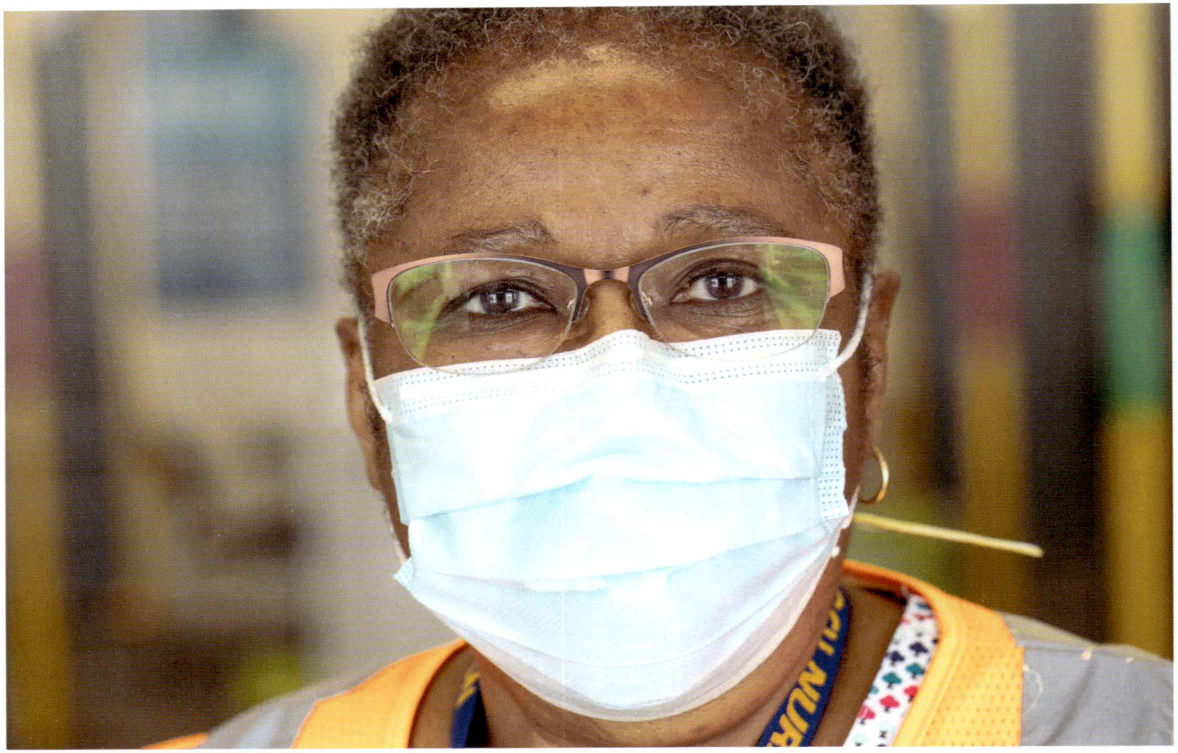

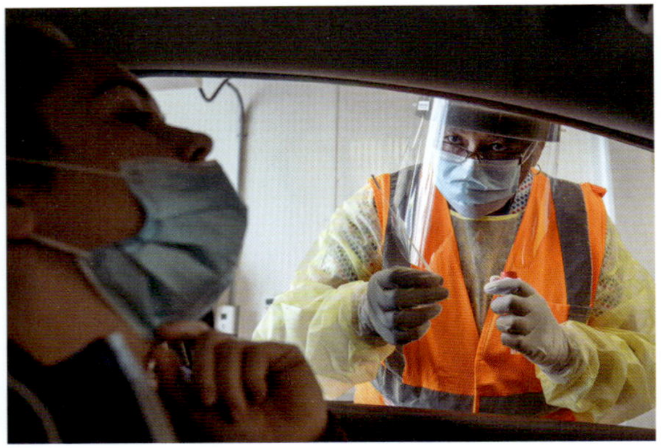

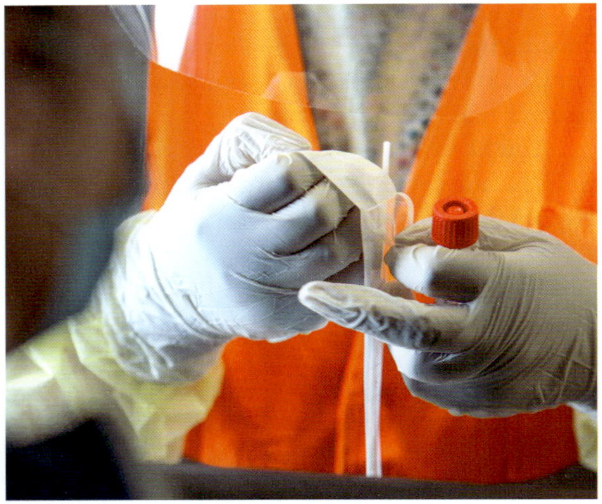

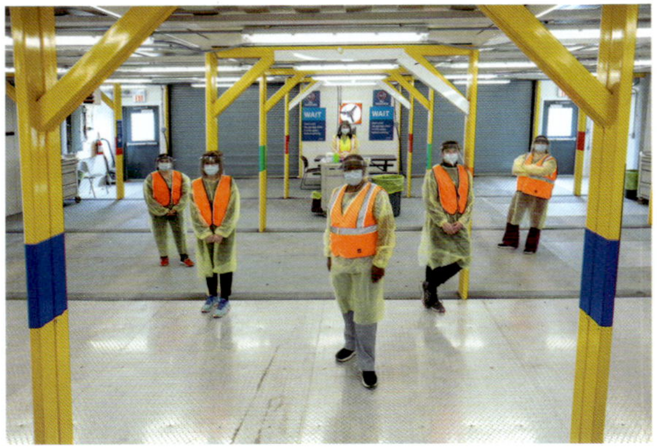

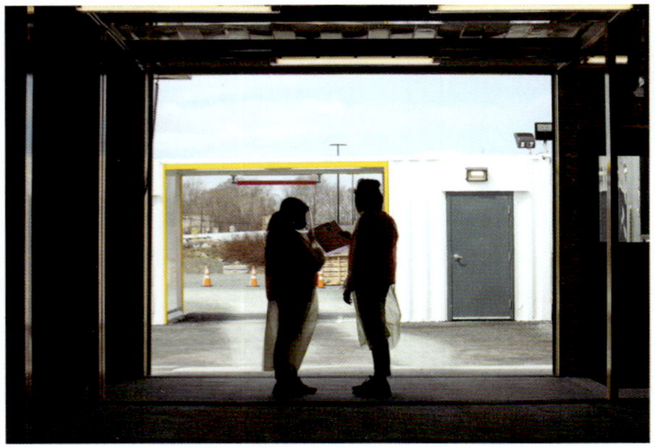

THIS PAGE: *Martha Brown, RN, came out of retirement to help run the drive-through COVID testing unit at the Dartmouth General Hospital.*

BOTTOM LEFT: *Brown and her team; front row, from left: Reena Pappachan, RN; Annabelle Rideout, RN; Martha Brown; Tiffany Dicks, PT; Nicole Lidstone, RN; back row at centre: Bev Bowers, LPN.*

SOMETHING TO CONTRIBUTE:
Martha Brown

Martha Brown, RN, hears a tap-tap-tap on the door of her tiny Dartmouth office and swivels around in her chair. As a nurse with a question opens the door, the rumble of metal garage doors washes into the room and four cars pull into the space just outside her office. The cars stop, the garage doors go down, and several workers in full PPE—gowns, gloves, masks, and face shields—move in, swabs in hand.

It's just another day at the Dartmouth General Hospital's drive-through COVID-19 testing facility, and Brown is the charge nurse leading the shift.

Not that she *has* to be there. Brown retired from nursing in 2010 and began mentoring African Nova Scotian students at the Nova Scotia Community College who were interested in learning to become continuing care assistants. She was also practicing nursing on a casual basis in March 2020 when the first case of COVID-19 arrived in Nova Scotia.

Brown stepped up and put her name forward at the QEII Health Sciences Centre. "I'm retired but I felt like I had something to contribute," she says. Since March 2020, Brown has worked at COVID-testing clinics in Halifax, Dartmouth, North Preston, and Cherry Brook. "I felt I could give something back to the Black Nova Scotian community by going to those special clinics in North Preston and Cherry Brook," she says. "It might not be on the same scale as these young nurses in their twenties and thirties that can go, go, go," she adds with a grin, "but it makes me feel valued because it's recognizing my experience and my knowledge." (For more on the Cherry Brook clinic, see "Making a Difference in Cherry Brook," page 26.)

It was that experience and knowledge that Dr. Todd Howlett, executive medical director of the Nova Scotia Health Authority's central zone, came looking for when he told Brown they were thinking of opening a drive-though testing unit.

In April 2020, Brown found herself working out of a trailer connected to a huge tent—a tent large enough for several cars to drive through. It wasn't feasible to work out of that tent through the winter, but with the help of a local business owner, a sturdier unit—one that could more adequately shelter both workers and patients from the elements—was built out of shipping containers.

The testing itself is a simple process: people drive in, they receive a test while seated in their car, and they drive out. Results are sent by email, phone, or text message within a few days.

Brown says her nursing experience often comes in handy with anxious clients—especially parents with young children. "I'm the type of person who likes to talk, so I just sort of turn it around and try and calm them down," she says. Judging by the coffees and kudos her clients offer, it's clear that most people are grateful for the service the team provides.

But it's not just the clients who are grateful. Last spring—"when Stephen McNeil was telling people to stay the blazes home" and Brown's workdays were very busy—she arrived home to discover a huge sign, made by her husband, her daughter, and her niece, outside her home. It read: "Thank you to all the front line workers and also to the one who lives here!"

"Well, the neighbours kept coming by and saying, 'Thank you, thank you, thank you.' It was really touching," she says.

Brown says she's happy she's been able to use her experience to help build an intergenerational team of newly graduated, mid-career, and retired nurses—and to feel like she's giving back to the community.

"This is where I'm supposed to be at this particular time in my life," she says. "It makes me feel good inside. It's like, gee, you know what? I am making a difference."

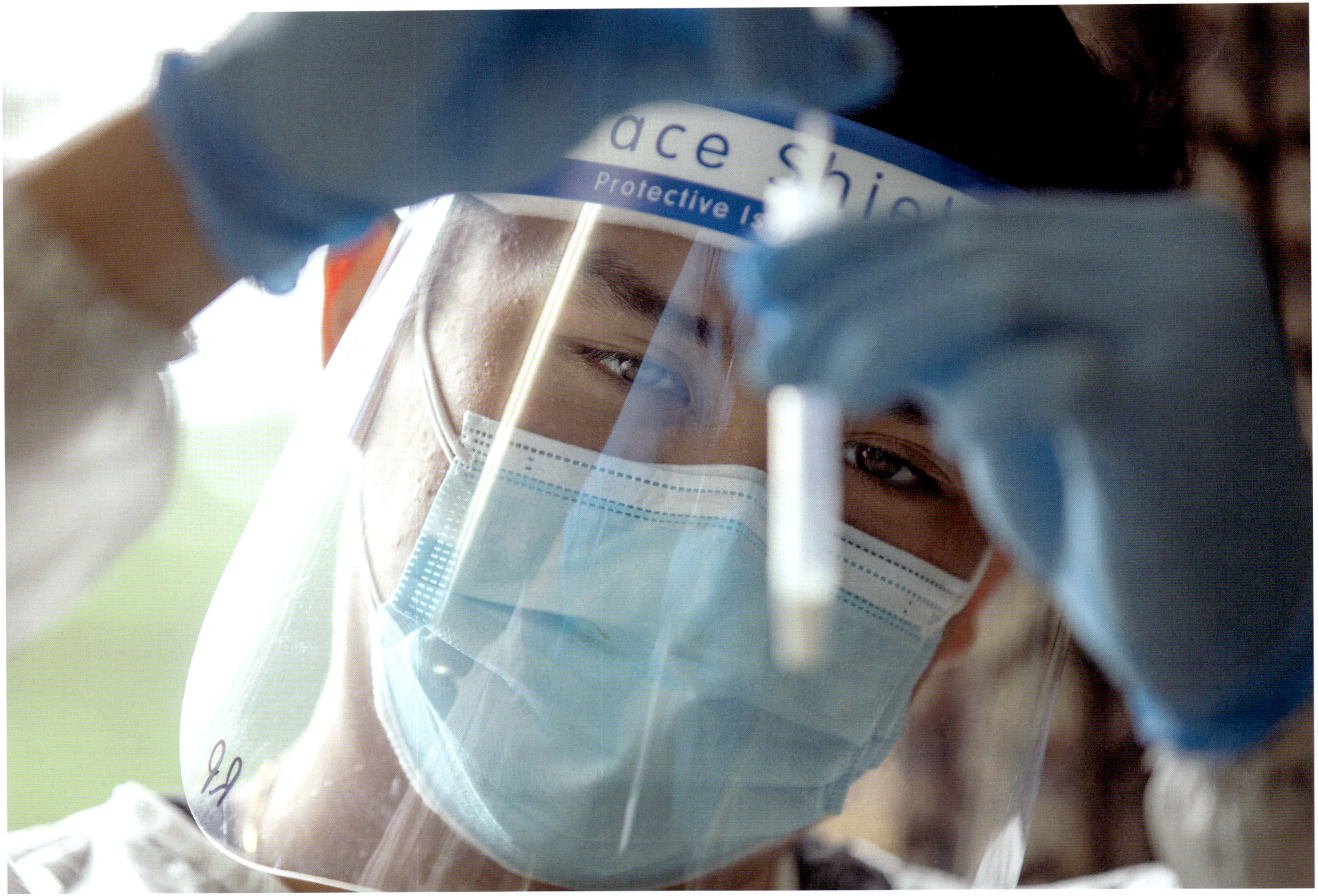
ace Shiel
Protective Is

THE POWER OF VOLUNTEERS:
Dr. John Ross and Harriet Wright

It takes a village to fight a pandemic—doctors, nurses, lab technicians, politicians, bureaucrats, and citizens —but one particular group of villagers has been key to Nova Scotia's winning battle against the third wave.

When he's asked how important the work of volunteers has been to Nova Scotia's pandemic response, Dr. John Ross, the medical director of PRAXES Medical Group, which coordinated a portion of the rapid testing in the province, doesn't hesitate.

"Super easy answer," he says. "We could not have done it without them."

He ventures that his group did something like four hundred thousand rapid tests during the third wave, and says 85 percent of all those tests were done in a single month at the peak of the third wave response. "We scaled from two- to three hundred on a busy day to close to two thousand per day," he says. "There's no way we could have scaled and provided the number of test sites that we were doing without volunteers—period."

PRAXES began providing pop-up testing at sites in Halifax and in smaller communities outside HRM in December 2020 as awareness around the value of rapid testing grew. At first, he says, there had been a sense that rapid testing had little value, but as the second wave broke, it was discovered to be very useful in catching people who were unaware they were infected. "We were taking people out of circulation early, and we were inviting back people who lived with those folks who ultimately would have become positive," he says.

As COVID case numbers grew, Nova Scotia had to scale up its rapid testing capacity quickly, and that, says Ross, is where the volunteer part comes in. "This had to be community embraced and community driven and accessed by the community," he says. "And when things get locked down, there are people who happen to have a little bit of time on their hands, and they also want to be involved and empowered."

Instead of being home, locked down and afraid, he says, people stepped up to help keep their communities safe. And when the third wave struck, those people really stepped up.

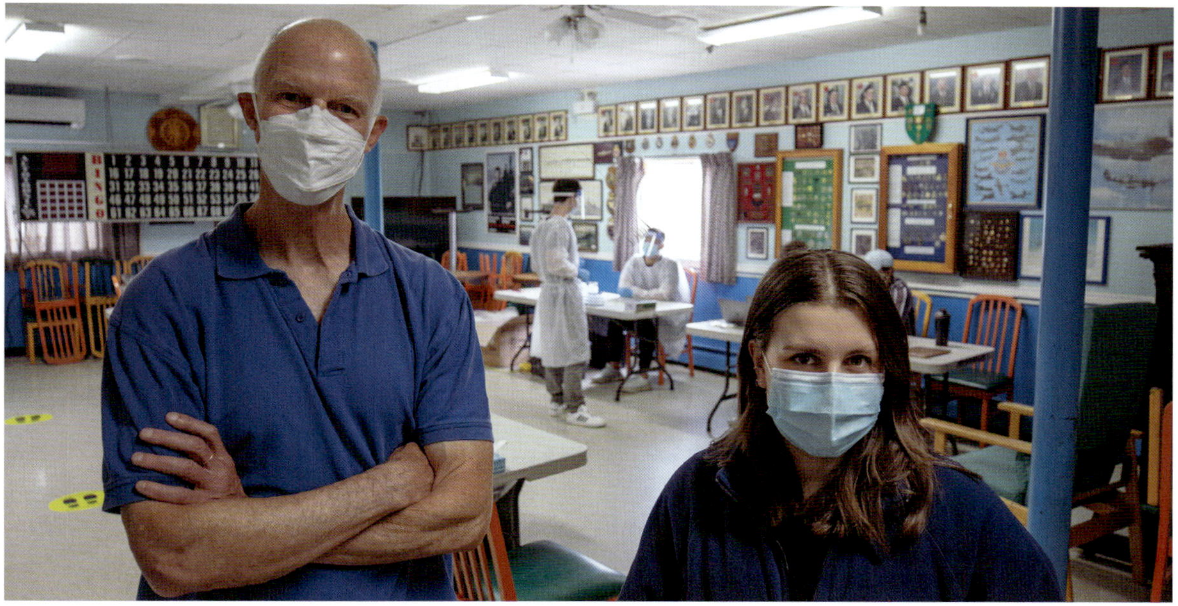

Dr. John Ross (left) is medical director of PRAXES Medical Group, which coordinated a portion of the rapid testing in the province. The sites rely heavily on the work of volunteers. Harriet Wright (right) started out as a volunteer and was quickly promoted to a paid position as a volunteer coordinator.

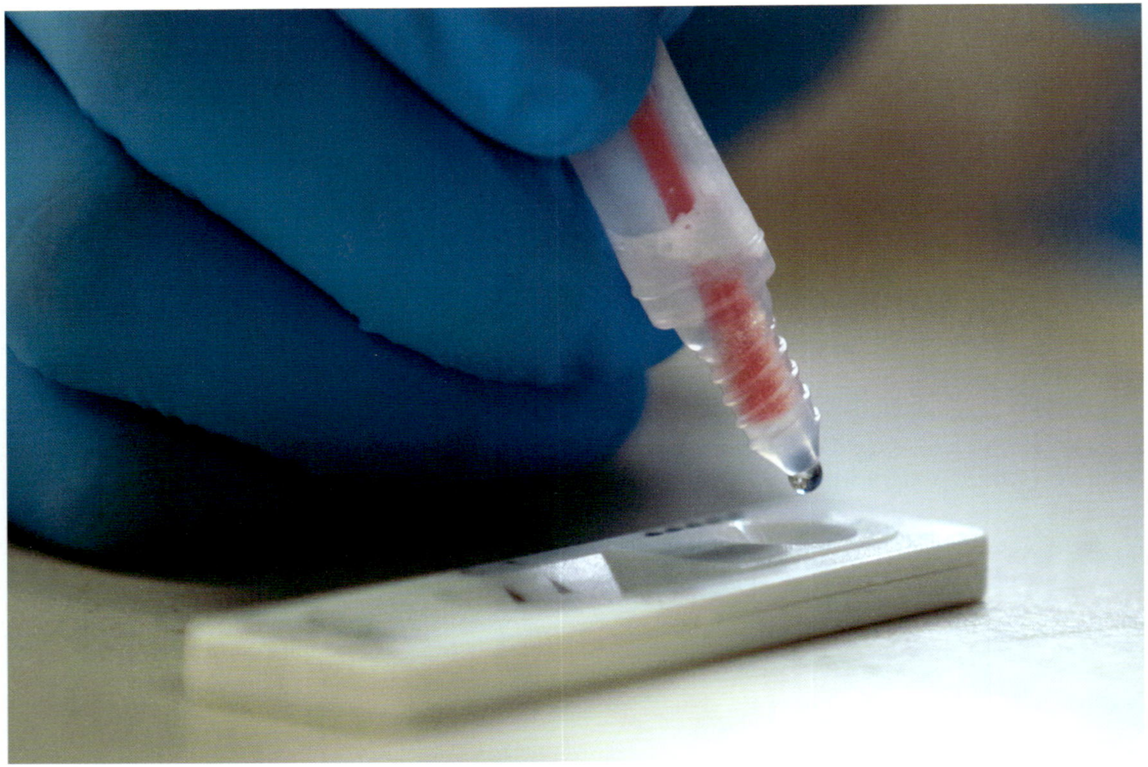

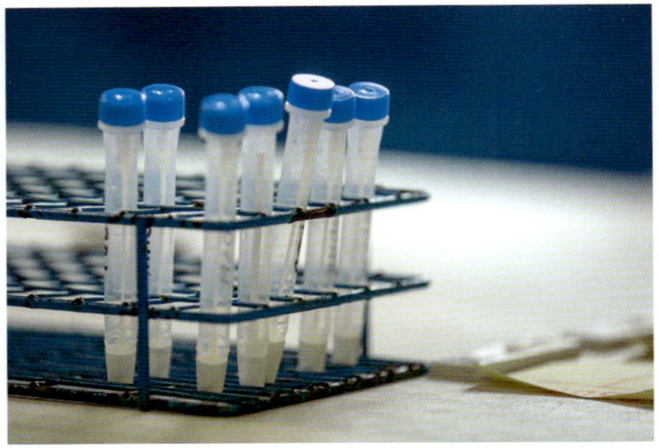

PAGE 10, AT LEFT, AND ABOVE: *Team lead Roman Pruski tests the swab from a rapid test that was performed at the Bedford Legion in July 2021. He explains the process: "The rapid tests used at our sites are the Abbott Panbio COVID-19 AG Rapid Test Devices, which are in vitro diagnostic rapid tests for the detection of SARS-CoV-2 antigens in humans. On the test cassette, if two lines appear, this indicates a positive test result, whereas one line on the test cassette is indicative of a negative result."*

"We took on a ton more testing," he says. "All we required was more volunteers to go and swab and to do the processing of the tests."

Harriet Wright had just finished her degree in health promotion at Dalhousie University in Halifax when she started out as a volunteer; she was quickly promoted to a paid position as a volunteer coordinator. She says Nova Scotia would not have had the capacity it had for testing without volunteers. "There were some days we were testing over two thousand people at some of our sites within seven hours," she says, "and without volunteers that just wouldn't have been possible."

"It was nuts," Ross laughs. "We went from two or three or four people doing swabs on a routine kind of day, to ten or twelve sometimes. Yeah, it was massive, and it was totally exhausting. It was like bone-marrow exhausting."

But he says Nova Scotians deserve credit, not just for volunteering at testing sites, but for coming out and getting tested. "Nova Scotia *rocked*," he says. "We were united around our concern about this virus, and people got united around a potential solution to it, which was to get out and get tested on a regular basis.... I think that empowerment can not be underestimated or underappreciated."

Ross adds that when people were asked why they came out to get tested, the response generally came in two parts. "They said, 'I want to know [if I'm positive], but I'm also here because I want to be part of keeping my community safe.' That was almost a tear-generating response for me," Ross admits, "and I heard it many, many, times."

Wright puts it simply: "The volunteers pretty much made it possible for us to really slow the wave in Nova Scotia."

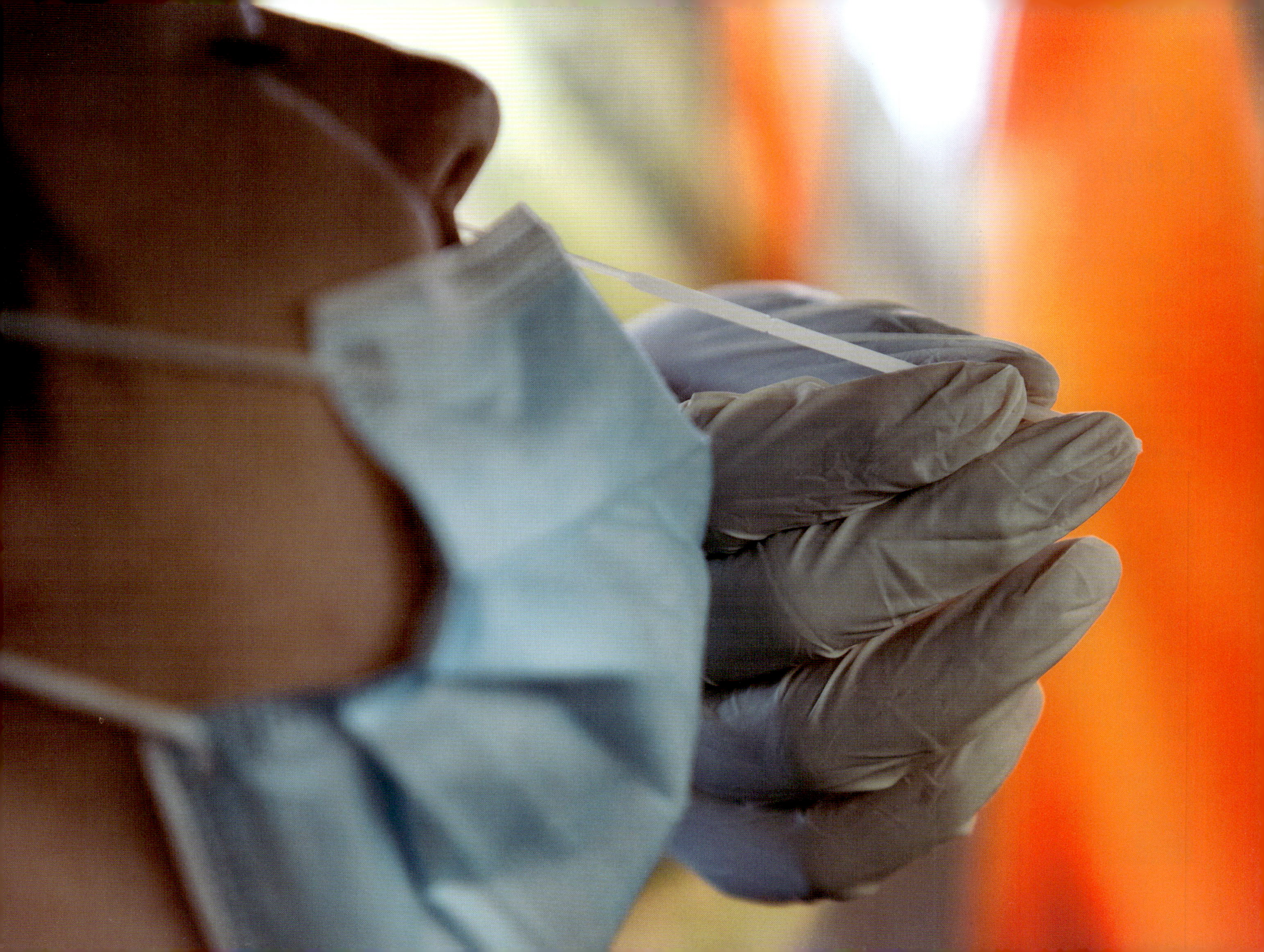

GRACE UNDER PRESSURE:

Charles Heinstein, Diagnostic Microbiology Laboratory

As COVID case numbers crept up through the second and third waves of the pandemic, and as Nova Scotians dutifully heeded the call to get tested as a way to prevent the spread of the virus, perhaps no single department was under more pressure to expand and adapt its practices than the Diagnostic Microbiology Laboratory at the QEII Health Sciences Centre in Halifax. That team was responsible for analyzing COVID-19 tests from across the province and getting the results back to people as quickly as possible—a critical factor in identifying outbreaks and helping slow the spread.

Charles Heinstein, the technical manager for the microbiology lab for the central zone, described the situation as "controlled chaos."

"There's a huge pressure, right?" he says. "We were testing for pretty much everywhere across the province, so the responsibility was that we needed to get these results, we needed to get them out quickly, and they needed to be accurate. And the volume didn't matter because we had to meet those criteria, regardless of the volumes."

The big question was—how could they keep up with the exponentially increasing demand? In the early days of the pandemic, the lab had been routinely processing between 200 and 300 tests per day. At one point, the largest number of tests they handled in a day grew to 1,500. Then it rose again to 2,500.

Heinstein says the key to expanding capacity lay in brainstorming and being open to fresh ideas. The entire staff was asked—what are the barriers to doing more tests? "Regardless of how crazy an idea was on how we were going to accomplish that, we needed to consider it," he says. "You just had to completely free your mind and pretend that barriers weren't barriers, because once you did that, you were able to think about how to overcome those barriers."

One barrier identified was data entry, so a new data-entry system was brought online in April 2021; it allowed to staff to scan a sample's barcode instead of typing the data in. Another barrier was staffing, which at the outset of the pandemic was approximately 60 full-time employees. By the time the third wave had peaked, the lab had 110 full-time employees, plus numerous volunteers including NSHA physicians, Dalhousie University graduate students, lab staff from the IWK Health Centre, IT staff from the NSHA, and others.

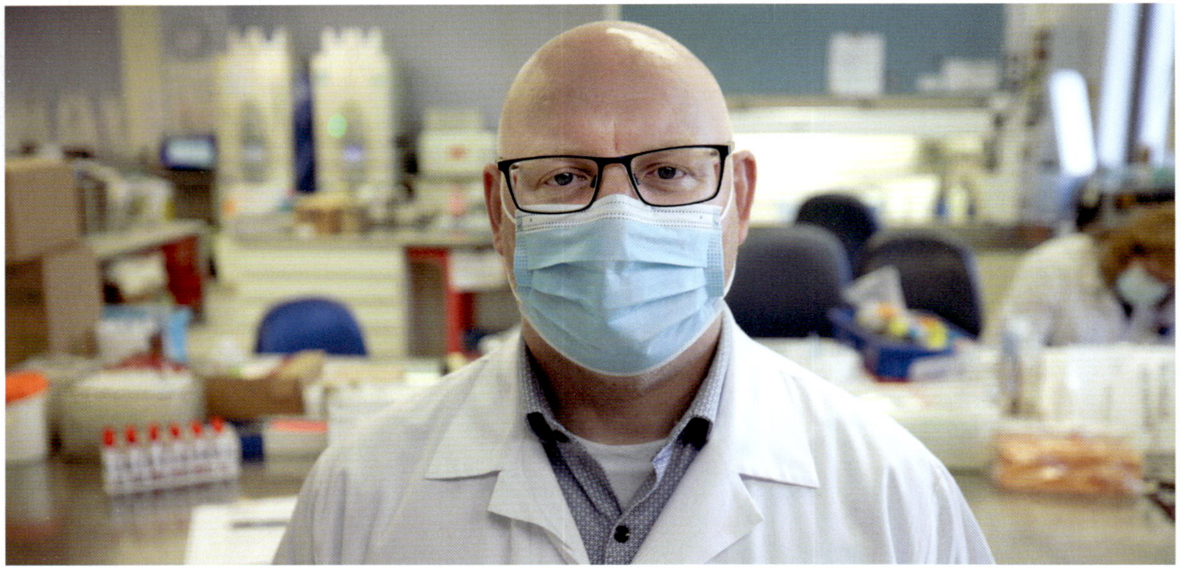

Charles Heinstein is the technical manager for the microbiology lab for the central zone, which was responsible for analyzing COVID-19 tests from across the province.

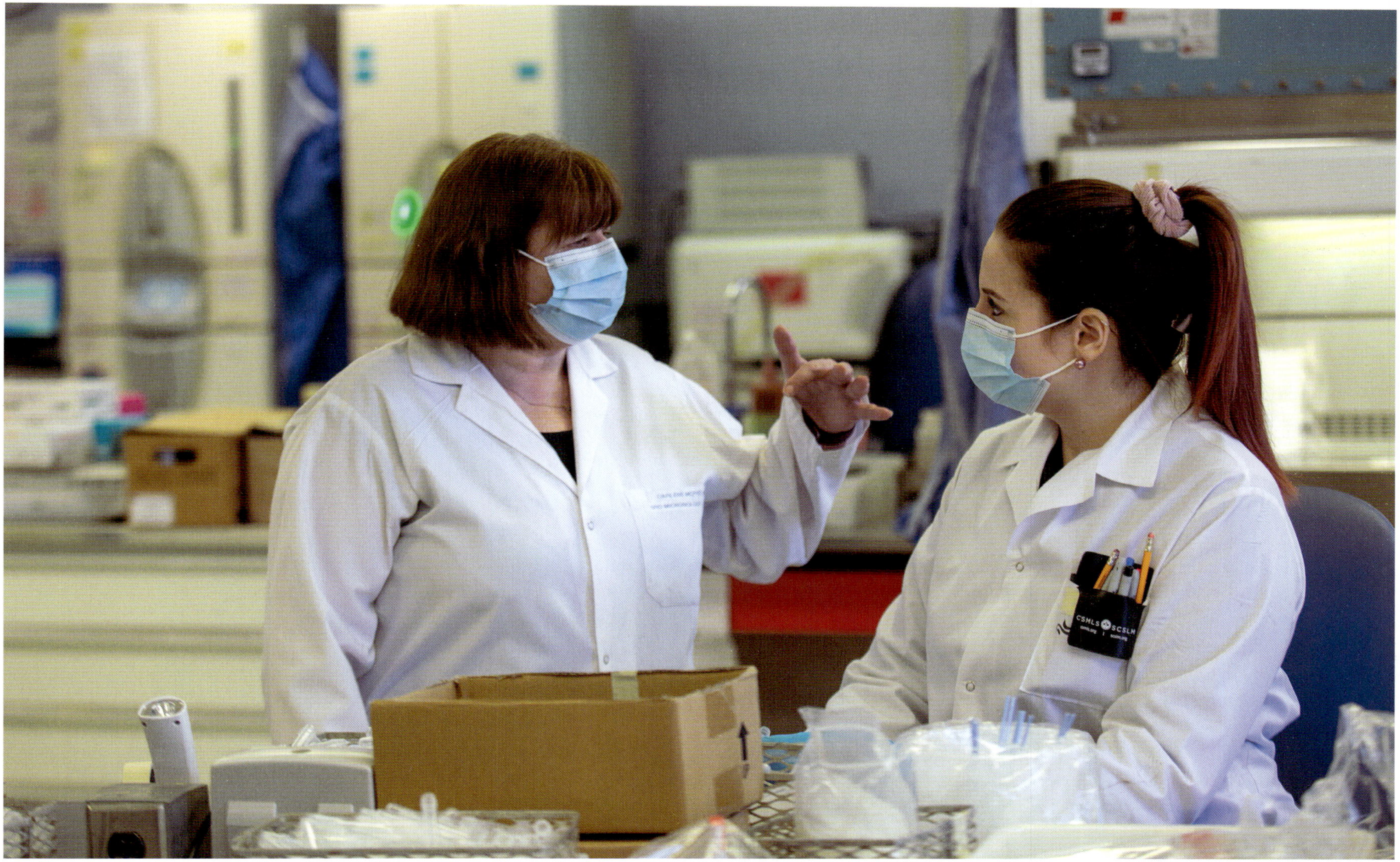

Darlene McPhee (left) is technical supervisor of the microbiology lab. She says, it's all about "supporting the province and keeping the numbers low. The quicker we are able to turn around specimens, the more we are able to get people out of isolation, or to let them know that they aren't sick with COVID." Angela Derby, (right) is a medical lab assistant. "I feel like I am part of a team that is really making a difference in the province of Nova Scotia right now with COVID-19," says Derby. "We all are working together to do the best we can to help the patients and to put people's minds at ease by getting testing done quickly and efficiently."

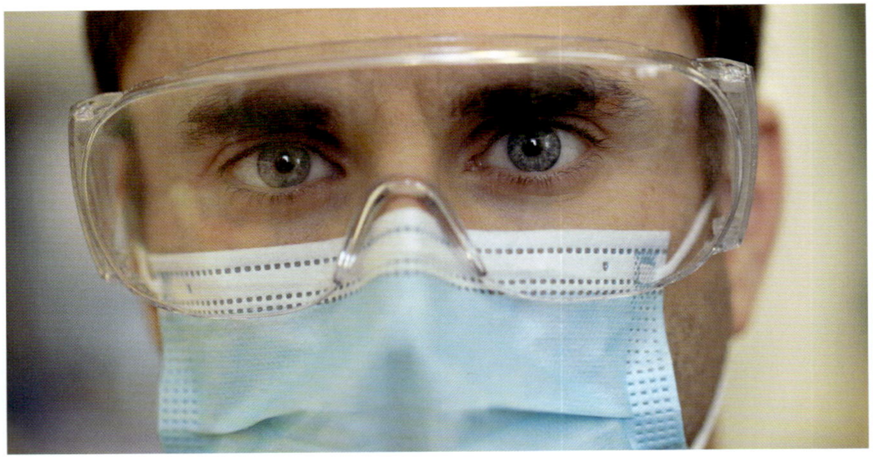

Darren Sarty is a technical specialist at the lab. "Across Canada, COVID is running rampant in the hospitals," Sarty says, "but in Nova Scotia, because of our testing and our public health protocols, we've been able to actually keep COVID at bay. It gives me great pride to be able to come here and say that I'm a piece of that puzzle and part of the solution."

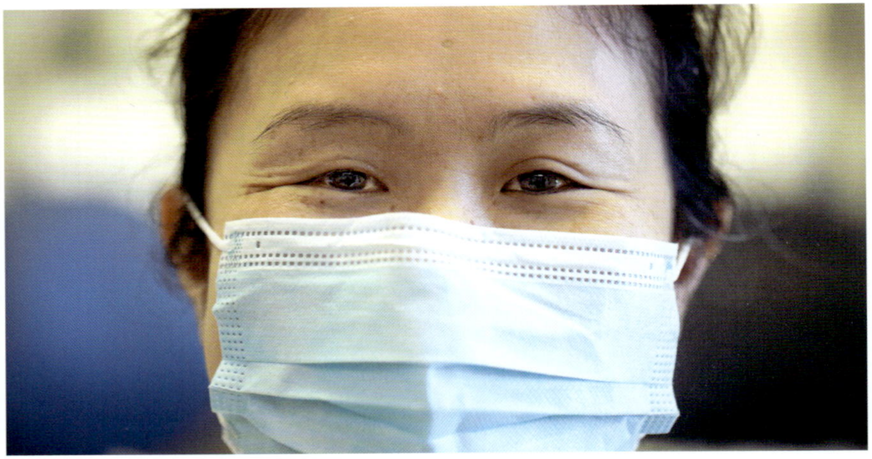

Grace Lee is a medical lab technologist at the lab. "I'm one of the MLTs that works through the microbiology lab. I'm happy to be here and to be part of the COVID testing [that is] helping people out; I just feel very accomplished in my job."

The lab began running twenty-four hours a day as the tests kept pouring in and the results kept pouring out. "More than a few of the medical directors and management staff worked twenty-four–hour days," says Heinstein. "Technical staff put in lots of overtime and the volunteers helped where their skill sets allowed."

But in late April 2021, Heinstein says, there was a lot of worry. The lab had plans in place to handle up to 8,000 samples and he says there was confidence they could push above that level. "But, like anything, until you test a plan you never know if it will work." At one point, the lab was receiving upwards of 15,000 samples per day. "Added to that was the pressure of the 45,000-test backlog that was being announced daily, so it was a stressful time," he admits.

The lab hit its highest number at 19,306 on May 5, 2021. Heinstein says during the days leading up to the peak they were breaking the highest-number-tested on a daily basis. Fortunately, case numbers gradually began to fall after that peak in May, and numbers of people getting tested slowly returned to more manageable levels.

"I must say, I've never been more proud of a group of people than I was during this period," Heinstein says. "Everyone did all they could to make the lab come together to hit these numbers. There were some rough patches, people got upset with each other, staff were tired, but at the end of the day we all came together and made it work."

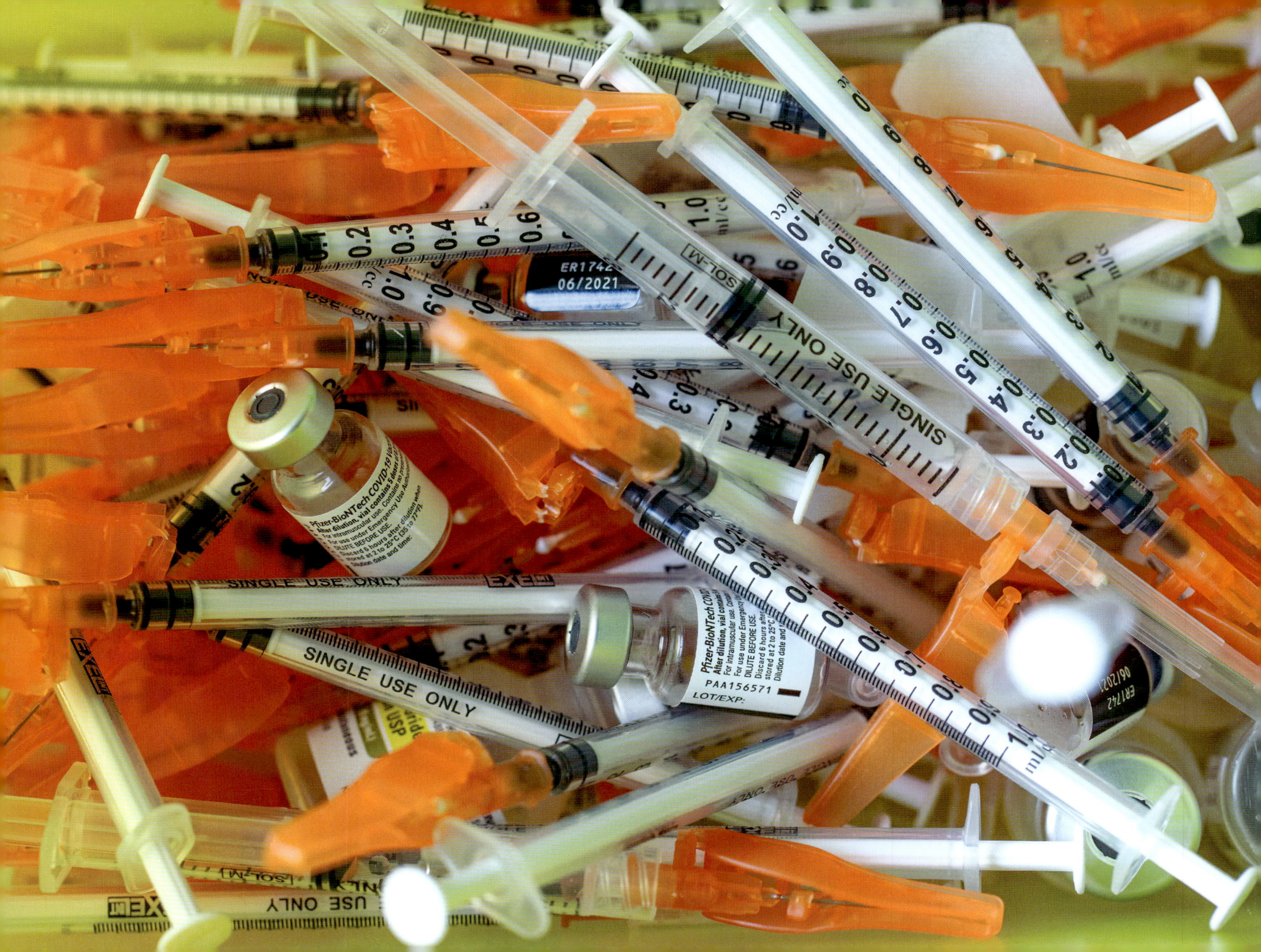
ER1742
06/2021
SINGLE USE ONLY
SINGLE USE ONLY
Pfizer-BioNTech COVID-19
DILUTE BEFORE USE.
PAA156571
LOT/EXP:
SINGLE USE ONLY

DETECTIVE AT WORK:
Contact Tracer Holly Kennedy

"Today, Nova Scotia is reporting four new cases of COVID-19 and three recoveries. Three cases are close contacts of previously reported cases and one is under investigation."

By now, Nova Scotians have heard words like these hundreds of times in the context of the day's COVID-19 case numbers. But what does it actually mean for a case to be "under investigation"?

It means someone like public health nurse Holly Kennedy is on the job, working to uncover the source of that infection in order to ensure that any people who may have come into close contact with the infected person or the source get tested—limiting community spread.

Kennedy, who lives and works in Sydney, Cape Breton, is a specialist in tracing communicable diseases. "Way before COVID, I was looking after things like tuberculosis, meningitis—things that crop up every once in a while—and then everyday things like your sexually transmitted blood-borne pathogens," she says matter-of-factly.

"So when COVID hit, it made sense that the communicable disease nurses would technically be the front line for case management while we got other public health nurses and other staff up to speed."

It often falls to Kennedy and her team to deliver the news that someone has tested positive for COVID-19—news that sometimes comes as a shock. Immediately afterward, she and her team go into "detective mode."

"We walk through questions about who's in the house, what type of elements are around them, like their workplace, where they been over the last fourteen days, were they at an exposure site? We flesh all of that out."

She says people are often surprised when they realize how many people they've actually been around. "It's like, hey, you worked on that day. Did you drive yourself? Yes? Okay—when you arrived, did you punch a clock? Take me through your whole day," she says. "A lot of people get overlooked [if] you don't approach it like that. So if they had to punch a clock and they walked past the secretary, did they stop and talk to that secretary for five, ten minutes?"

She acknowledges that people are sometimes nervous about disclosing who they've been in contact with if they've contravened the province's social distancing guidelines, because they're concerned about being reported to the authorities.

"Our first and foremost priority, regardless of how many people were at your party, is to protect each and every person at that party and to control the spread of disease amongst the public," Kennedy says. "If we don't know all the details, we can't do our job."

After all the possible exposures have been identified, Kennedy does a risk assessment to determine whether an exposure notice—"if you were at location X between the hours of Y and Z"—needs to go out to the public.

One of the hardest parts of her job, she says, is learning that a person she and her team have been following has died as a result of contracting COVID-19.

"You were following that person, you understand their family dynamics, they've talked to you, you're talking to their nurses, you're following them in the hospital, and then all of a sudden they pass away," she says, adding that she and her team often find it necessary to debrief on a personal level when that happens. "I'm not allowed to talk about those cases with my spouse. I'm not allowed to talk about those cases with my friends or family. So you really have to lean on your fellow nurses."

The entire process is very much a team effort, and their job is a critical one in the fight against COVID.

"We are kind of the 'front' front-line workers," says Kennedy. "Without us, there would be community spread." She admits it feels good to know that her work has made a difference.

"I'm proud of the work I do, and I think I do a very good job," she says. "You can choose to let yourself get beat down by COVID—or you can choose to allow yourself to rise above."

Public health nurse and COVID contact tracer Holly Kennedy, of Sydney, works to uncover the source of COVID infections.

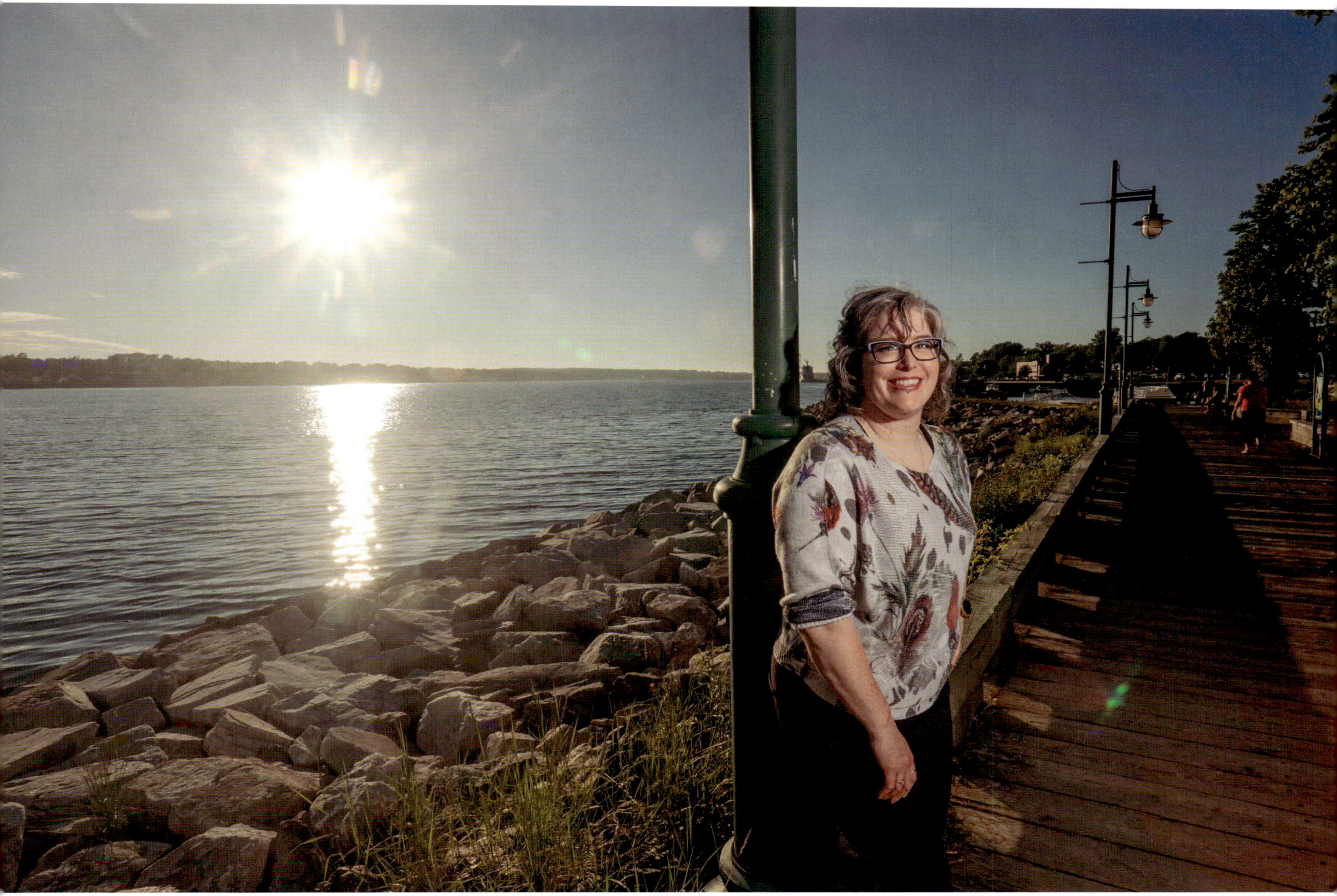

TESTING ON ARRIVAL:
Halifax Stanfield International Airport

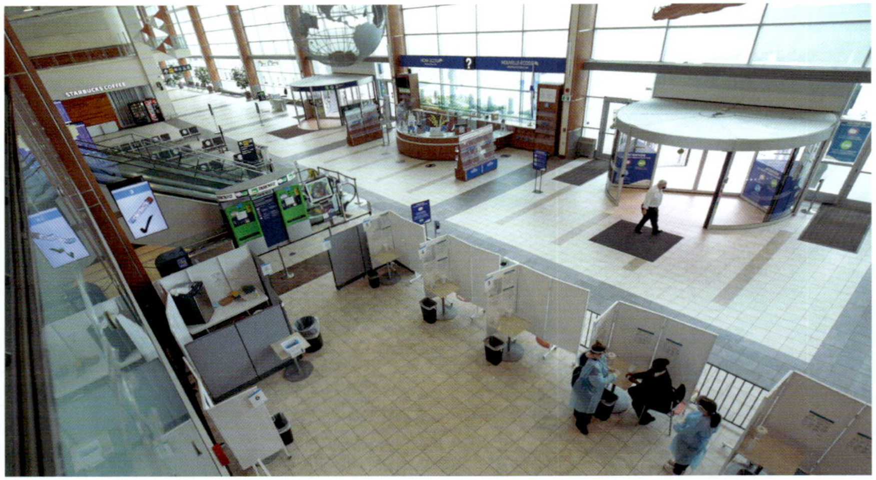

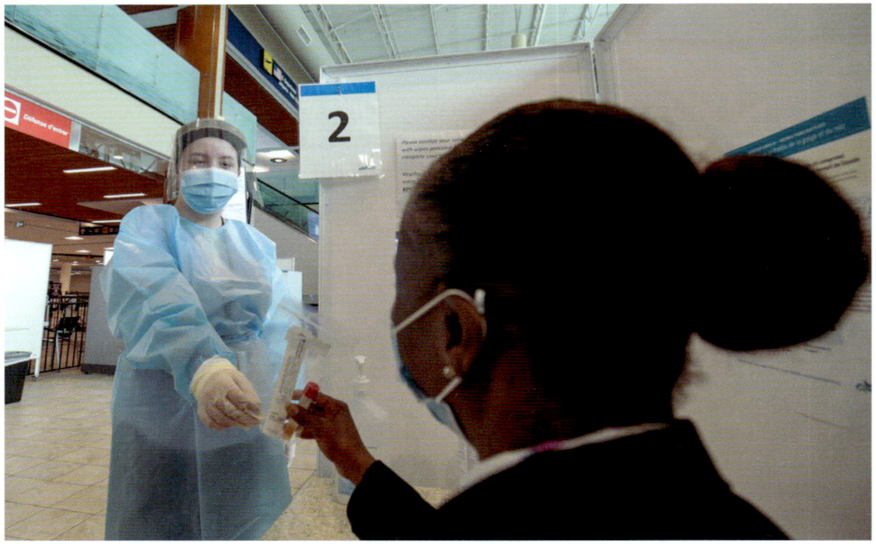

With no international traffic and very little domestic travel, business at the Halifax Stanfield International Airport has been way down since the start of the pandemic. Self-isolation requirements for people who travel from other Canadian provinces or territories are based on vaccination status and testing. In early June 2021, on-site testing was made available to passengers arriving at the airport.

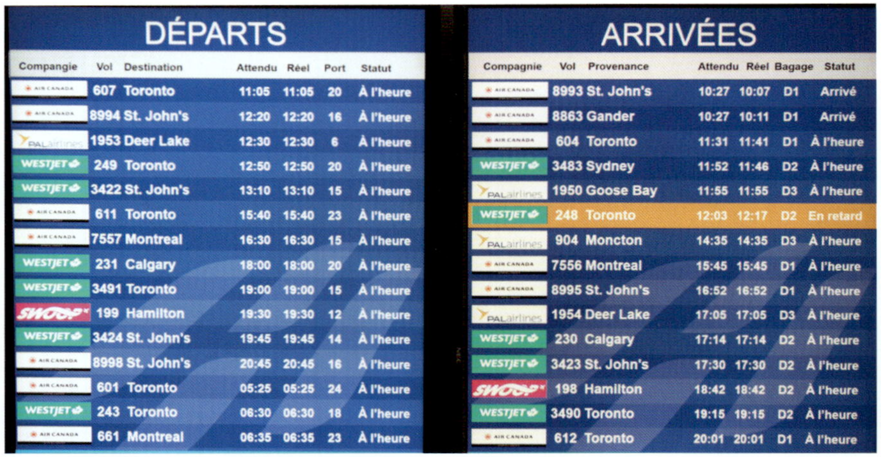

ABOVE: *The airport did not accept international travellers during the pandemic. All incoming and outgoing flights, with the exception of cargo flights, were from within Canada, as seen on these arrivals and departures boards in early July 2021.*

TOP AND BOTTOM LEFT: *Alexandra Mallan (left), an emergency support aide with the Nova Scotia Health Authority, helps out a client at the voluntary COVID-19 testing centre at Halifax Stanfield International Airport.*

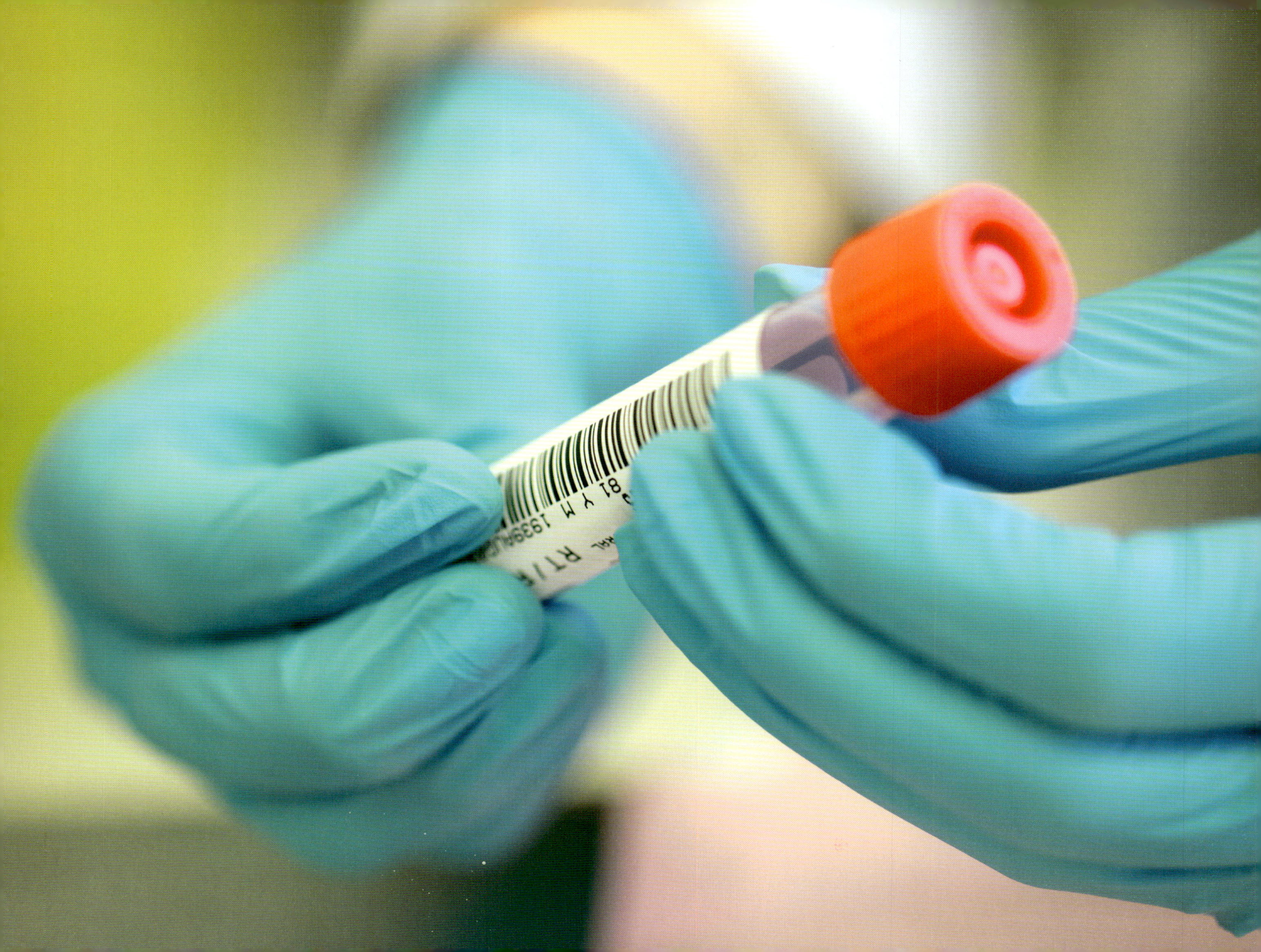

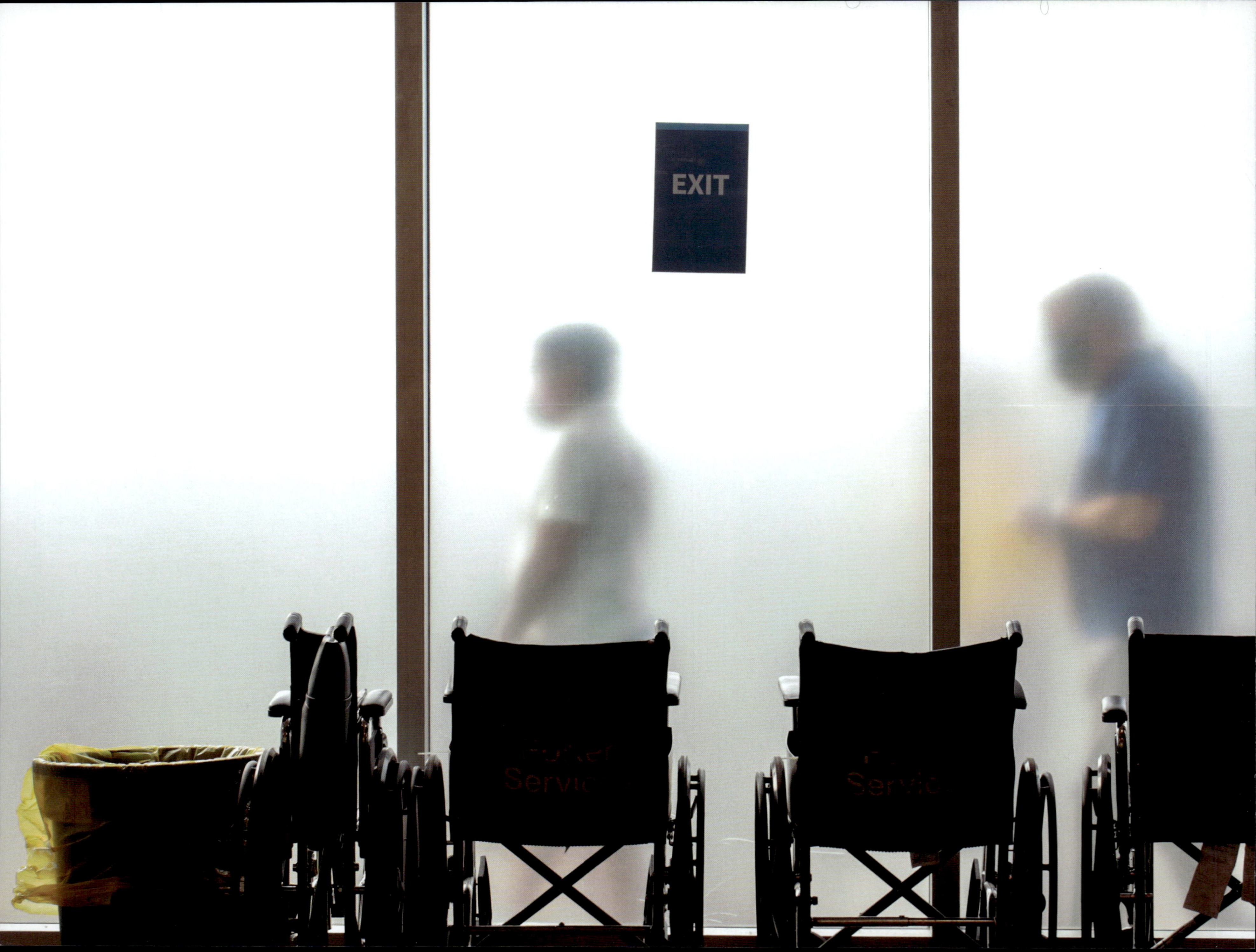
EXIT

Part Two: A RAY OF HOPE

VACCINE QUEEN: *Tracey Barbrick*

In the before-times, Tracey Barbrick had been enjoying a fairly typical career as a high-level provincial government bureaucrat. She had been an associate deputy minister for the Government of Nova Scotia for about seven years, most recently at the Department of Community Services. She'd also been the assistant deputy minister for Labour and Advanced Education, and she'd worked for a stretch at the Department of Health and Wellness.

But her career took a dramatic turn when her phone rang on December 6, 2020, and she was called on to become the associate deputy minister responsible for the COVID-19 vaccine rollout.

"By December eighth I was there," Barbrick says. "By December fifteenth, we had our first shipment of vaccine." She laughs. "It was a whirlwind."

Even she finds it a little unbelievable. "If anybody had told me in December that we would be at the point where we are, in two weeks time, going to exceed 180,000 doses in arms in one week"—[we spoke in early July 2021]—"if anybody had ever told me we could do that, I would have not believed it, considering that flu clinics deliver less than 500,000 doses over six months and we will deliver 1.5 million."

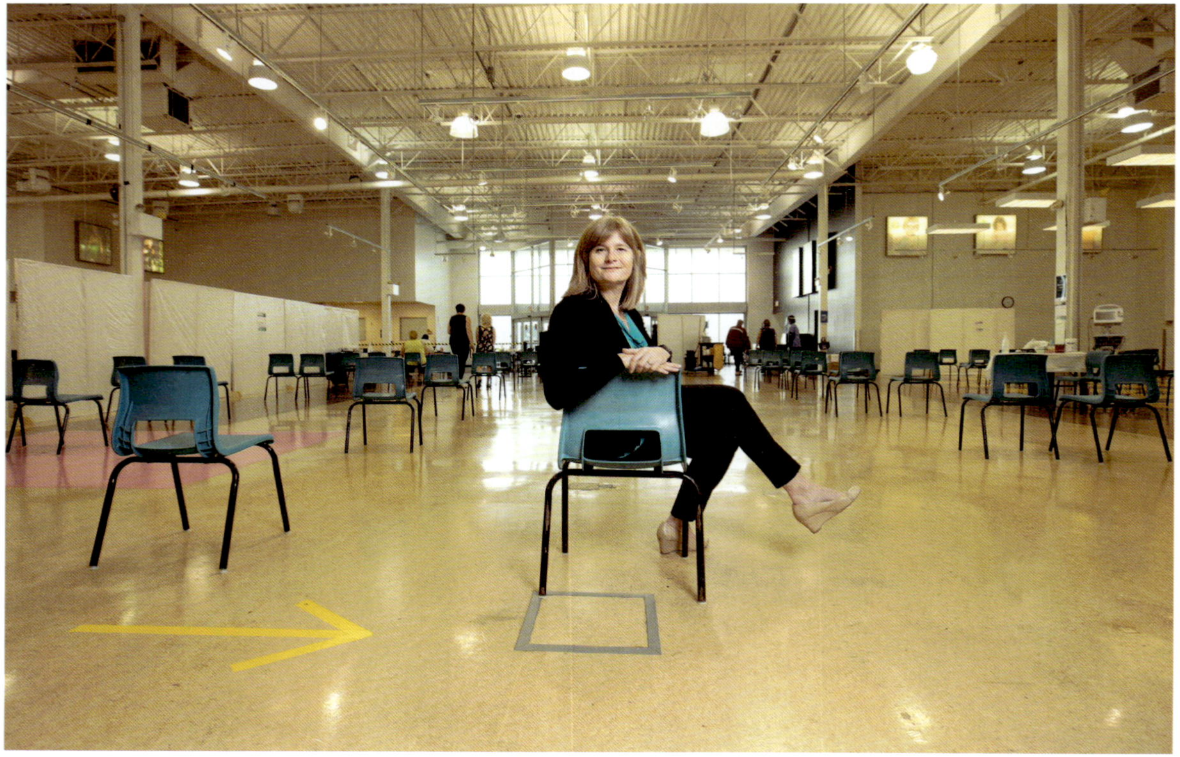

She hasn't done it alone, of course. She coordinates the numerous teams that work together to deliver the vaccines—pharmacies, community clinics, digital services, and many, many others. It's a feat of logistical wizardry, especially considering that the supply of vaccines is a constantly moving target. "We never have certainty on when we're going to get it, how much we're going to get, what it will be. We are constantly re-jigging," she says, adding that the whirlwind of supply is not anyone's fault. "It's just a function of demand for a vaccine that the entire globe wants."

She says, and she's not kidding, she hasn't slept much since December. The upside: the job is a little more rewarding than the average day behind a desk as an assistant deputy minister.

"I just feel so privileged," she says. "It's not very often in government that you get a mission like this, where you've got a goal as clear and as tangible as: We need to get at least 75 percent of this province vaccinated with two doses of vaccine and it has to be done as fast as we possibly can."

Tracey Barbrick is the associate deputy minister responsible for the COVID-19 vaccine rollout—which was truly a feat of logistical wizardry.

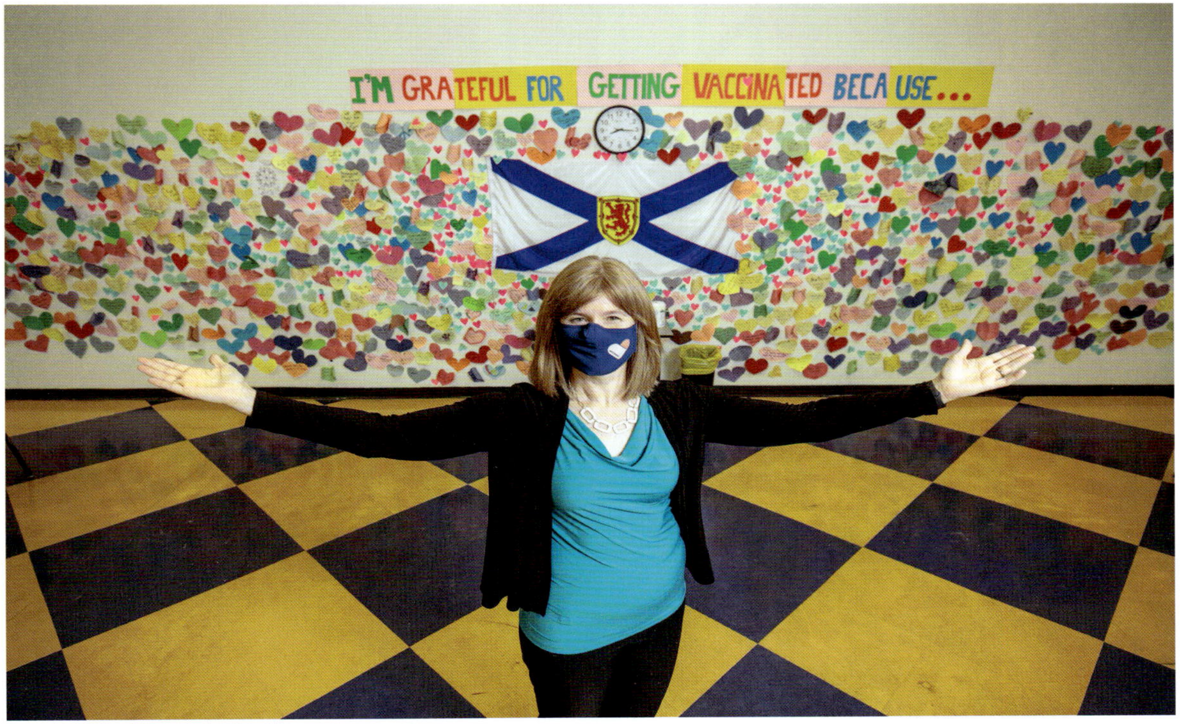

Tracey Barbrick stands in front of the "wall of gratitude" at the community vaccination clinic at Mic Mac Mall in Dartmouth.

In early July, her team administered its one-millionth dose of COVID-19 vaccine; Nova Scotia stood as a national leader in vaccine uptake. By November, Barbrick predicts, we'll be in a "steady state. There will always need to be a COVID vaccine in the province, just like flu or other vaccine programs, but it'll likely be readily available and people can just make appointments and go in and get it." And she says she's paying close attention to whether we'll need an annual booster.

Despite all the challenges, Barbrick says her role has given her some rare opportunities to make connections with the citizens she works for. She tells the story of an elderly couple who had called the premier's office because they were struggling to get physical copies of their vaccination records; when she personally delivered the records to their door, they were beyond grateful.

"It reminds me of how we have to be so mindful of citizens at the front of everything that we do. I could see it on their bodies that they were actively relieved that I had those receipts for them," she says. "And I just thought, I need to do more of that, because it was so lovely.... It was the most warm thing I've had my direct hands on for a while."

She's looking forward to the day when we've all been double-vaccinated.

"It just means so much. It means our own personal safety; the likelihood of us becoming COVID-positive and the likelihood of us transmitting it to our loved ones and our community will be significantly reduced," she says, adding, "I am forever mindful that there are so many countries that have not even had a whiff of vaccine yet, so we are just so incredibly privileged."

Barbrick is also looking forward to someday knowing the worst is behind us, and she acknowledges that her team's contribution toward getting the province vaccinated will forever be part of the story.

"There are thousands of people, and I could list each one of the team leads that have worked around the clock every day. It's been such a huge effort. I am just so grateful to be with this team every day. The recognition of what they have all given up personally in order to be able to achieve this for Nova Scotians almost takes the legs out from underneath me," she says. "It's thousands of people doing everything they can to get this done for Nova Scotians.

"It will be the most meaningful work of my life forever," she says. "The most meaningful work of my life."

MAKING A DIFFERENCE IN CHERRY BROOK

"This pandemic involves us all, so we come together as a community, as a society. That's really important," says Shauna Crawley-Jordan, an RN and a community health-care worker from North Preston and East Preston.

Crawley-Jordan is delivering vaccinations at a community clinic in Cherry Brook, a predominantly African Nova Scotian community outside of Halifax. The province held similar clinics across the province, recognizing the disproportionate risk of adverse COVID-19 outcomes on those communities, and acknowledging the systemic racism that has contributed to mistrust of the health system within Black communities.

"I think it's really important that people see people they know," Crawley-Jordan says. "They can come to me with any question, no matter how small, and they're acknowledged and listened to, and their concerns and fears are validated."

Liette Williams, RN, of East Preston, says it feels great to give back to the community and to help make sure everyone is safe. "I never, never thought we would be in a pandemic and I'd be on the front line, working," says Williams. "It's very important because I think the community members like to see people who represent them. It makes them feel more comfortable seeing someone who looks like them."

Crawley-Jordan says this is not just where she *needs* to be. "This is where I *want* to be—to be able to positively affect my community's health and wellness. I am very proud after thirty-nine years. At the age of fourteen I wanted to be a nurse," she says, "and I don't believe I'm going to stop anytime soon."

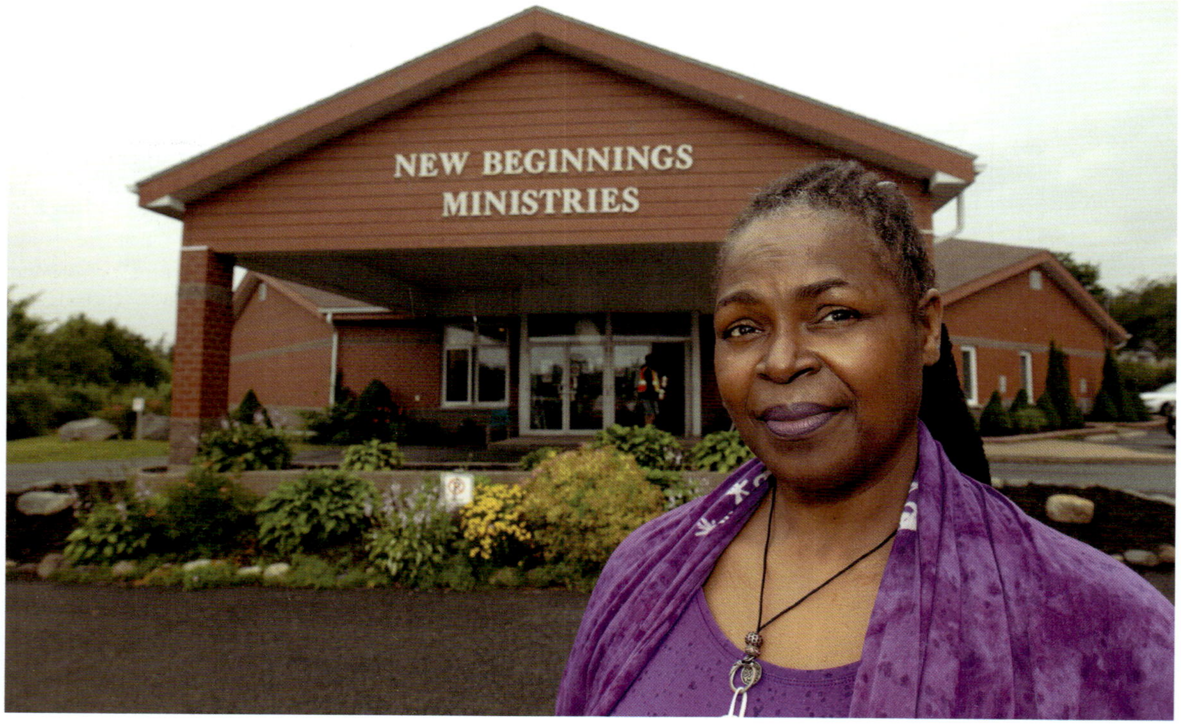

Shauna Crawley-Jordan, RN, is a community health-care worker from North and East Preston, working at the Cherry Brook vaccination clinic. "This pandemic involves us all, so we come together as a community, as a society," she says.

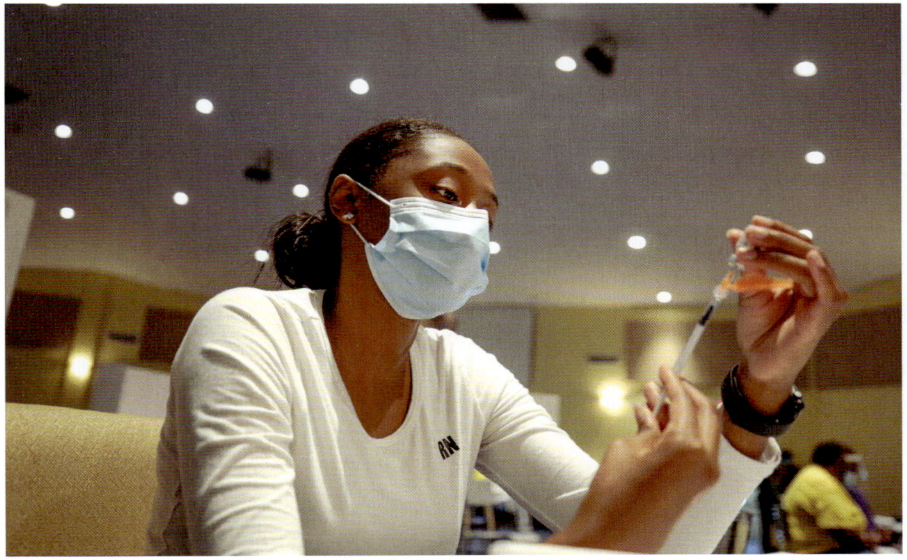

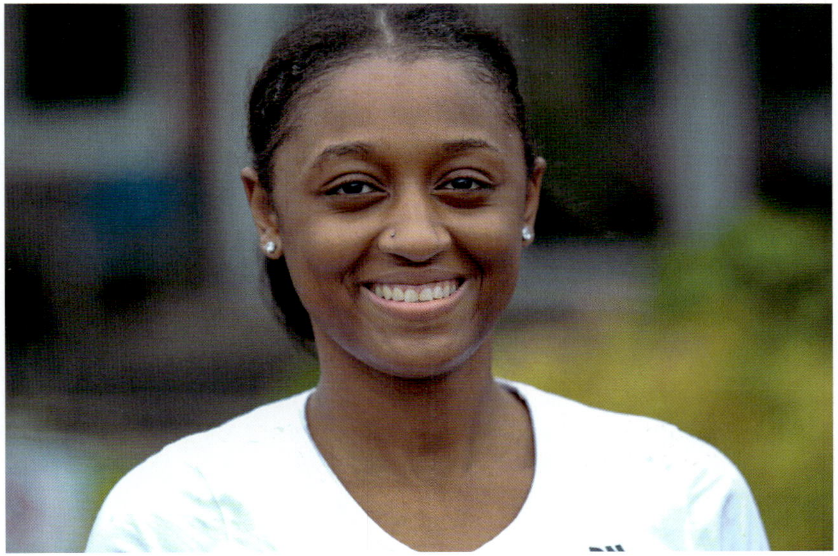

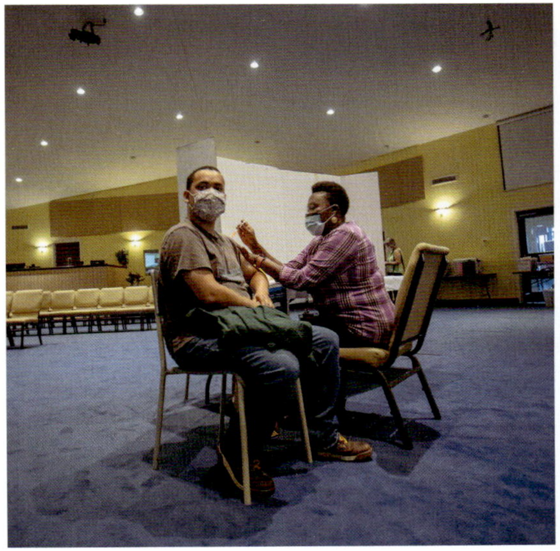

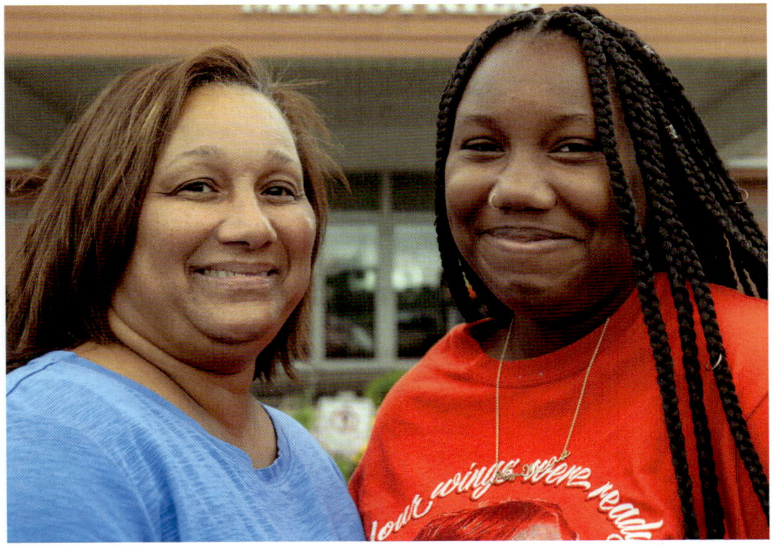

TOP RIGHT AND LEFT: *Liette Williams, RN, of East Preston, says it feels great to give back to the community and to help make sure everyone is safe.*

BOTTOM LEFT: *Christopher De-Kock receives his COVID-19 vaccine from public health nurse Alexcia Amoah.*

BOTTOM RIGHT: *Kathy Williams and her granddaughter Nyia Harrison, both from East Preston, smile after receiving their vaccinations at New Beginnings Church.*

DELIVERING THE VERY FIRST VACCINE: *Jennifer Turcot*

Jennifer Turcot had wanted to be a nurse ever since she was a little girl. Now a licenced practical nurse (LPN), she says she never wavered in her goal, except during the brief period when she wanted to be a police officer —"because I'm bossy," she laughs. So she was more than thrilled when she had the opportunity to give the very first COVID-19 vaccination in Nova Scotia on December 16, 2020.

"I was very nervous because there were a lot of people watching," Turcot says, referring to the reporters and camera crews that looked on as she prepared to inject fellow nurse Danielle Sheaves.

"It was exhilarating. It was nerve-racking. This was the first time I'd drawn up this vaccine and it's extremely sensitive," she says. "So, to be honest, my first thought was, 'This has to be done well,' and I had to get all the cameras out of my head so I could focus on doing it. And then once I gave the vaccine I was like, 'Ahhh! We did it!'"

She acknowledges that the public health team at the Nova Scotia Health Authority had to do a lot of work behind the scenes to make that moment happen, but she never doubted that it *would* happen.

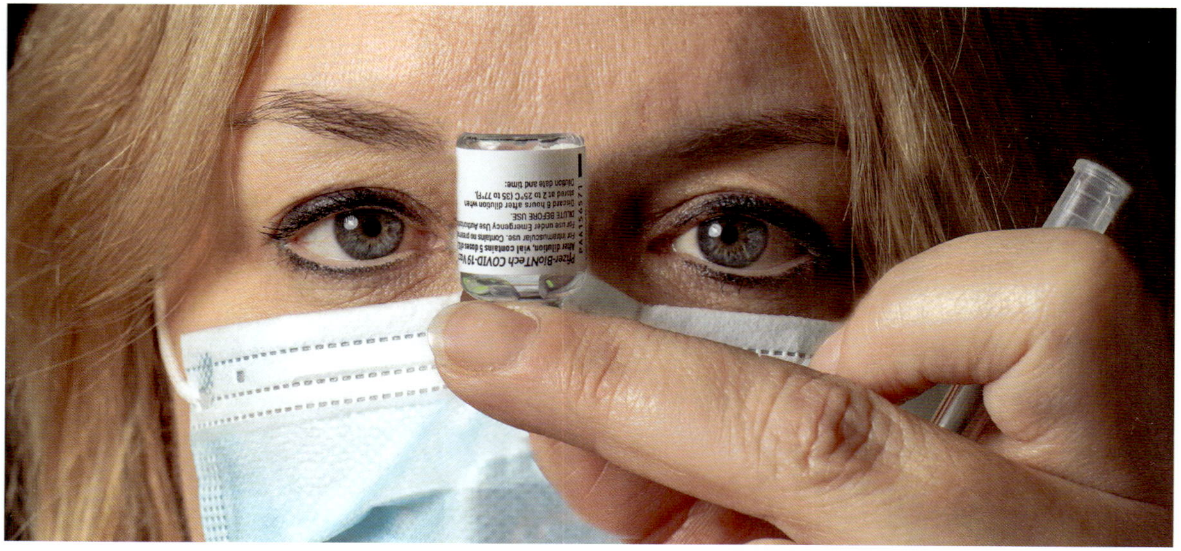

"That is what we advocate for all the time, so it was a proud moment," she says. "History in the making."

Turcot then joined the team at the Halifax Forum to begin delivering vaccines every day. "We started with health-care workers," she says, and pauses to wipe a tear from her eye. "I'm sorry. I get welled up thinking about it because, especially with the health-care workers, they've been so happy. They're grateful. Some of them feel slightly guilty that they're getting it before someone who might be at higher risk, but they're at risk every day, too, although they still feel that real sense of responsibility to their patients or clients."

Turcot was also there on March 17—the day members of the general public aged eighty and up became eligible for vaccination.

"You don't realize people truly haven't been out of their houses. Some people have not left their house in a year, not even to go to the grocery store—their family members have been going for them," she says, noting that many seniors had not even seen their grandchildren because their families were concerned

Jennifer Turcot, LPN, delivered the very first COVID-19 vaccination in Nova Scotia.

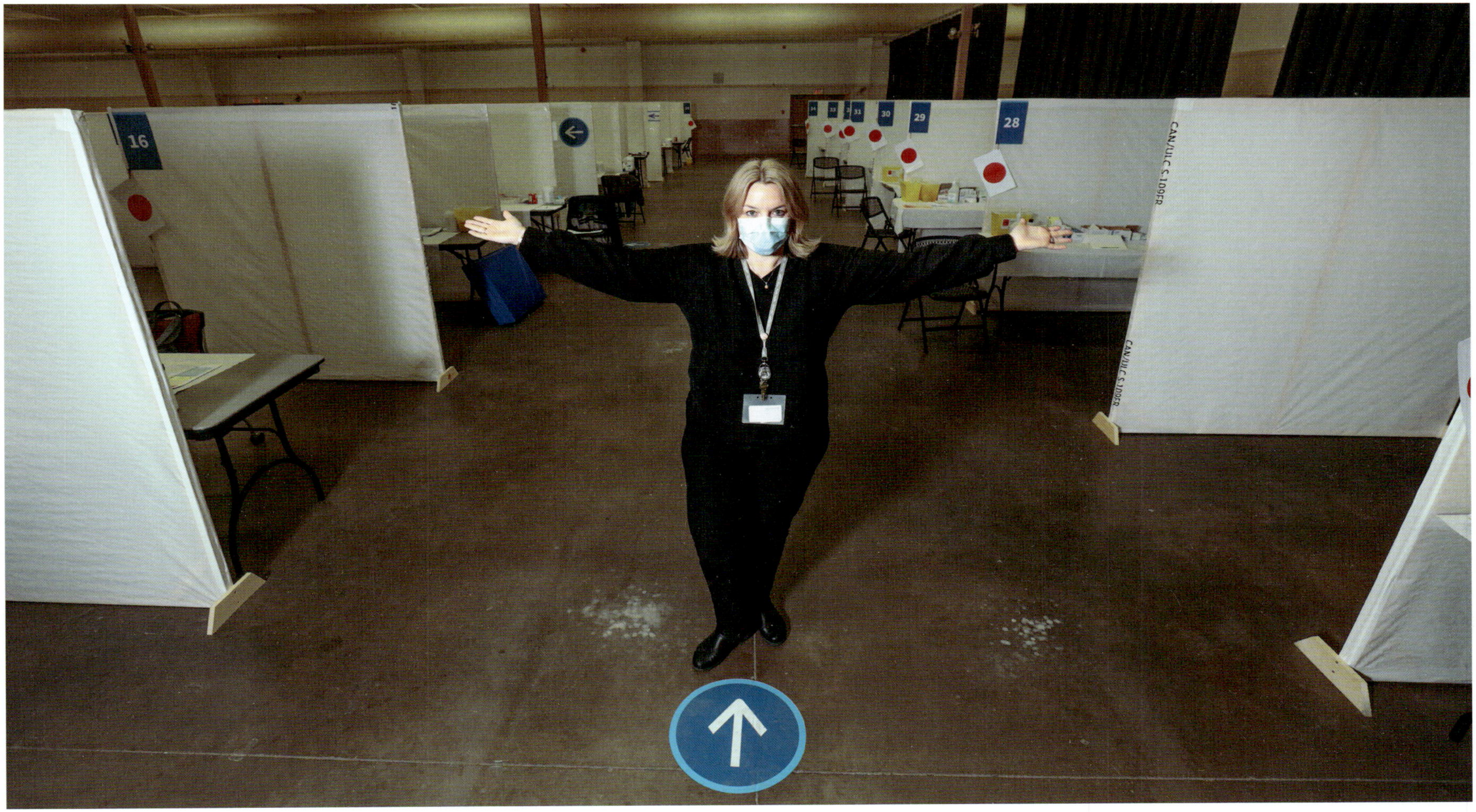

Jennifer Turcot shows off the community vaccination clinic at the at the Halifax Forum.

about COVID. "So they're coming here and they're dressing up. This is a huge deal because this is like being able to go out again.... Those first days of those clinics were powerful."

Those moments brought home to Turcot the importance of what she and the Public Health team had achieved over the last year. "I just felt really proud of all the work we had done to pull this first clinic together so quickly. A lot of people worked really hard," she says.

"People were truly afraid, so I was very proud to be their light at the end of the tunnel."

A HAPPY VACCINATION DAY IN SYDNEY

THIS PAGE: *As the province rolled out its vaccination strategy, clinics like this one were held at the Canada Games Complex at Cape Breton University in Sydney.*

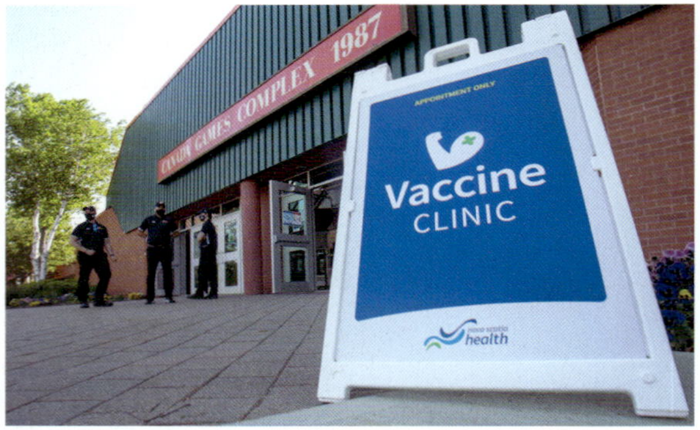

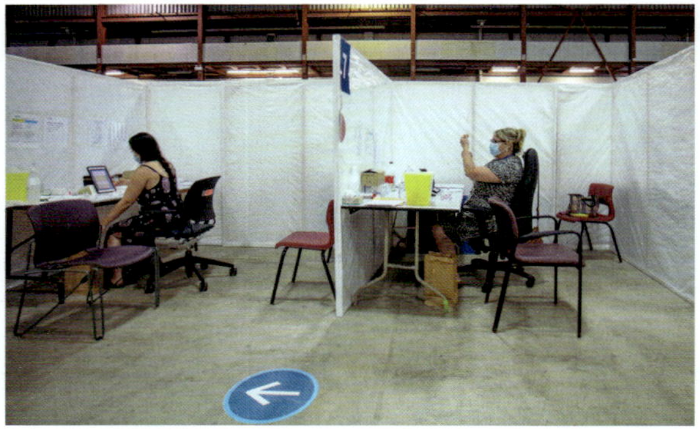

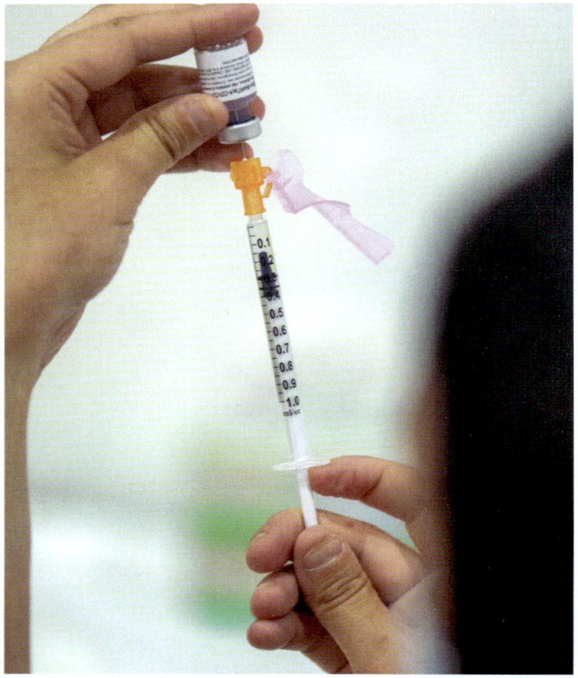

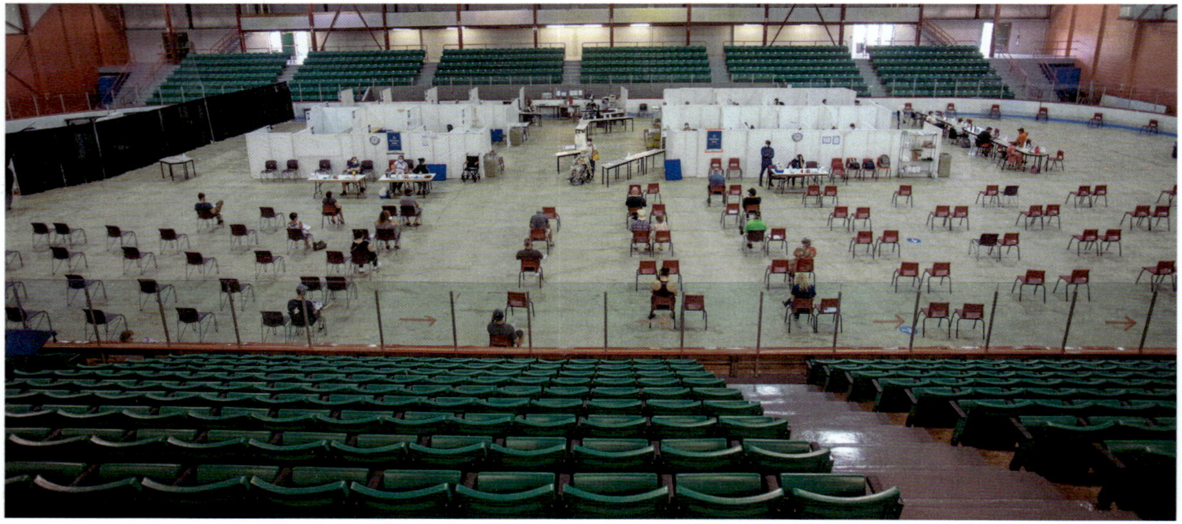

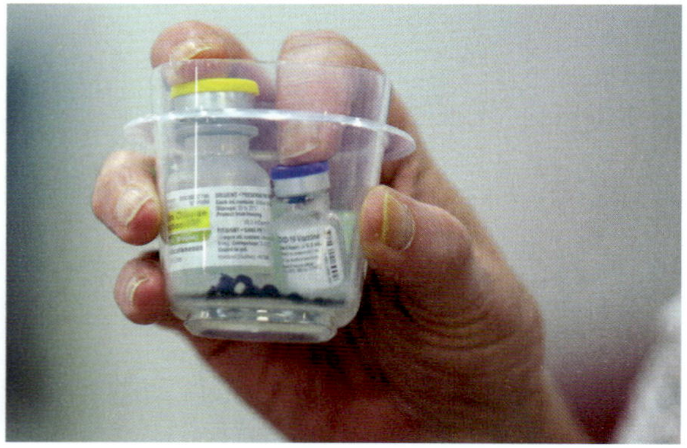

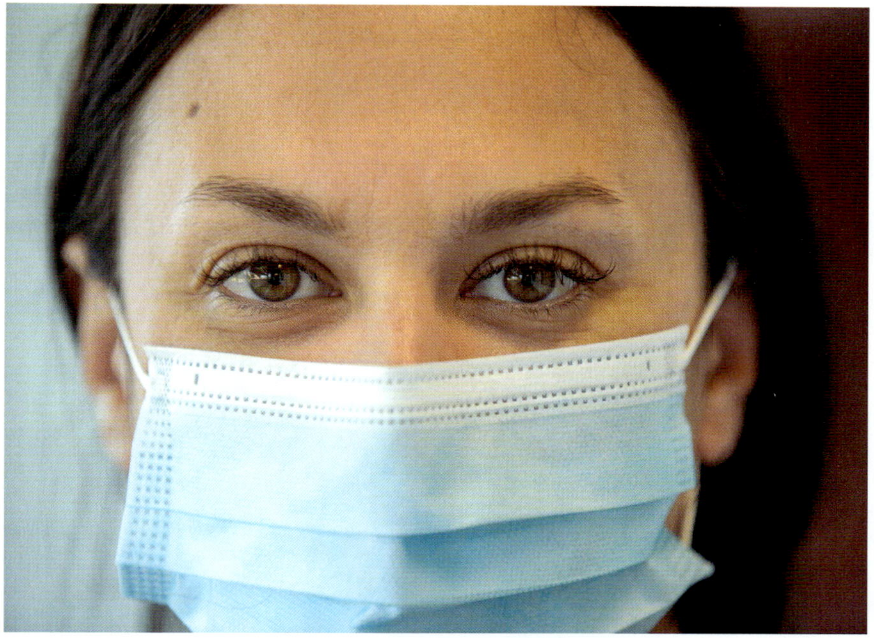

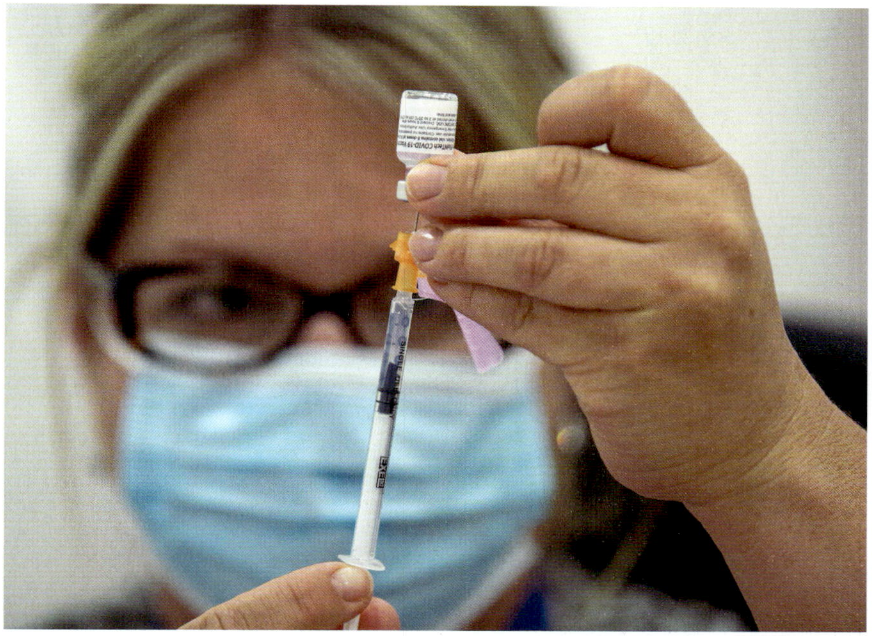

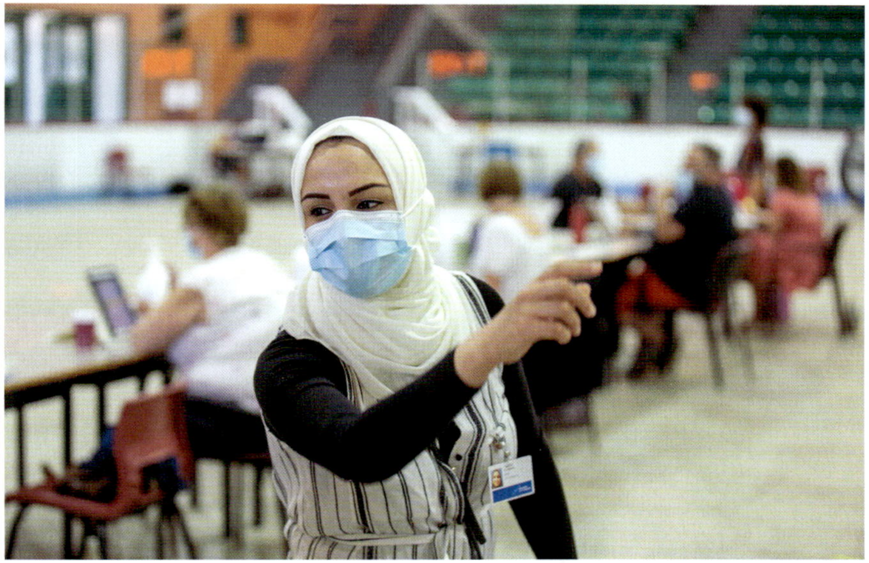

TOP LEFT: *Ashley Sullivan, LPN, worked at Sydney's community vaccination clinic. "It makes me feel good to help clear out this pandemic and vaccinate people. And it's nice to see people's faces when they're so happy to receive the vaccine," she says. "On days when you're tired, it's just nice to see people [who are] so happy and who say, 'Thank you for being here.' I think when we're hopefully past this, years down the road, it will be nice to look back and know that I was part of that.*

TOP RIGHT: *Andree Poirier, RN, at the community vaccination clinic, Cape Breton University Canada Games Complex, Sydney: "When the children started coming in, they were so excited and they were really a good example for all the adults that were hesitant," she says. "It's an honour to be out here and to be doing our part to beat COVID-19."*

BOTTOM LEFT: *Ayha El-Darahali was the site screener at the community vaccination clinic at CBU's Canada Games Complex in Sydney. "I'm very fortunate to be part of such an amazing team," she says. "I feel like I'm able to give back to my community here in Sydney and that is something that I really want to do."*

NOVA SCOTIANS GETTING THE JAB

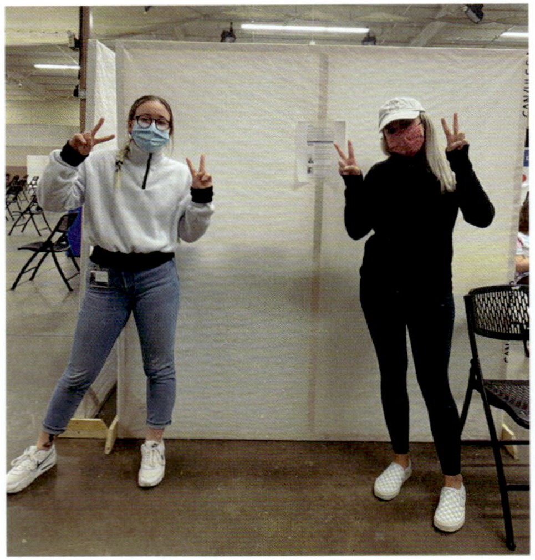

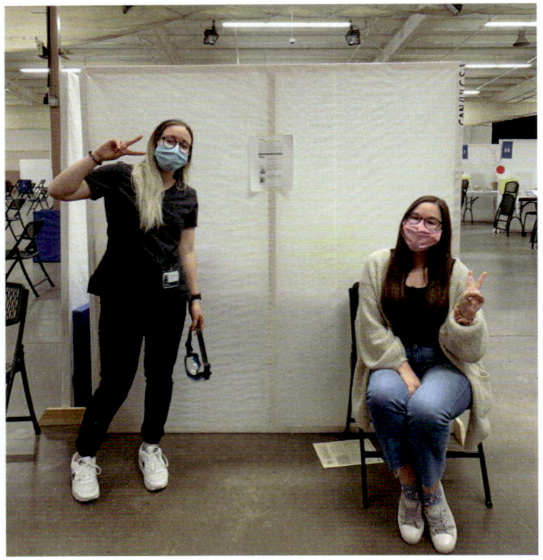

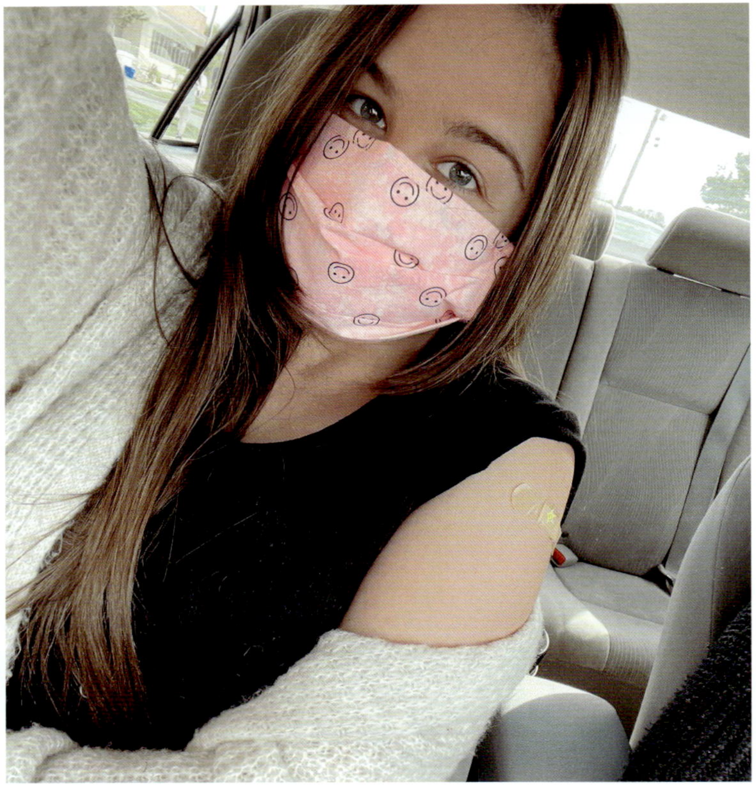

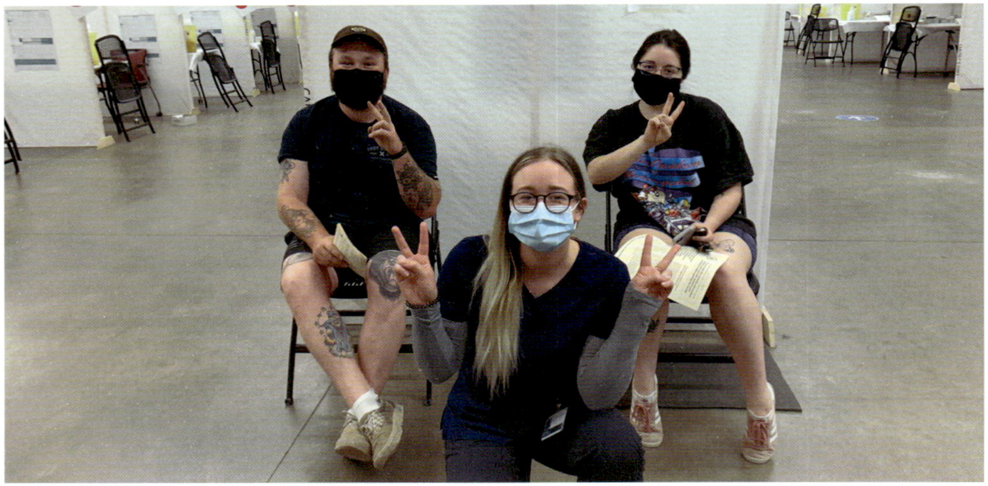

THIS PAGE: *Nicole Dalrymple of Halifax sent some images of her vaccination day. Nicole (in the pink smiley-face mask, which she says is "indicative of my mood that day") writes, "I'm also including a few—with enthusiastic permission of all involved—taken with one of my best friends, Jessica Savoie, who works at the vaccination clinic at the Forum. She's made a point of taking photos with every friend that comes through! Once again, the pink mask is me, and standing in all black is Cailin Boyce. The couple is Regan Zscheile and Alec Crowell. BTW—the peace sign is a 'V' for vaccine."*

She adds, "I couldn't be more excited to get this vaccine and help this beautiful city and all its local businesses rebuild (and then go see my mom without worry of infecting her)! As somebody who works in history, I'm also so ready to be a part of something bigger and to contribute to the story of how we beat this virus. We're all going to look so cool in a hundred years!" (**NICOLE DALRYMPLE**)

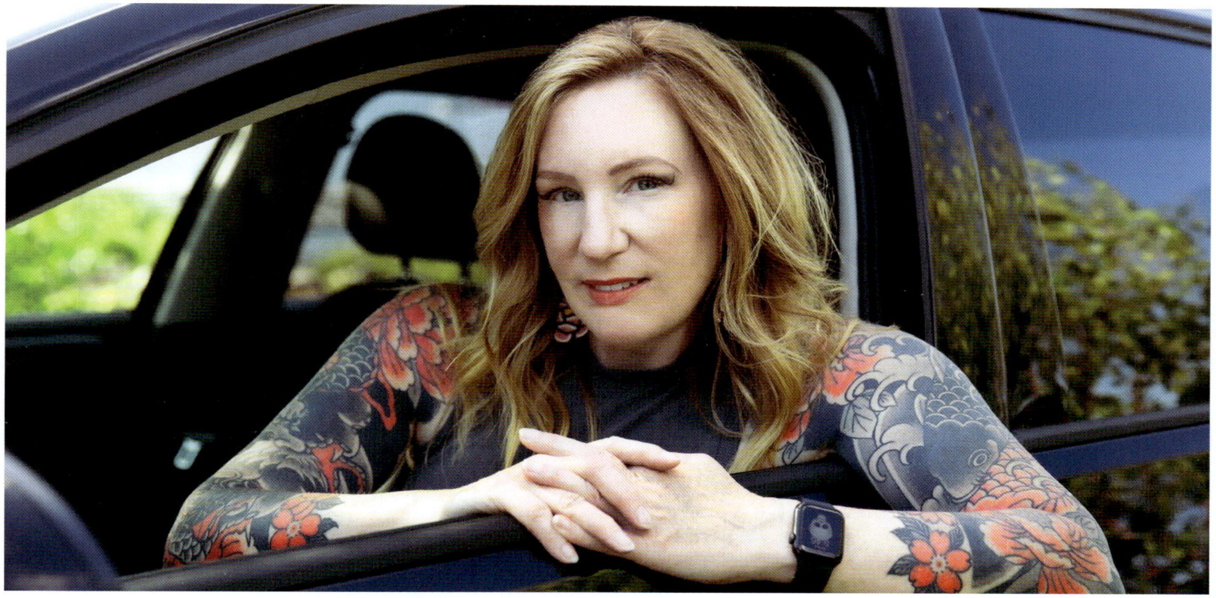

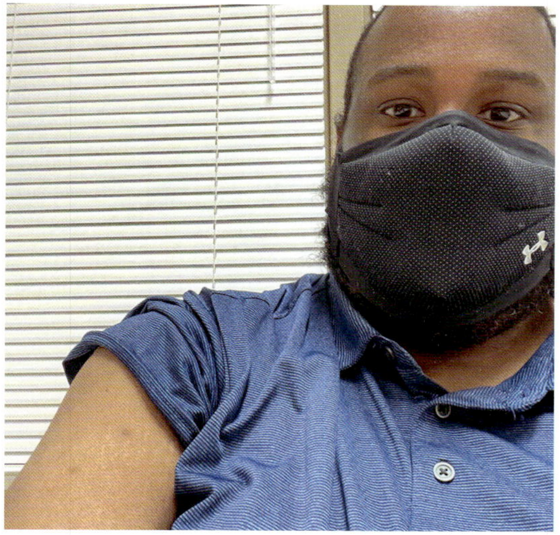

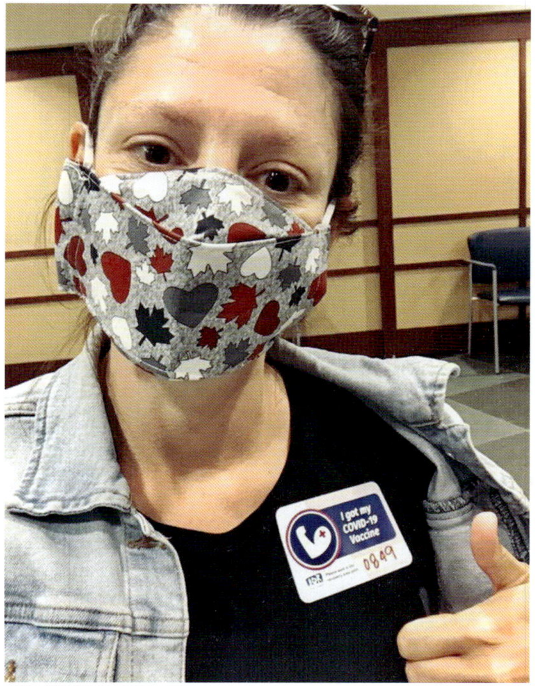

ABOVE: *"My name is Kelly Clark and when the opportunity arose to become a role model for Nova Scotia's vaccine campaign, I happily stepped up to the plate. Or drove up, I should say! I was one of the first people to be vaccinated through the Dartmouth drive-through vaccine clinic and became the subject of a Nova Scotia Health video and media campaign that saw my image published across Canada and around the world. I might just have some of the most famous arms in Nova Scotia!*

"To publically step forward and do this was personally important—not just because of the COVID-19 pandemic—but to promote vaccination in general. My father, Walter, contracted polio as a child and it affected him his entire life. He suffered, but never complained, as he always said there were many who had it far worse. My dad was part of the generation that was held back due to the physical ailments brought on by the polio virus. . . .

"Fast-forward sixty-six years later and here Canada is, in the midst of fighting a deadly virus in a similar county-wide effort. Although my dad is no longer with me, I feel in my heart that he would be proud—I made a difference by volunteering and stepping up to promote an important and necessary step to getting our lives back to normal, one shot at a time.

"Someday people will look back in history books and see me, getting that shot in my tattooed arms and being excited to be one step closer to hugging my family, seeing my friends, and living my life." (KELLY CLARK)

TOP RIGHT: *Andrew Paris took this photo of himself after receiving his vaccination in Truro on May 31.* (ANDREW PARIS)

BOTTOM RIGHT: *Sarah-Jane Arsenault of Bedford sent this shot of herself taken right after she receivied her first dose of the Pfizer vaccine at the IWK Health Centre in Halifax.* (SARAH-JANE ARSENAULT)

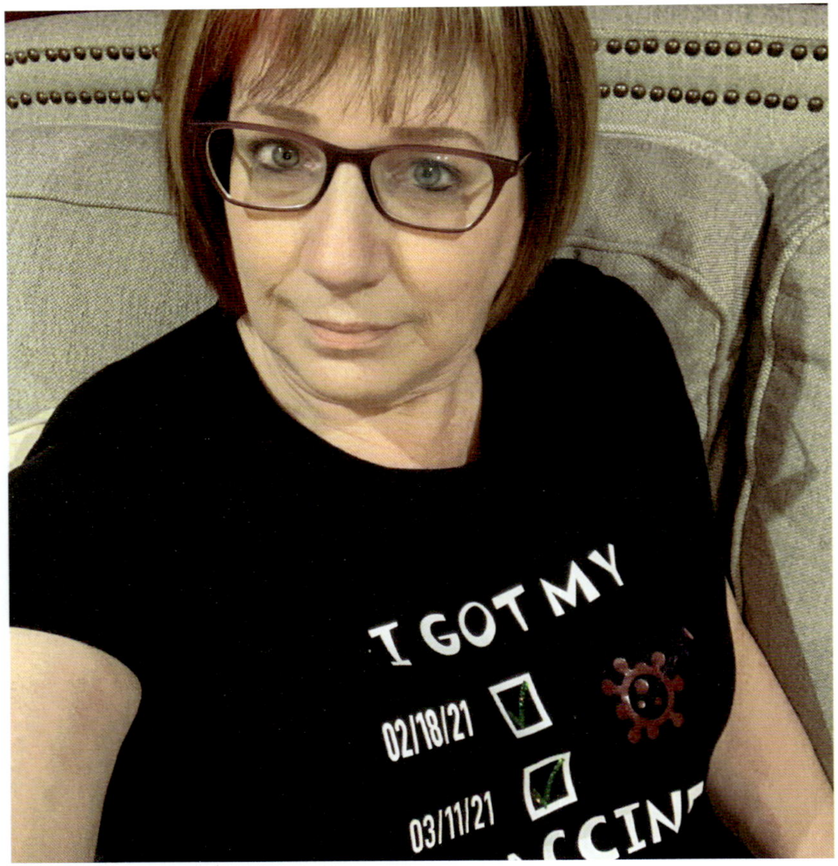

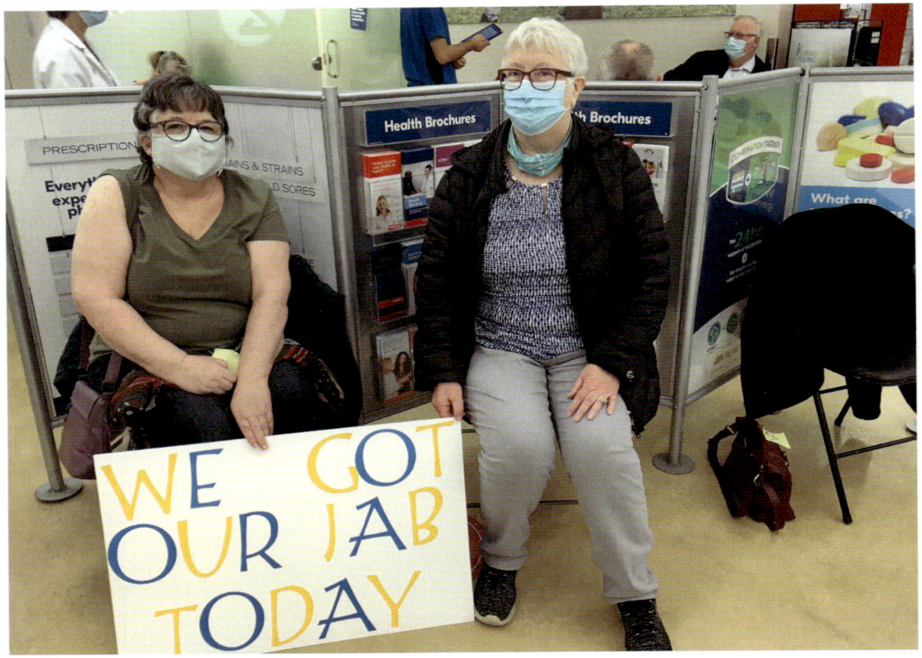

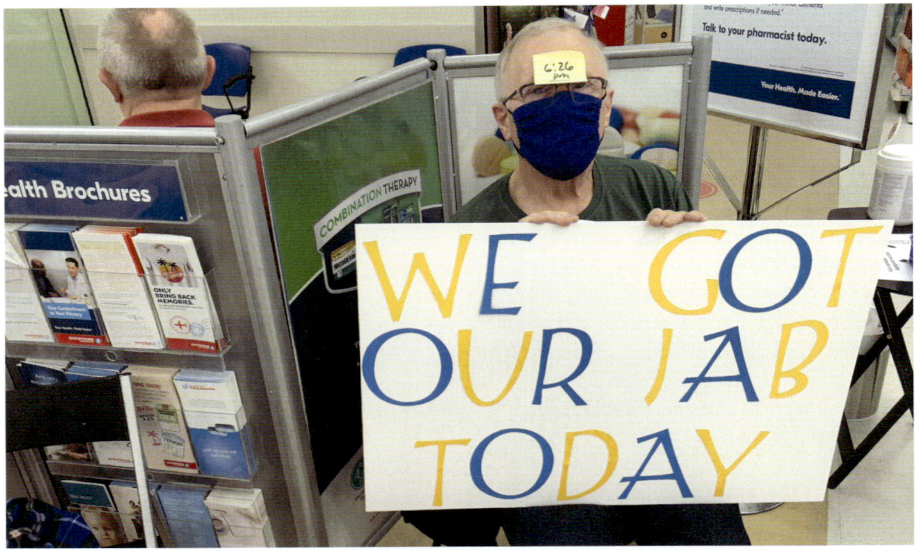

ABOVE: *Vicki MacBain, a continuing care assistant who works in long-term care and lives in Sheet Harbour writes, "I feel very privileged to be able to get both shots—not only to protect myself but also the many people I care for on a daily basis. Thank you, Nova Scotia!"* (**VICKI MACBAIN**)

TOP RIGHT: *Phyllis Murray (right), who works in the Nimbus office, was more than thrilled to receive her first dose of the vaccine. She's shown here with her friend Marge Pettipas of Shad Bay.*

BOTTOM RIGHT: *Phyllis's husband, Leonard Murray, says, "Note that Phyllis won the lottery, but she was more excited to get her COVID vaccination!"* (**PHYLLIS AND LEONARD MURRAY**)

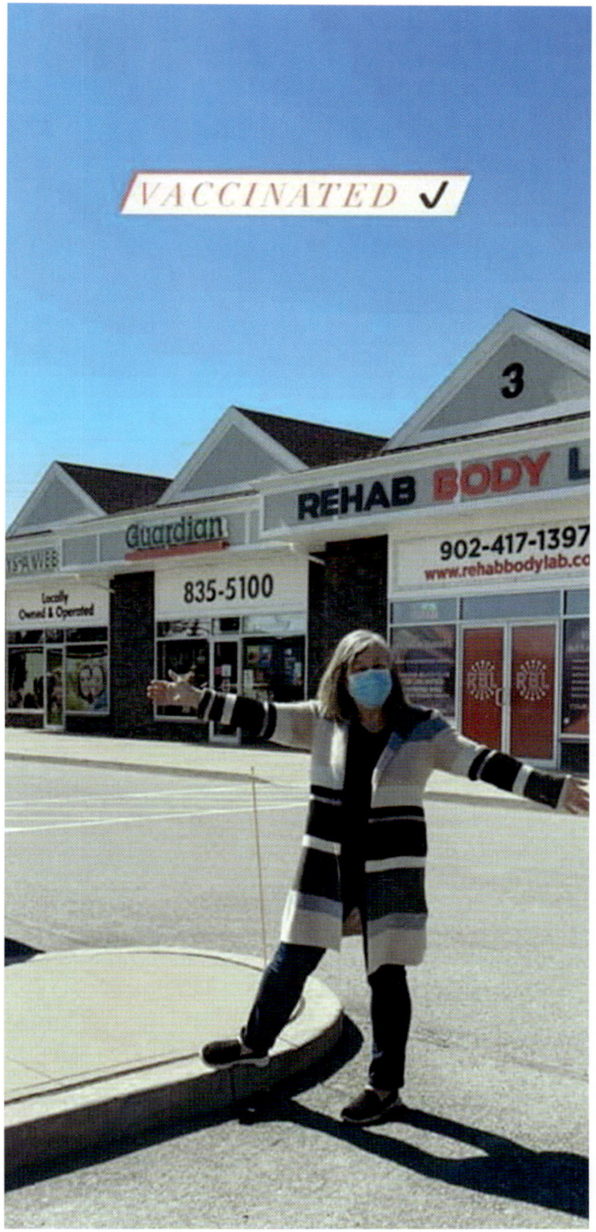

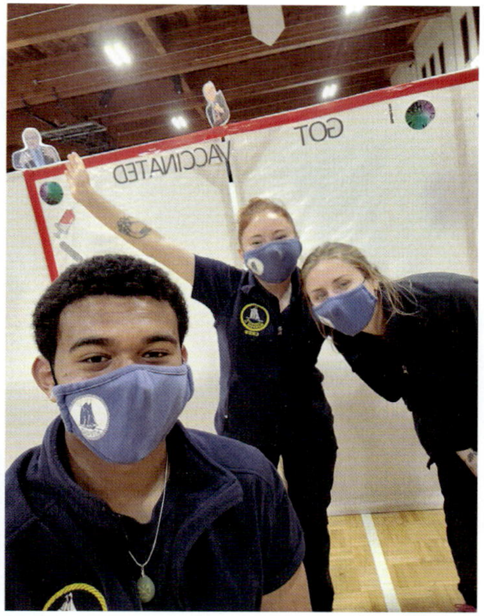

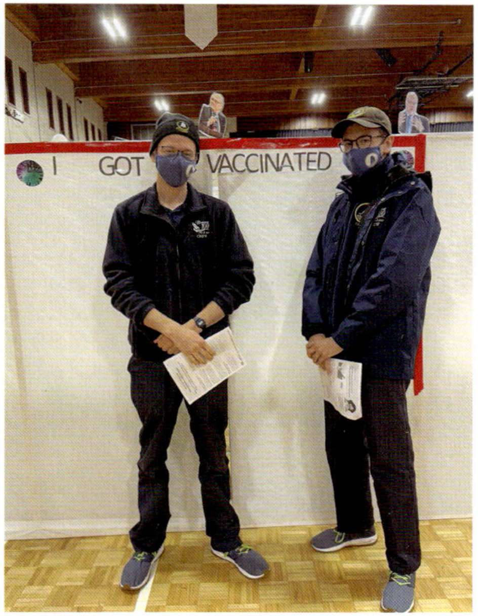

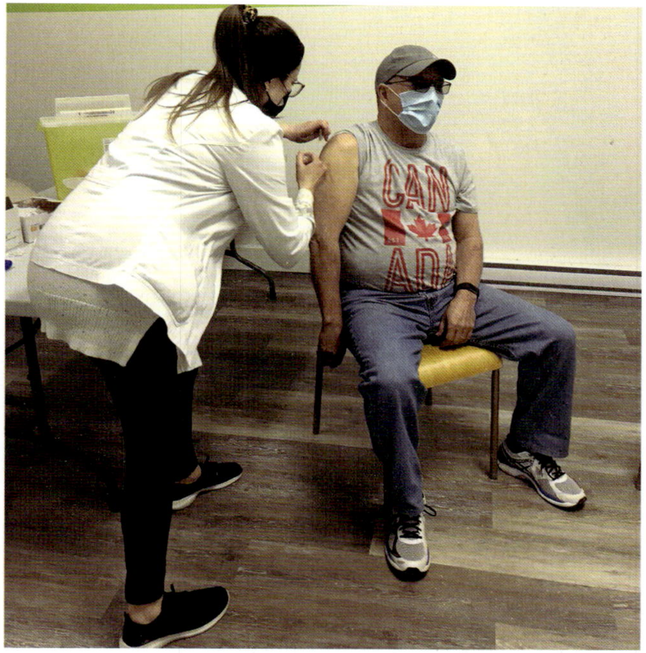

FAR LEFT: *Monique Tempelaars, of Bedford sent this image of herself after receiving her first dose of the AstraZeneca vaccine at a pharmacy in Hammonds Plains.* (**MONIQUE TEMPELAARS**)

CENTRE: *Emily Sollows, who does communications for* Bluenose II *wrote: "Here are some photos of the* Bluenose II *crew getting their first dose of the COVID-19 vaccine. Luckily, all crew members were able to receive their first dose just in time before setting sail for the* Bluenose 100 *Sail Past season."*
CENTRE TOP: *Maxwell Te-Scott (left), Leticia Taylor (centre), and Megan Milette (right).*
CENTRE BOTTOM: *Liam Oland (left) and Will Traves (right).* (**EMILY SOLLOWS**)

ABOVE: *Don Pottie of Halifax "got the jab" at Forest Hills Fellowship Baptist Church in Dartmouth.* (**DON POTTIE**)

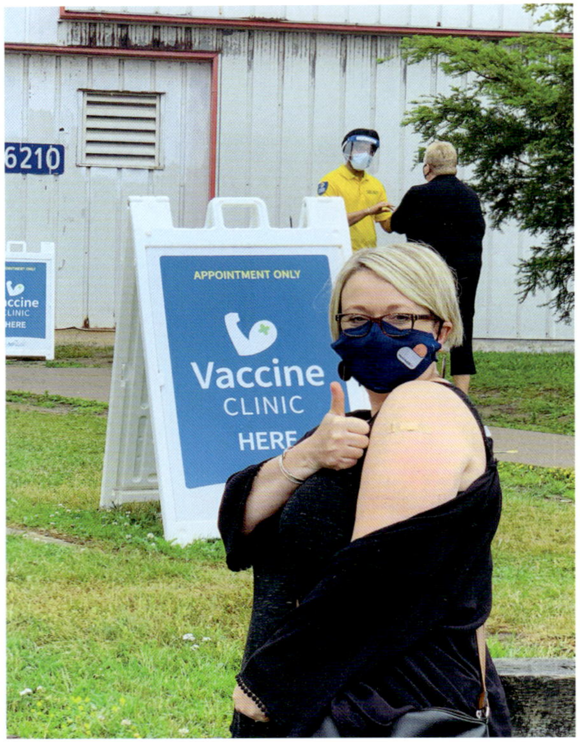

Angela Campbell of Halifax received her second dose at the Halifax Forum Multipurpose Room on July 9, 2021. "Today I received my second dose of Pfizer," she wrote. "To say I am happy is an understatement. I am the youngest of twelve siblings, and all of us have been 'double-dosed,' as has our eighty-six-year-old mother. This means more family gatherings are on the horizon, and more hugs from Mom. Things we took for granted sixteen months ago, but never will again. Happy? Yes!" (**ANGELA CAMPBELL**)

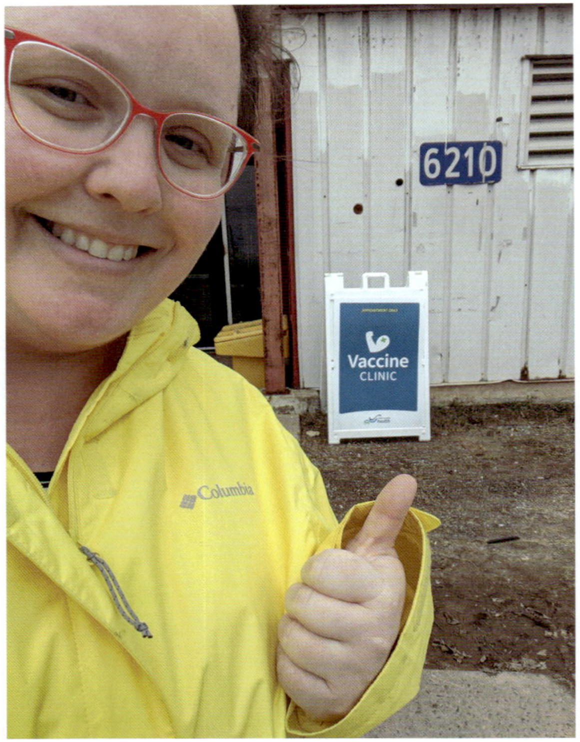

Grace McCreight, a public health nurse in central zone, writes, "For a month in the spring of 2021 I was deployed to give COVID-19 vaccines in Halifax and Dartmouth. This was a picture my first full day, where I was honoured to give eighteen first-dose vaccines, and to receive my own first dose as well. This was my favourite month worked since the pandemic began. In a career where I have worked in many different public health roles, both COVID-19 related and not, this was the most joy I had been around in a long time. Staff and clients alike were all filled with a buzz and a promise of the future." (**GRACE MCCREIGHT**)

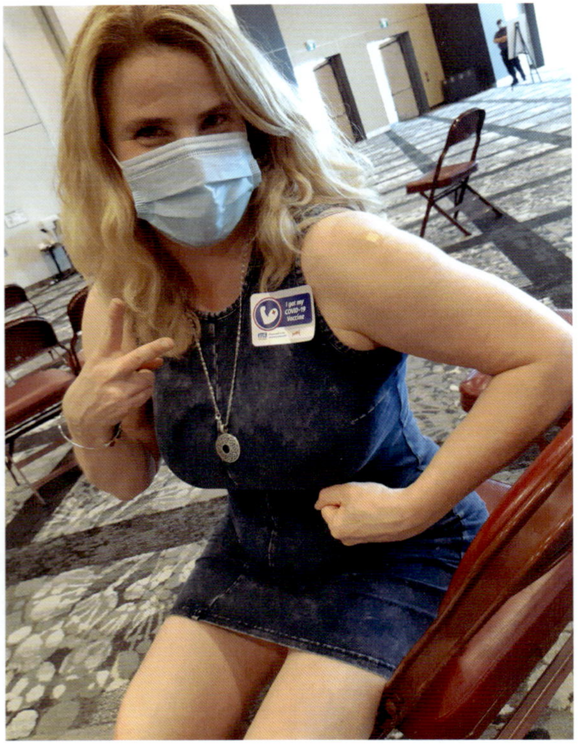

Terrilee Bulger is the co-owner of Nimbus Publishing. She received her second dose of the COVID-19 vaccine in late June. "My sister lives in a hotspot in Ontario," she says, "and she and her family caught COVID. Luckily for her, she had received her AstraZeneca vaccine a few days prior to testing positive. Her husband had not yet received his vaccine and had, therefore, not been so lucky. She had cold-like symptoms, while he ended up in ICU, so I took the first shot I could get, since even a few days can make a difference. I started with AZ and then followed with Moderna. I never would have guessed that I would be so excited to get a vaccine!" (**ANGELA MOMBOURQUETTE**)

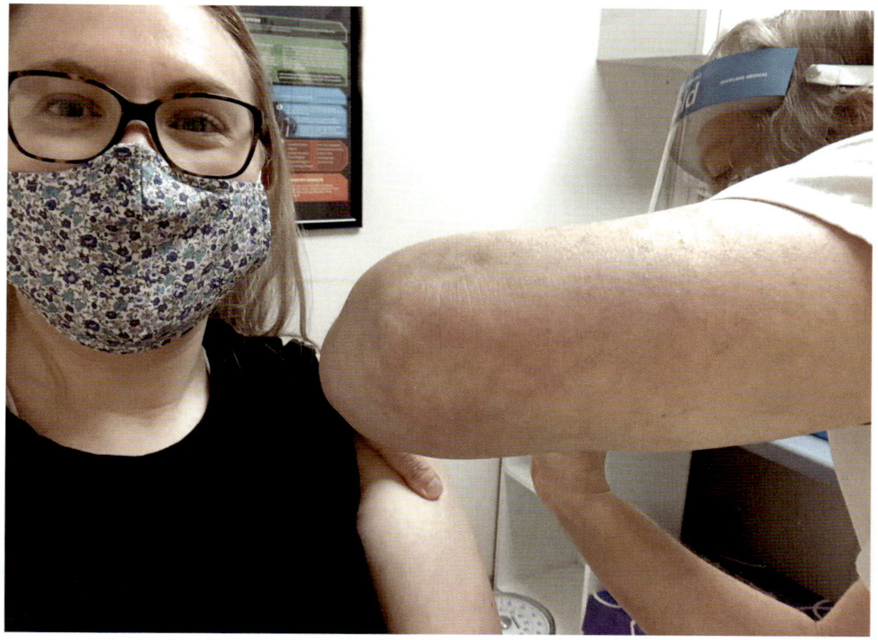

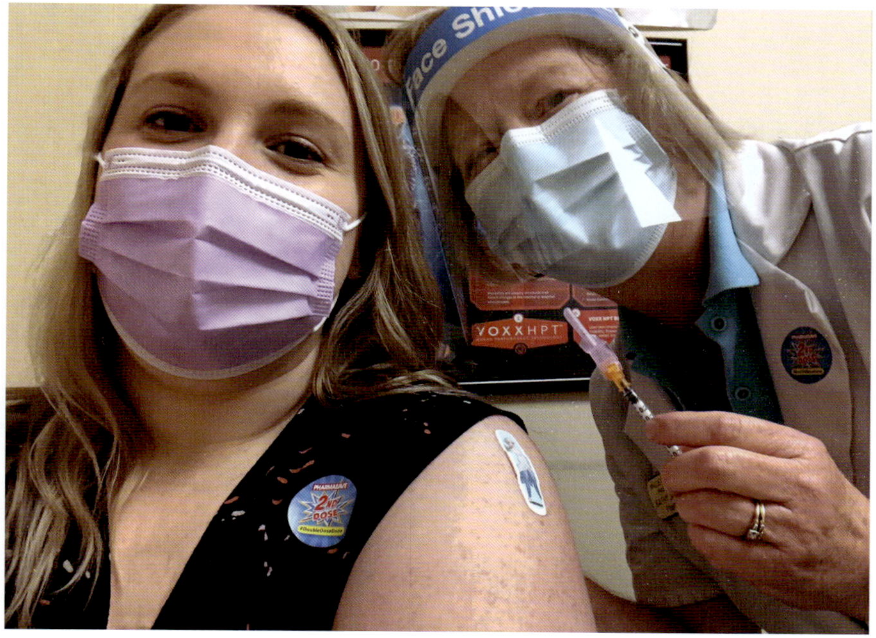

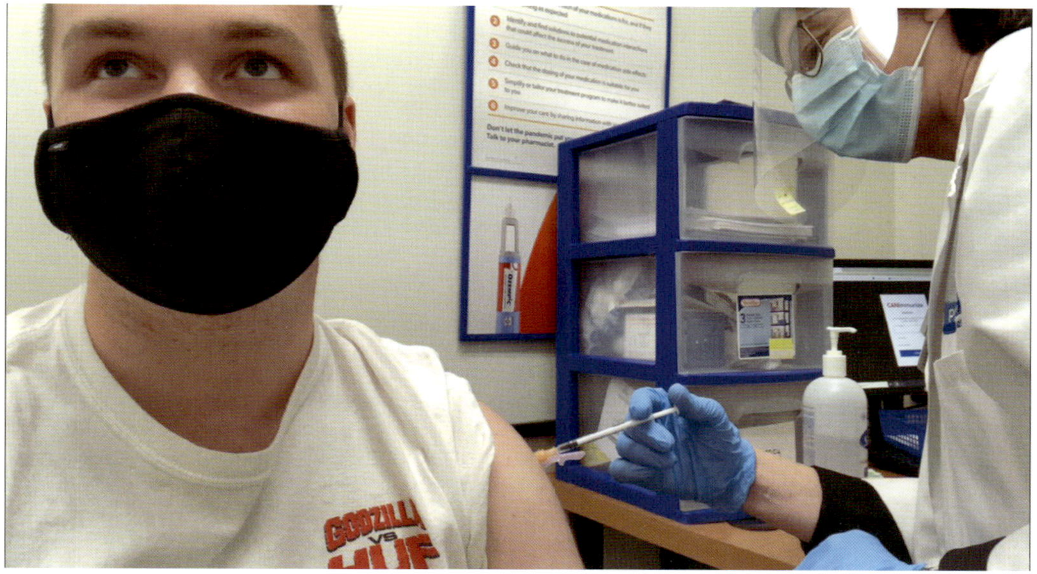

ABOVE LEFT AND RIGHT: *Adam Spurrell of Dartmouth writes, "The photos are of my mom (Kathy Spurrell) administering first and second doses to my sister (Amy Spurrell) at Kingston Pharmasave in Kingston. The year 2020 was my mom's fortieth year as a pharmacist there, and she was supposed to retire. When the pandemic hit and vaccines began, my mom continued to serve her community as she has for over forty years. She plans to continue until their vaccine clinic closes. She's the absolute best."* (**ADAM SPURRELL**)

LEFT: *Luke Ruelland from Eastern Passage writes, "Here is an image of me receiving my first dose of the vaccine on June 4, 2021, at Walmart in Bridgewater from a kind woman named Dawn. This was a special moment for me because it marked what seemed to be the start of the end of what was more or less a terrible time in our lives."* (**LUKE RUELLAND**)

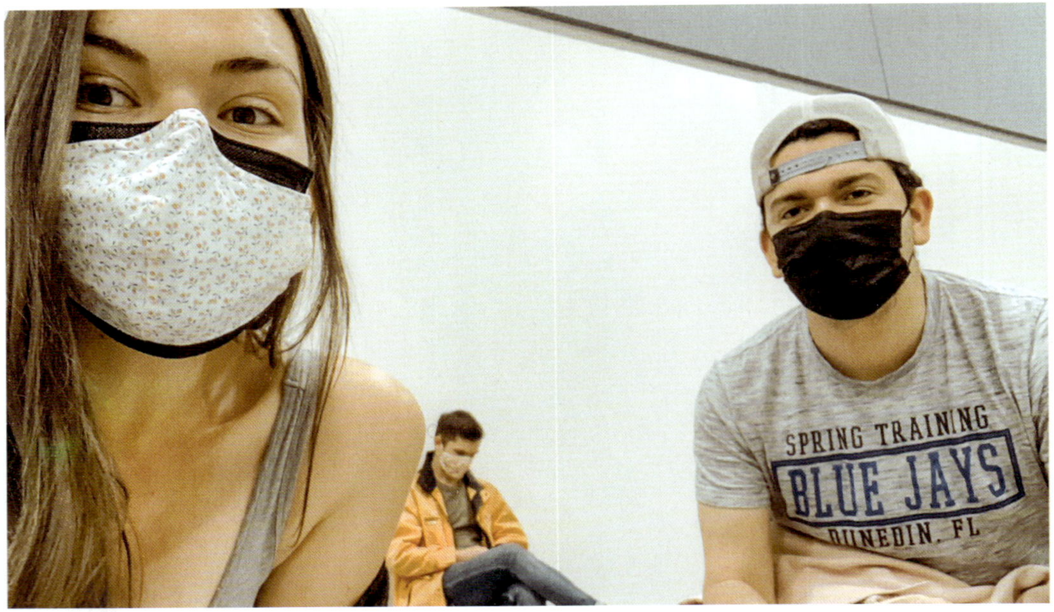

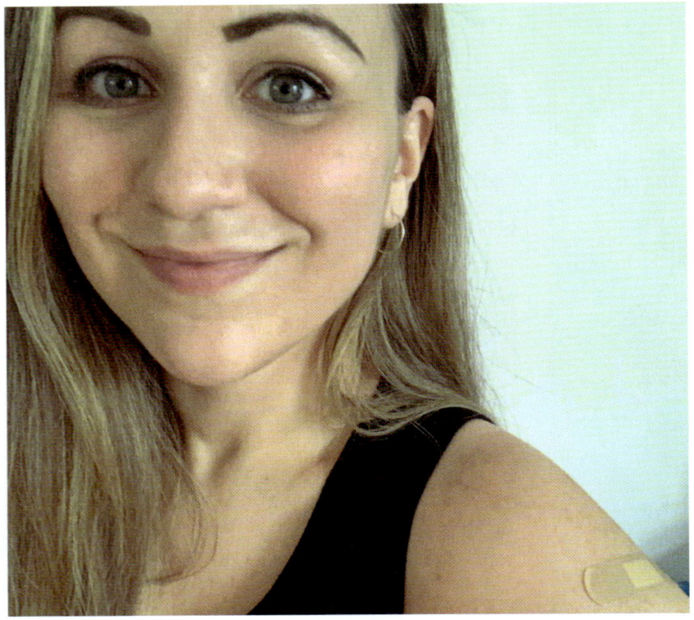

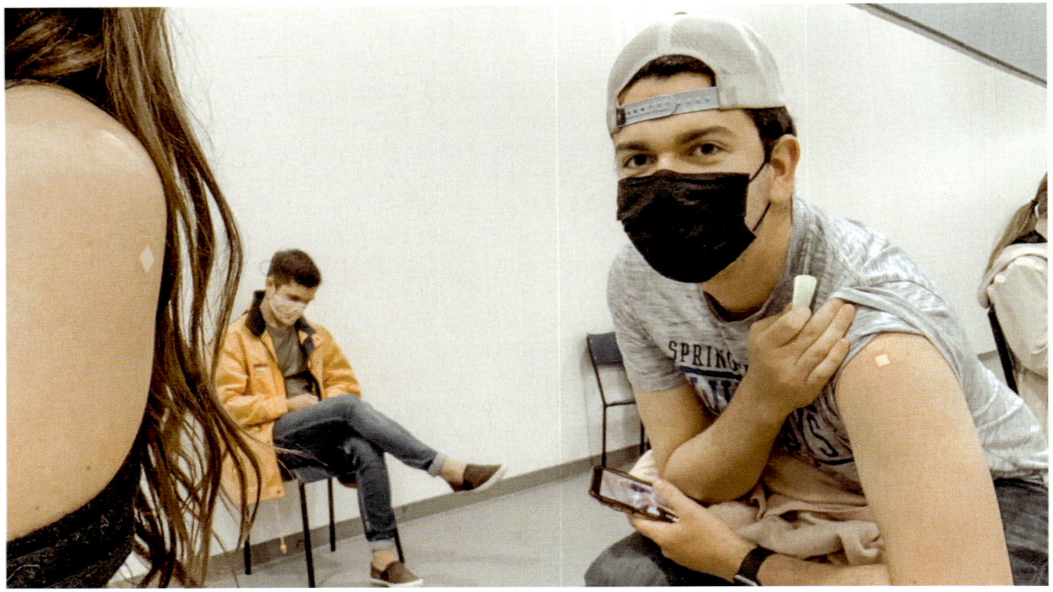

TOP LEFT AND BOTTOM LEFT: *Kaitlyn Cormier writes, "This is me and my boyfriend, Eli Moscovitch, proudly and excitedly showing off our fresh vaccines in Bridgewater, May 29, 2021—a date I'll remember forever!!"* (**KAITLYN CORMIER**)

TOP RIGHT: *Sacha Smith of Halifax writes, "This picture was from May 31, when I received my first dose of the Pfizer vaccine. Even now, trying to describe what getting this vaccine meant to me is difficult—there are a lot of thoughts and emotions packed into it. The third wave of COVID (and our third lockdown in HRM) was emotionally tough; personally, this was the hardest lockdown yet. Getting the first dose of the vaccine felt like a huge wave of relief; like gaining a sense of security. More than that, it brought about immense hope. Hope that I could see my family and friends again. Hope that our small businesses would be able to re-open and stick around as part of our communities for many years to come. Hope that we, as a province, a country and a global community, could overcome the pandemic together. ...It may have been gray and raining the day I got my first dose of the vaccine, but things sure felt pretty sunny when I left my appointment!"* (**SACHA SMITH**)

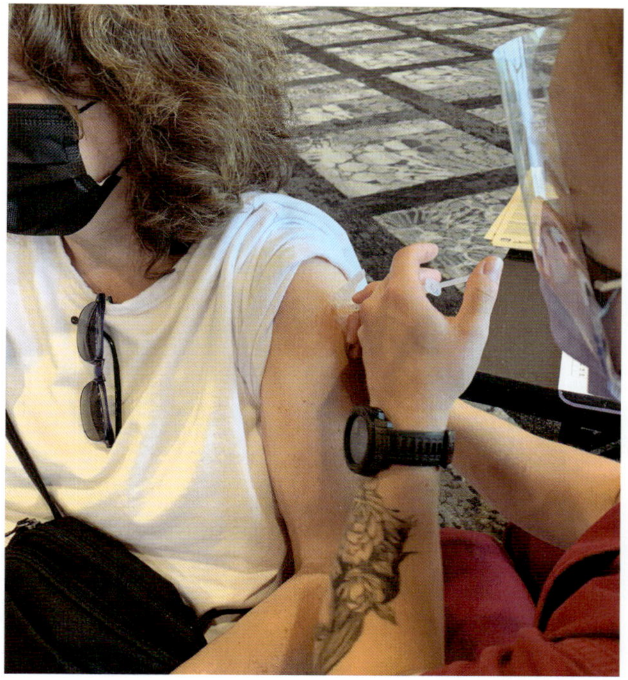

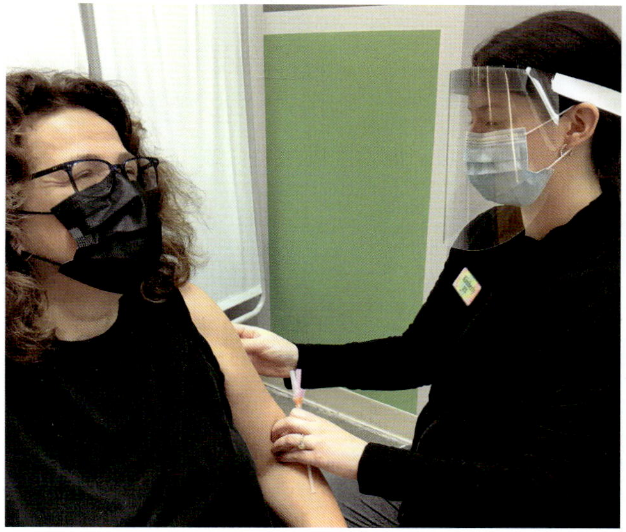

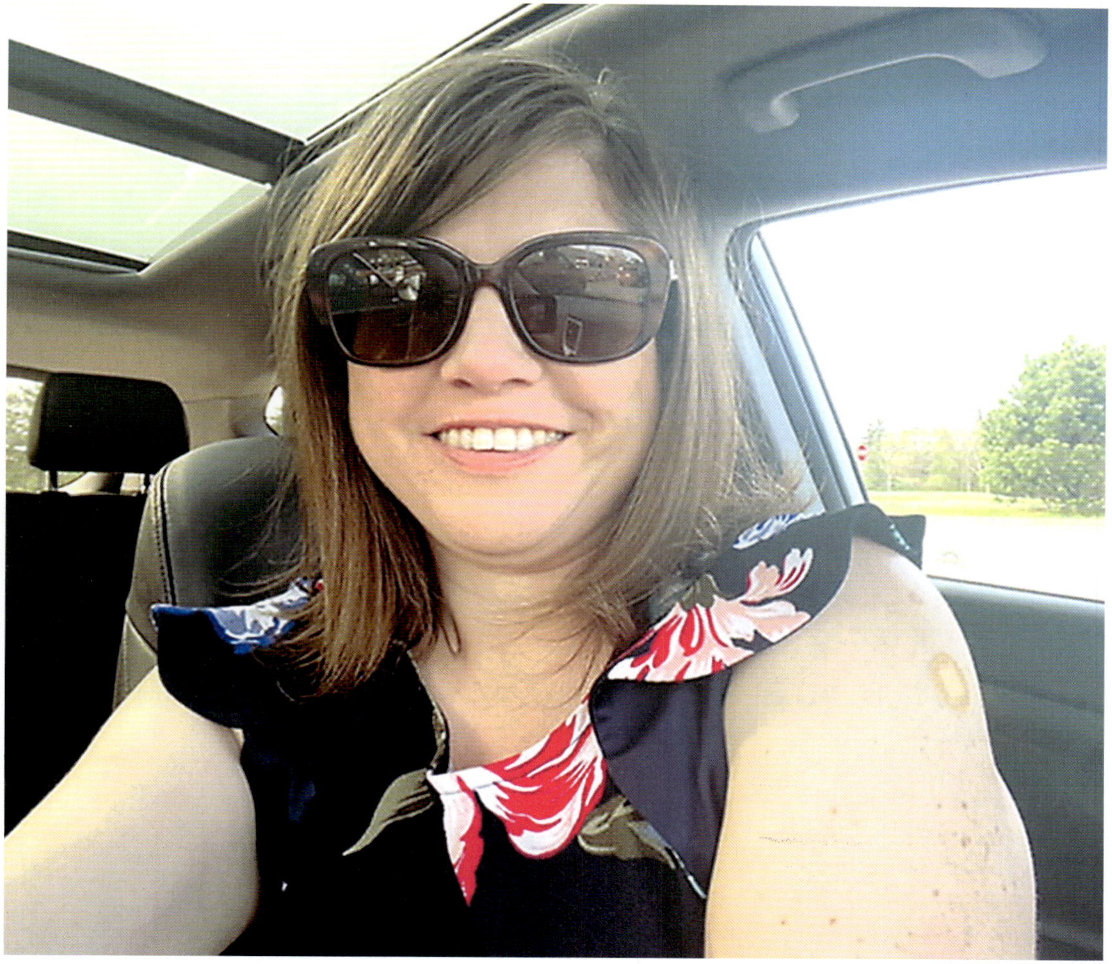

TOP LEFT AND BOTTOM LEFT: *Wendy Purves of Halifax was thrilled to receive her first and second doses. "I couldn't wait to receive my first dose of the vaccine—I knew how many people had died and how hard everyone in health care was working. I wanted to do my part to help not only myself but my community. When I received my second dose, I felt a huge sense of relief to be double-vaccinated and to live in a country where that was available to me.* (**WENDY PURVES**)

ABOVE: *Tina Thibeau of Tantallon says, "I was so excited to get my vaccine on May 20th and be part of our way forward."* (**TINA THIBEAU**)

IN THE DRIVER'S SEAT:
Allison Flemming

A lineup of cars snakes between the orange pylons in the parking lot outside the Rath Eastlink Community Centre in Truro. Workers in fluorescent safety vests approach each vehicle, and after registration and a few quick questions each car moves ahead to the vaccination area. The car door swings open and a hypodermic needle is quickly poked into the driver's shoulder. If there are passengers who have also been screened, they, too, get poked. The car is then ushered to a parking area to wait out the fifteen-minute post-vaccination period. If anyone starts to feel unwell, they are told to let the workers know with a honk of their horn.

Allison Flemming, an emergency-room nurse for the last eighteen years, is the team lead at this clinic. She says the drive-through clinics were originally set up for people with reduced mobility, but they became popular for many other unexpected reasons.

"A lot of people are coming with small children. We had someone come through who had a seven-day-old baby with them—not something they wanted to bring into a clinic that has a lot of traffic. They felt safe, and that's somebody that probably wouldn't have been able to get vaccinated," Flemming says.

"We have other people who have sensory challenges, and we've had such great feedback from families saying it's been the best vaccination that they've been able to achieve for their family member or the person in their care."

For Flemming, her experience dealing with all kinds of situations in the emergency department enabled her to rise to the challenges of the clinic. She says she was flattered to be asked to take on the role and to be part of something so different from her regular job.

"We're just connecting with so many people every day. We have 420 appointments today," she says, looking around at the almost festive atmosphere in the parking lot. "It's a very positive environment around here as well; people are very excited to get their vaccines."

A nurse calls over and asks if the next tray of vaccines is ready. Flemming nods and heads toward the command trailer.

"I think it's wonderful for the people that wouldn't otherwise be able to get vaccinated, she says, a smile radiating from behind her mask. "I'm a part of them bettering their future."

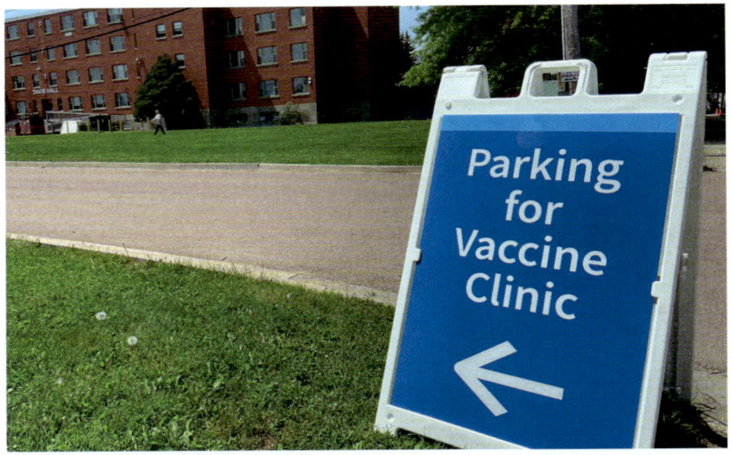

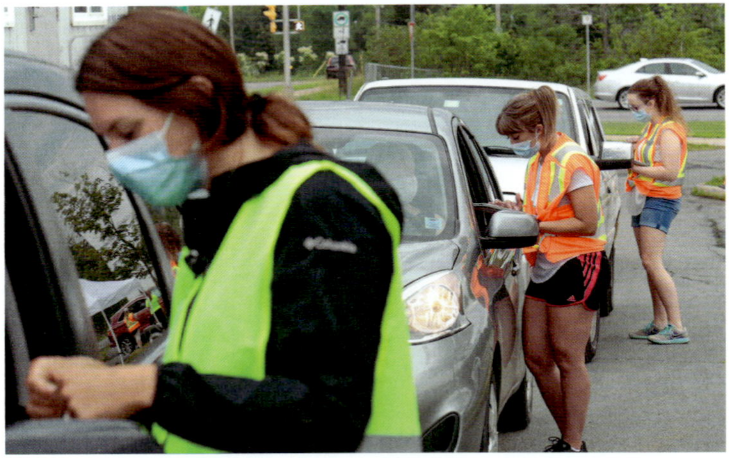

ABOVE: *From left: Hillie Smith, LPN, Alice Chaisson, RN, and Kimberly Brown, RN, greet clients as they arrive at the drive-through vaccination clinic at the Rath Eastlink Community Centre in Truro.*

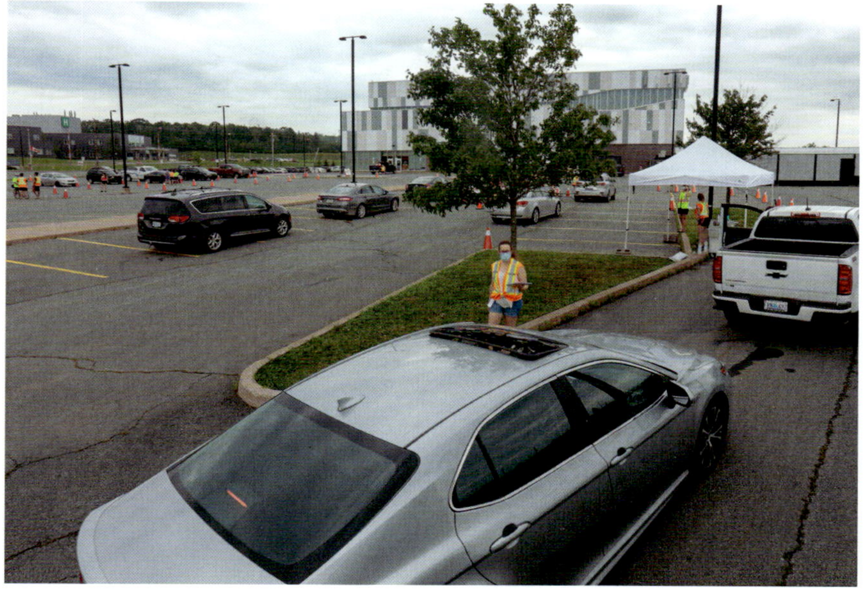

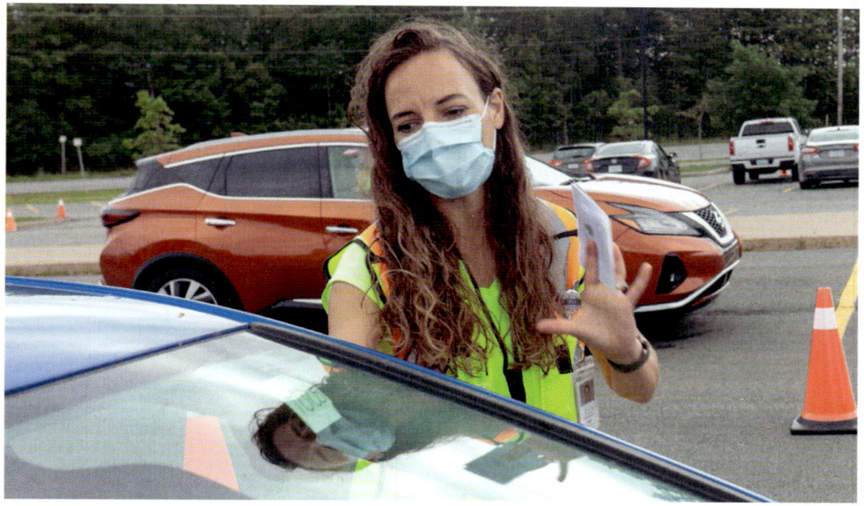

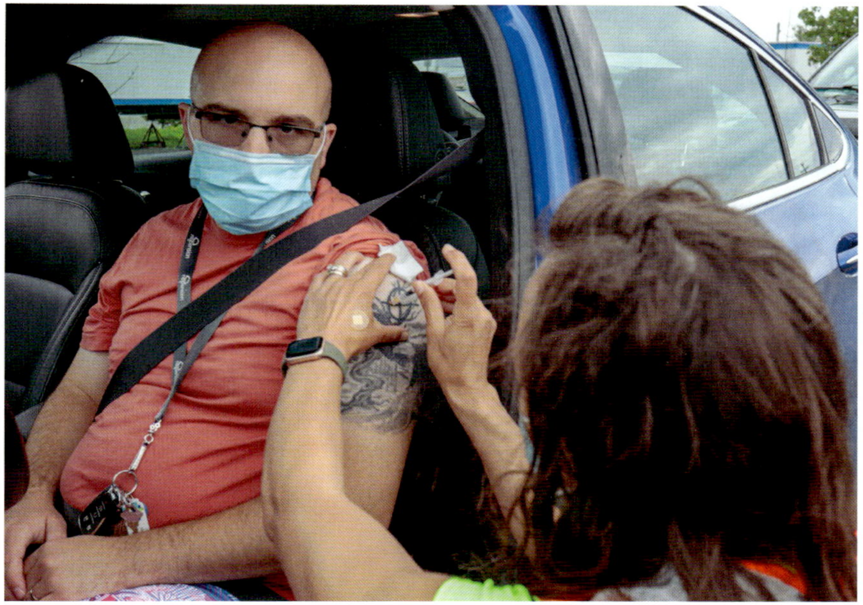

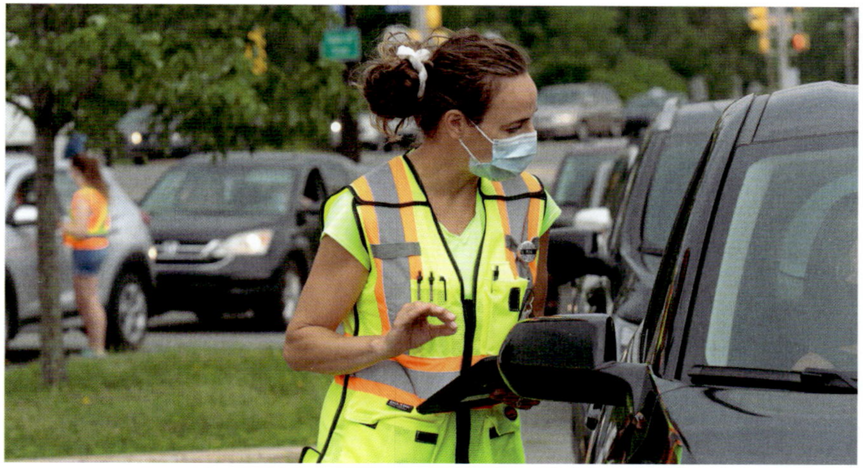

BOTTOM LEFT: *Joshua Creelman of Truro receives his COVID-19 vaccination. "It's important for members of society to vaccinate themselves against possible infection to make us all safe," Creelman says.*

TOP AND BOTTOM RIGHT: *Team lead Allison Flemming, RN, explains the procedure to patients as they arrive at the drive-through clinic in Truro.*

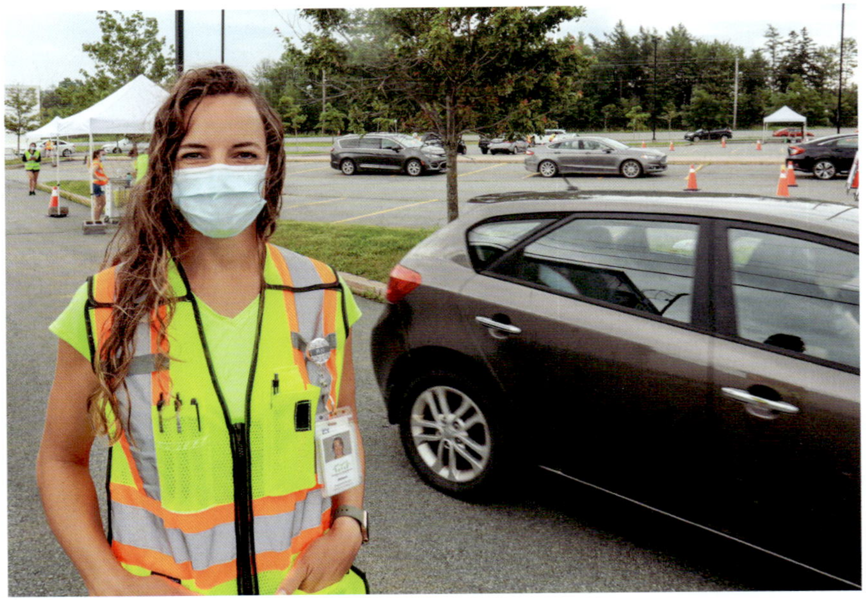

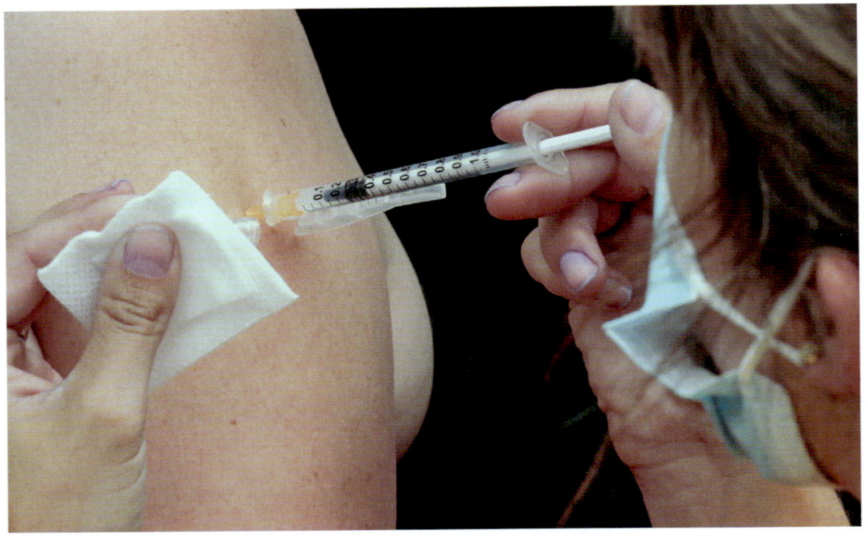

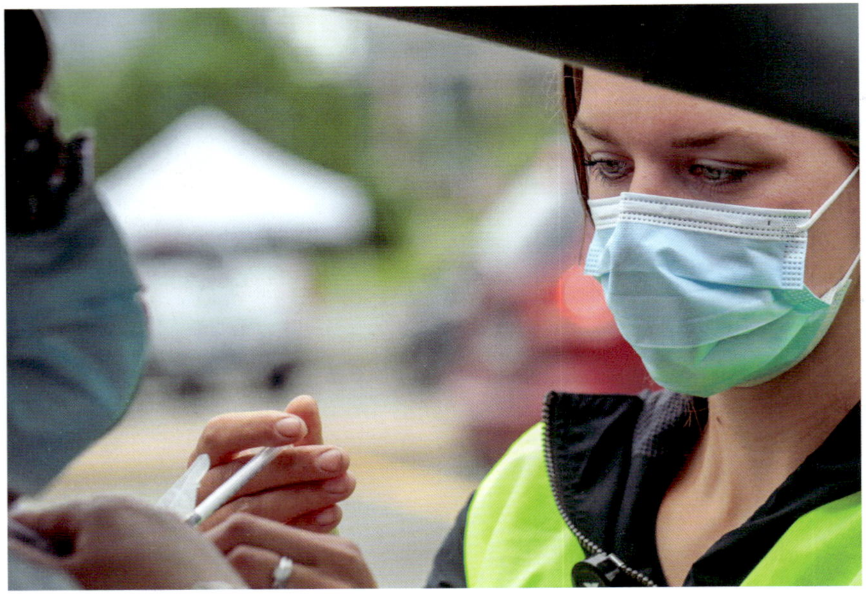

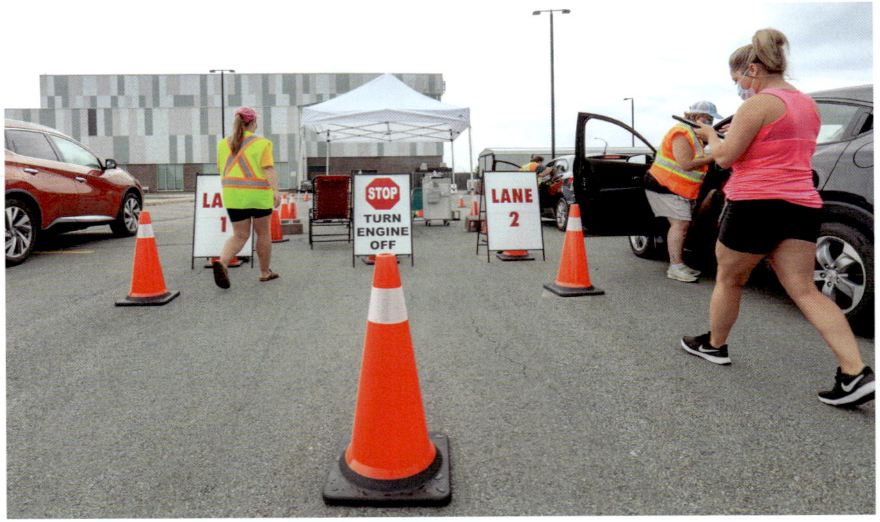

TOP LEFT: *Allison Flemming oversees the clinic.*
TOP RIGHT AND BOTTOM LEFT: *Hillie Smith vaccinates a client.*
BOTTOM RIGHT: *The busy drive-through vaccination clinic at the Rath Eastlink Community Centre in Truro.*

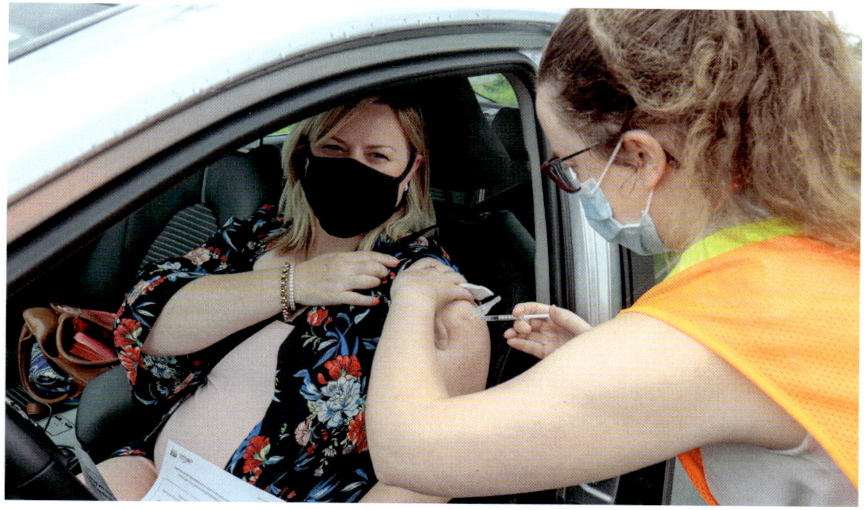

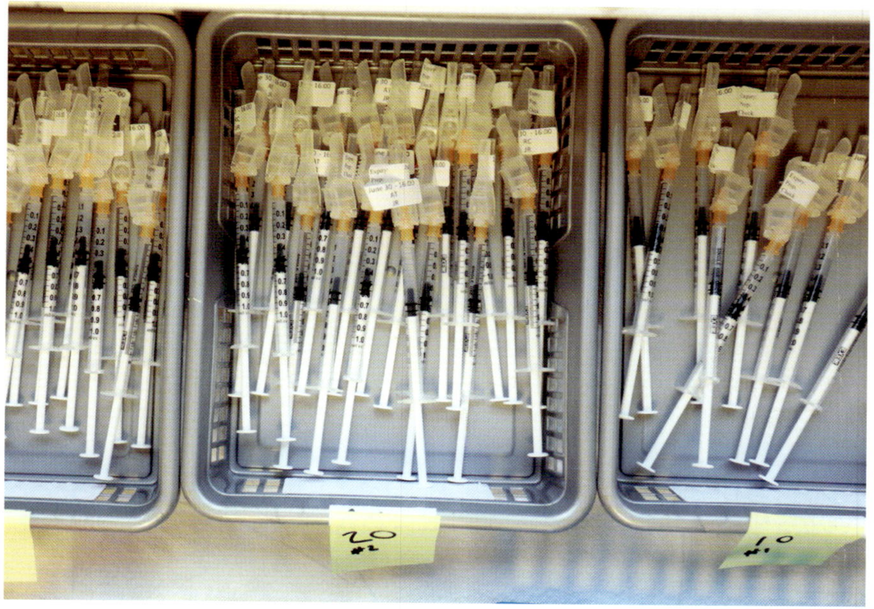

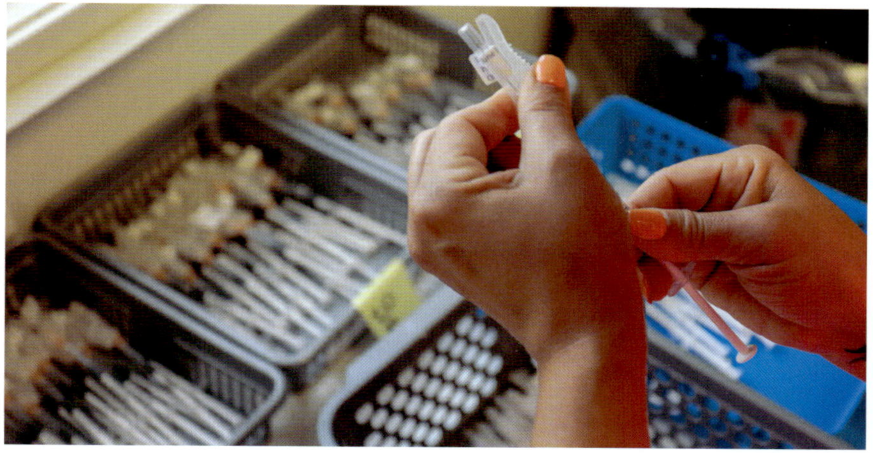

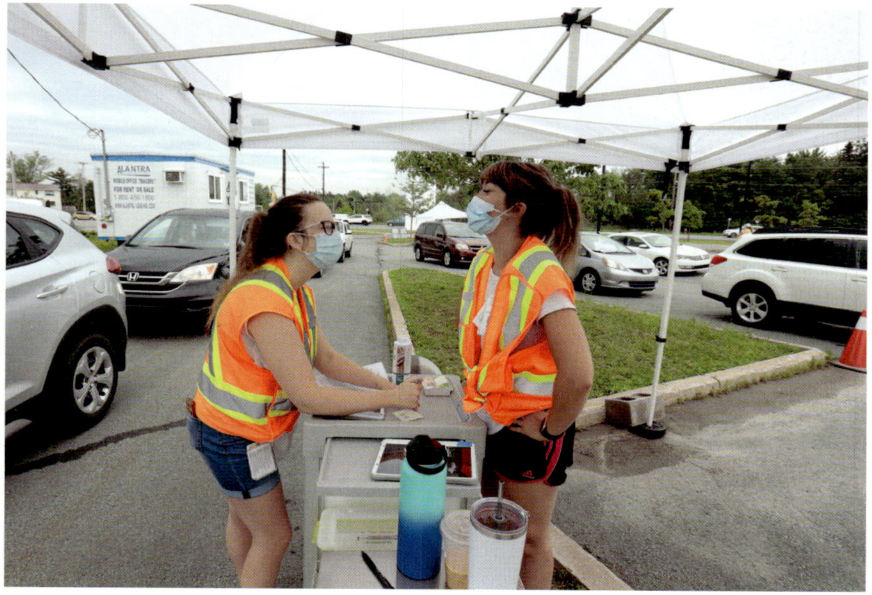

TOP LEFT: *Trish Langille of Elmsdale said she felt "free" after she received her second shot.*

TOP RIGHT AND BOTTOM LEFT: *A nurse prepares vials of vaccine in batches of twenty for use at the drive-through clinic.*

BOTTOM RIGHT: *Nurses Alice Chaisson and Kimberly Brown share a moment of levity.*

A VOICE FOR HIS COMMUNITY:

Athanasius "Tanas" Sylliboy

Registered nurse Athanasius "Tanas" Sylliboy was just finishing the student hours he needed to complete his Master of Nursing nurse practitioner program at Dalhousie University when COVID-19 arrived in Nova Scotia. Sylliboy is from the Mi'kmaw community of Eskasoni in Cape Breton, and was working at the community health centre in Eskasoni when the pandemic began.

Even before the entire province was put under lockdown in late March 2020, Eskasoni's chief and council had enacted a lockdown to limit movement to and from the reserve.

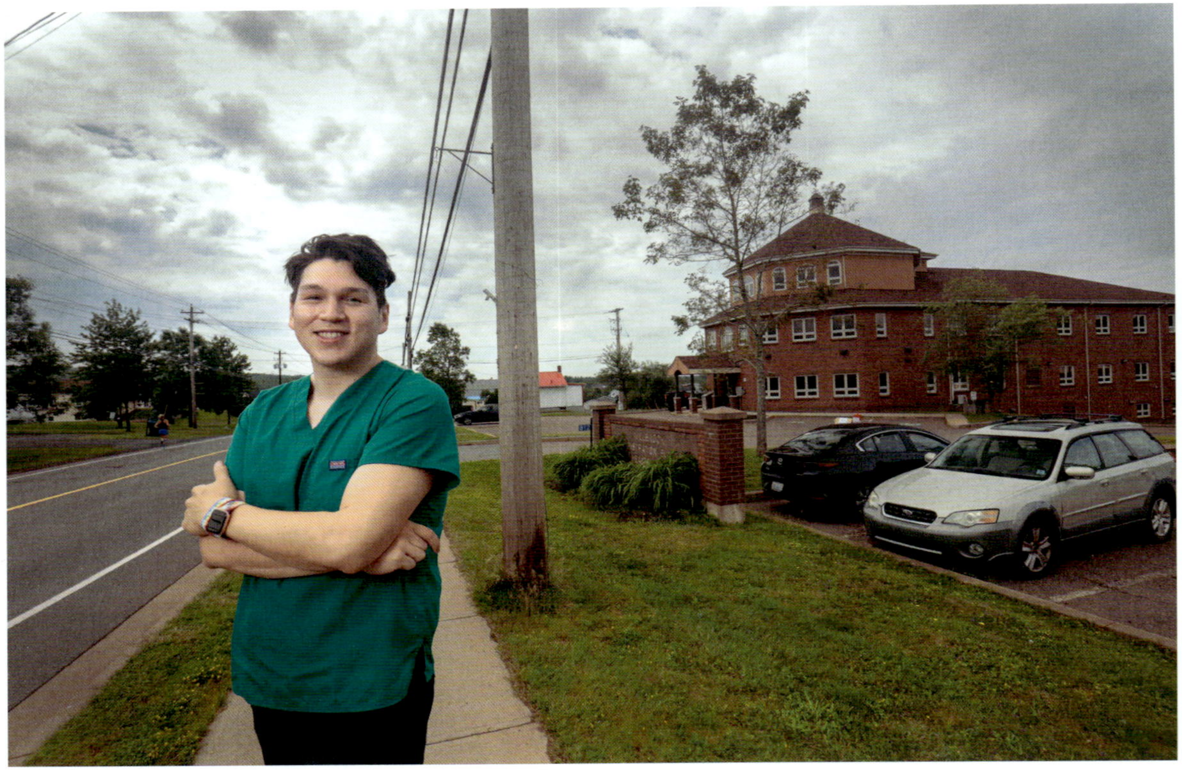

Sylliboy understood why. "We have overcrowding, inadequate housing, and poor access to health services, which is really a perfect storm for this virus to gain entry to our communities. We have people undergoing chemotherapy, people who are immunocompromised, people who have just had surgery," he says.

As a medical practitioner, he wanted to find a way to communicate to Indigenous communities how they could best avoid spreading the virus—and do it in a way that integrated Indigenous perspectives and knowledge with western knowledge.

So he designed a series of posters—like the kind we've all seen in hospitals that remind people to wash their hands or to avoid visiting high-risk individuals—using Mi'kmaw words. He and his mother then headed out to deliver those posters to the homes of Elders in the community. It wasn't long before the idea began to spread via social media; other communities began to request the posters, and Sylliboy had requests from as far away as British Columbia.

"I just thought it was one of those small ideas that turned out to be a big solution in terms of

Athanasius "Tanas" Sylliboy created signage using Mi'kmaw words to help communicate health and safety-related messages around COVID-19 in Indigenous communities.

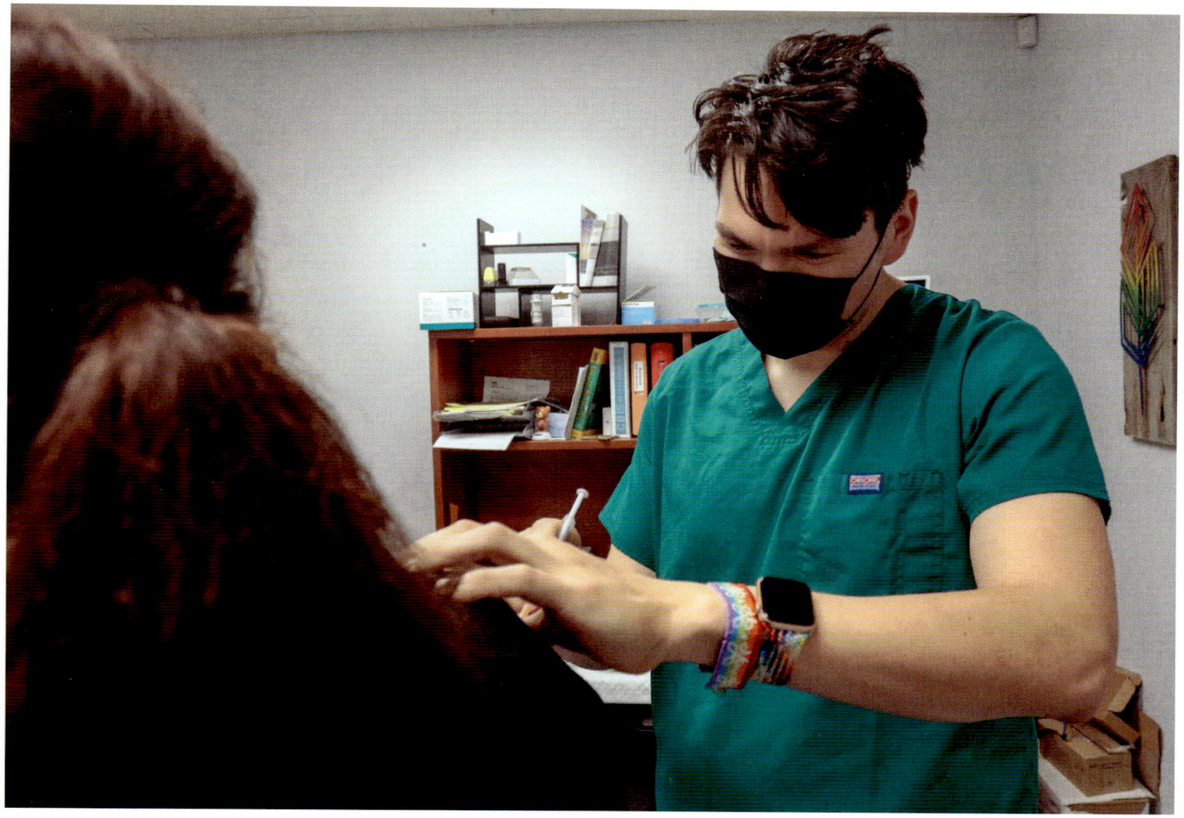

Tanas Sylliboy was working at the community health centre in Eskasoni when the pandemic began; he now works at the health centre in Millbrook First Nation.

protecting each other and working for each other. And everyone really bought into it," he says. "Everyone was putting their posters up to say, 'No visitors at this time.'"

He says he can't stress enough the importance of delivering health-care messages in the language spoken in that community.

"If information is dispersed in a language that is not the first language of an individual, there's potential for miscommunication. An example I heard for the case of COVID—'COVID' does sound similar to one of our words, which is 'beaver,' and the misinformation got to a point where one elder thought there was a virus being spread by beavers," he says.

"In the past, things have been done without consulting our communities. And when it actually gets to us, either it doesn't make sense or it's not purposeful, or it's not really valid in terms of what's being asked of our community."

Sylliboy says his passion has always been to decrease the barriers and improve the lives of the people in his community, and he acknowledges that the history of racism and discrimination in Canada has created a sense of distrust around health care.

"We don't need people coming into the community and saying, 'This is what we're going to do; this is what I think your needs are or what I think the solution to those needs is.' So I think being a voice for our own communities is really important. And I really feel like it's a valuable asset in terms of repairing this broken bridge between health care in Canada and First Nations people or Indigenous people in general."

Sylliboy was awarded a Dr. Robert Strang Community Hero Award in 2021 for developing his posters and creating educational videos in both English and Mi'kmaw; he also helped develop a COVID-19 community education hotline. He now works at the health centre in Millbrook First Nation, and he says he sees a similar sense of community there as people show up to get vaccinated.

"It's the communities that I'm very proud of. Anyone can make a poster. It's the willingness to be here for each other. And I always say, there's a word—apoqonmatimg—which means we are working together. We are here for each other," he says.

"As Indigenous people, we are a social community.... I think everyone really stepped up. That's the true value of how we protected ourselves in the end, because everyone was really listening to what was being asked of them."

COMING TO A COMMUNITY NEAR YOU: *Holly Gillis*

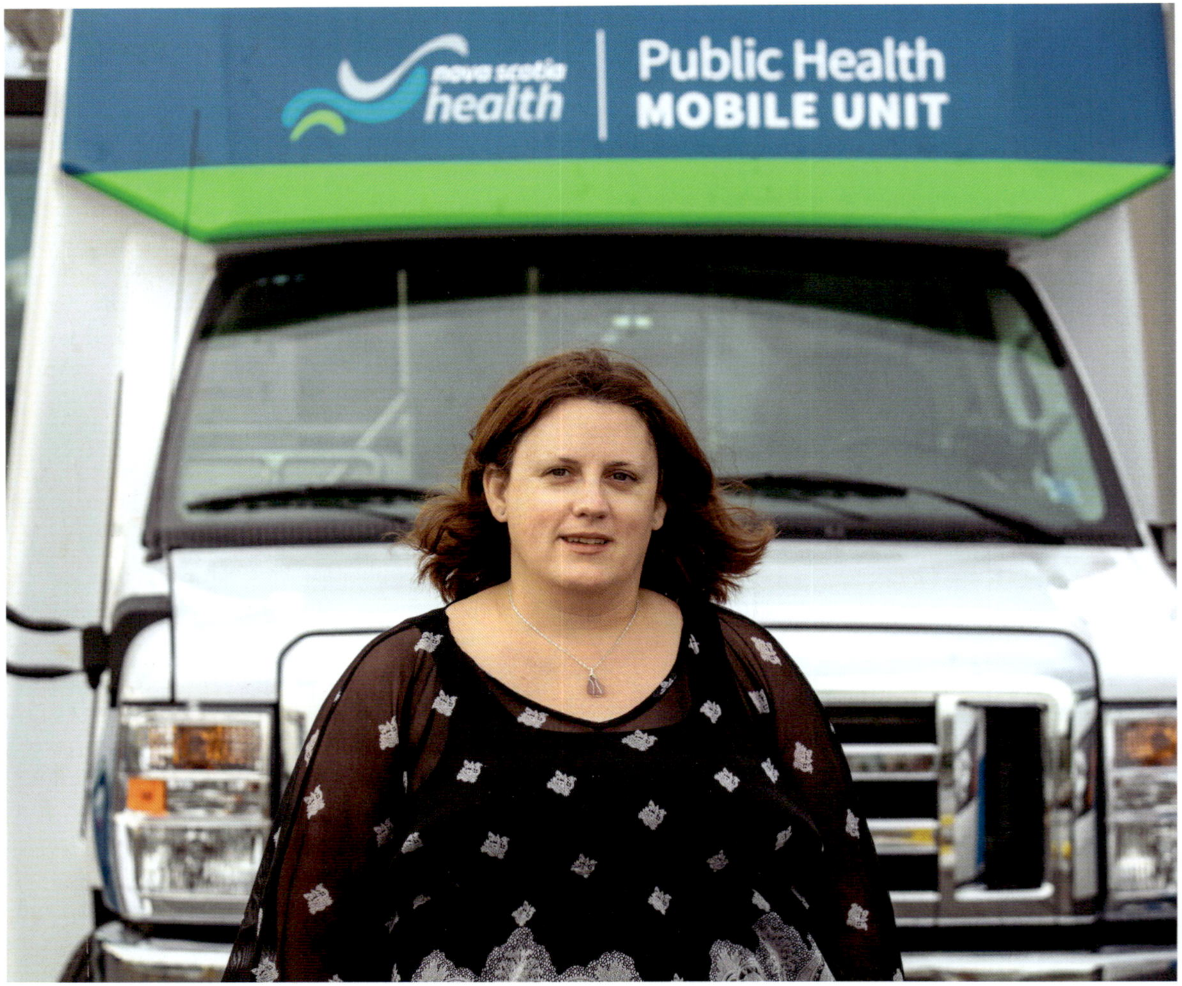

Testing and vaccination have been essential components of Nova Scotia's winning strategy in the battle against COVID-19, and for Nova Scotians who live in the Halifax Regional Municipality, it's been relatively easy to access both. But for those who live outside HRM, particularly in rural and remote communities, getting tested or vaccinated has not been quite as simple.

Enter the Nova Scotia Health Authority's Public Health Mobile Unit—a fleet of ten 20-by-22–foot vans that deliver community-based testing and vaccination to various locations across the province.

Holly Gillis is the director of the Public Health Mobile Unit. She agrees testing has been one of the huge successes of Nova Scotia's pandemic response. "The more hundreds and thousands of Nova Scotians that come out to get tested, that really helps us build the early warning system so we can see COVID activity and then clamp it down really quickly," she says. "The great thing about the mobile units is that we can go where the community needs us to go.... We can go to people's homes, we can go to multi-unit apartment buildings. We can go to communities, to playgrounds, to waterfronts, and bring testing wherever we think there might be some COVID activity."

Holly Gillis is the director of the Public Health Mobile Unit—a fleet of ten 20-by-22–foot vans that offer community-based testing and vaccination in various locations across the province.

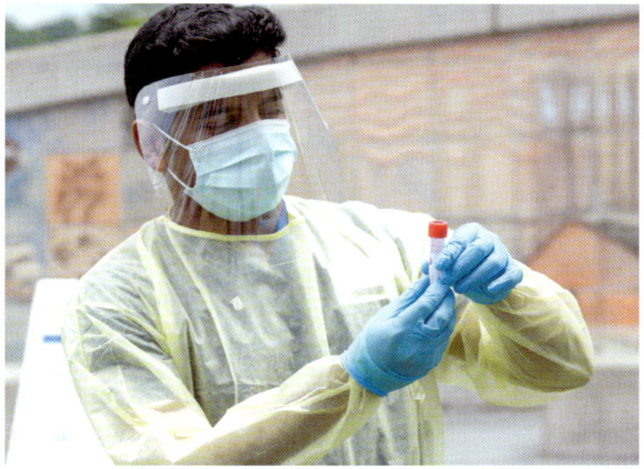

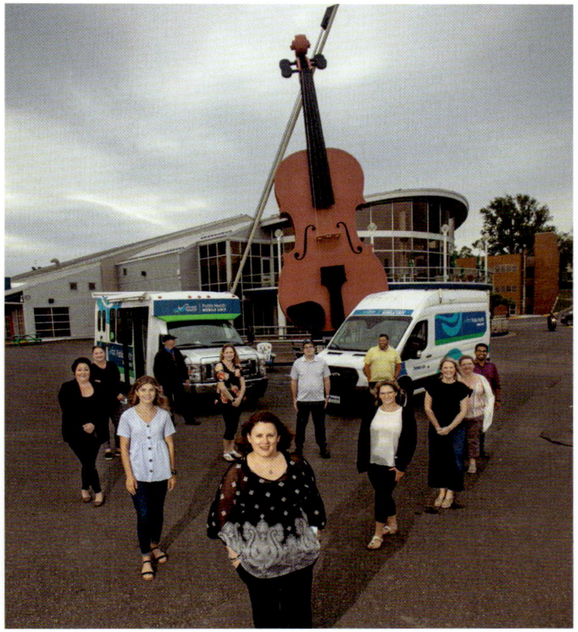

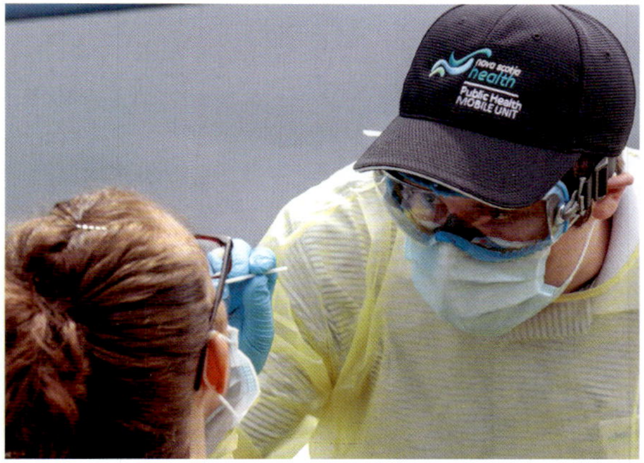

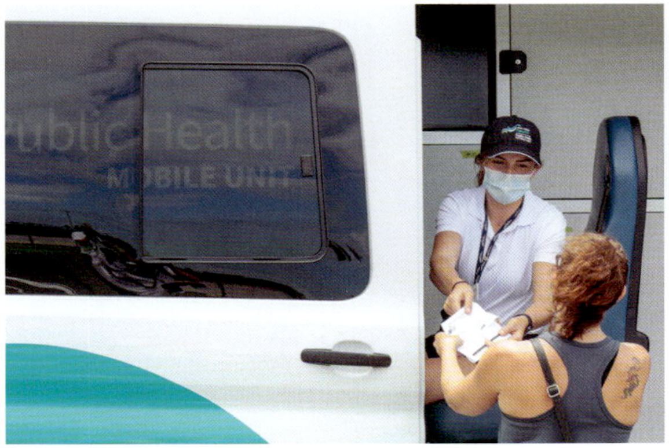

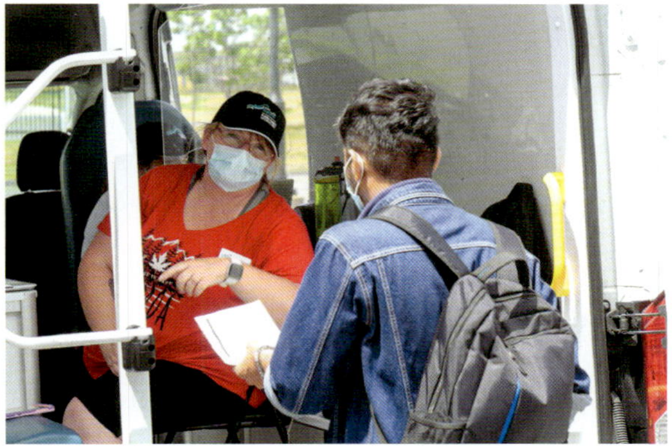

THIS PAGE AND NEXT PAGE: *The Public Health Mobile Unit performs COVID-19 testing in Sydney.* TOP LEFT: *Danny Joseph.* BOTTOM LEFT: *Hannah O'Callaghan.* TOP RIGHT: *Kory Coffin.* BOTTOM RIGHT: *Lisa Robinson.* NEXT PAGE TOP LEFT: *Patel Farhin.*

It's a tool that's been used before in Nova Scotia—but not for quite some time. In the 1940s, mobile health units travelled the roads of the province with x-ray machines, looking for patients with tuberculosis. Today, the ten vans—six for mobile testing and four for mobile vaccination—follow some of those same roads.

"Public health has always been a mobile workforce," says Gillis. "We go into homes to help with health protection, or for families that have had a baby. We spend a lot of time in community. So we've always had that mobile element."

Gillis has five teams that span the province and can "really go anywhere the epidemiology needs us to go," says Gillis. On this particular day there were four testing units around the province in communities testing between five- and six hundred people.

"The team is amazing. They're incredible humans who don't know where they're working two days down the road, but they're okay with that. They watch their email for our 'bat signal,' as we call it, and then they just go," she says. "They've travelled; they've left their families. They've slept in hotels, they've stood out in the -30° wind-chill and in the +30° temperatures. The people working on this program are incredible."

Sometimes when the units arrive in a community, they discover that the barrier to access isn't just location. "I remember one day we were at a fire hall in a community that had had some increased

COVID activity," Gillis says. She started chatting with a woman in her seventies who told Gillis it was her first COVID test.

"I asked her what brought her out, and she said it was the fact that we were set up in her community. She couldn't go to the hospital because her husband had died there in the fall and she didn't feel comfortable going there, but she felt comfortable going down the road. And she was doing her part because Dr. Strang said to," Gillis says, adding she's also had people with anxiety or agoraphobia express that they are more comfortable coming to the mobile units than to formal testing or vaccination sites.

She points out that it's the willingness on the part of Nova Scotians to step up that makes these efforts worthwhile.

"Testing is great, and it's awesome to be able to offer a health service, but it wouldn't exist if Nova Scotians didn't come out," she says. "We can build vans, we can build clinics, we can say you should get COVID-tested, but ... what keeps a lot of us going is that Nova Scotians keep showing up and keep rolling with what we ask."

Gillis says she's beyond proud of her team for making the mobile units work as a key part of the province's COVID response.

"I have a huge sense of pride for what we've accomplished, and I feel really honoured to be a small part of a great response to a really unknown time in our history," she says. "I think as we move through this into the 'after-times' of COVID and we reflect on things, a lot of what we remember will truly be the kindness and the compassion—how we've treated each other as a work team, but also as a community, at a really vulnerable time."

She smiles. "I'm extremely proud to be a Nova Scotian right now."

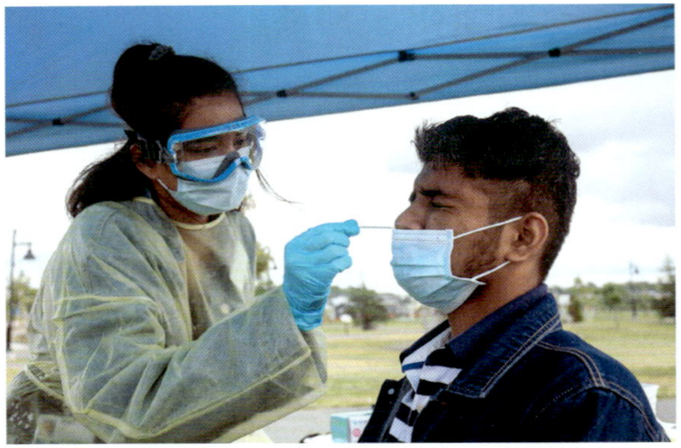

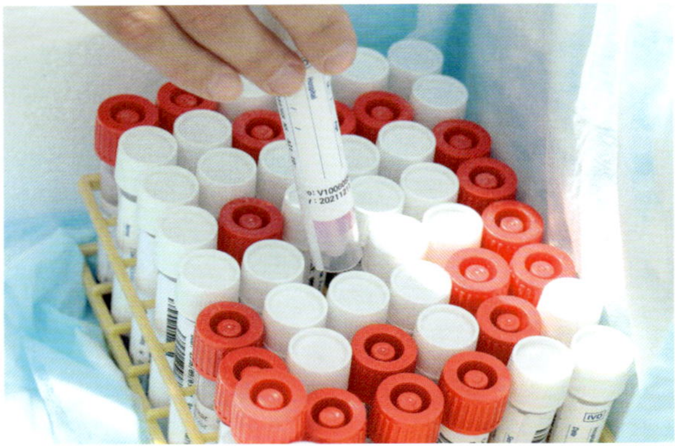

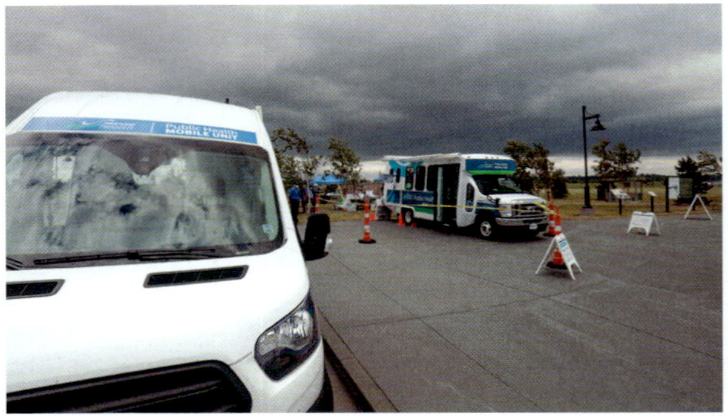

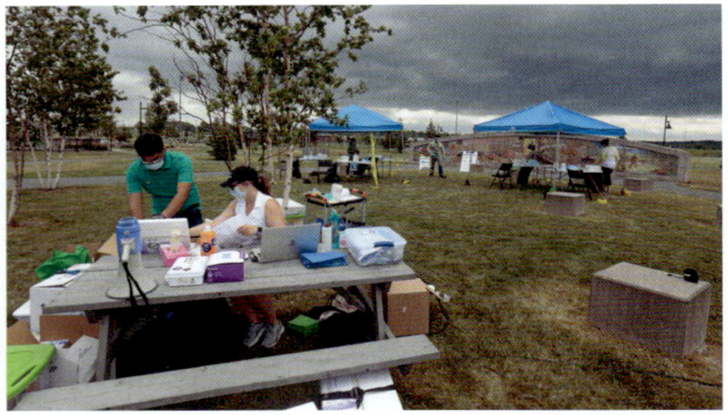

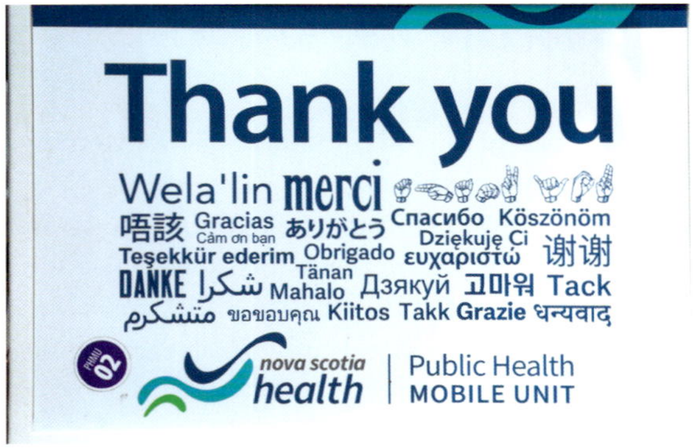

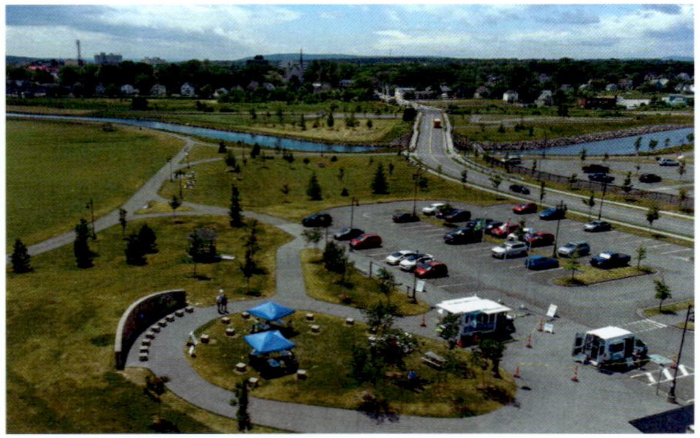

THE PHARMACY SOLUTION:
Diane Harpell and Tiffany Savary

Like thousands of Nova Scotians, pharmacist Diane Harpell waited anxiously for an opportunity to book a vaccination appointment—but this appointment would not be for herself. On this particular morning at 7:00 AM, she was looking for appointments for her seventy-two-year-old parents: her mother, Sharon Hodder, a retired nurse, and Arthur Hodder, himself a retired pharmacist.

Finally, she was in, and she snagged appointments for the location she was looking for: The Medicine Shoppe on Baker Drive in Dartmouth—which she happens to own. But just because she owns the pharmacy doesn't mean she was able to jump the queue; she had to use the same system as everyone else to get the booking. "That was the moment that, through all of this, was the most real for me," says Harpell. "I was booking a vaccine for my parents in the middle of this craziness, and when I got those appointments, it was pretty incredible."

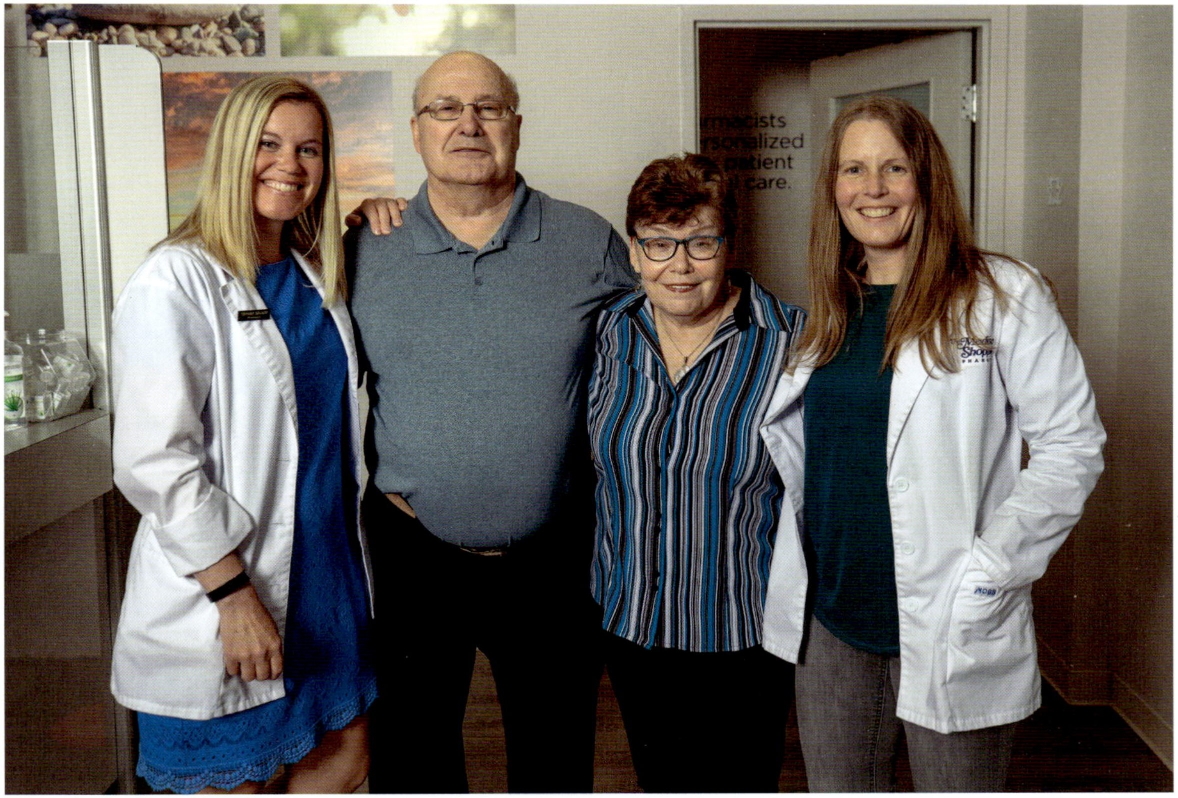

She immediately called her sister, Tiffany Savary, who is also a pharmacist and who is the Professional Accountability Manager for the Nova Scotia College of Pharmacists. The two made plans to get together on the day Harpell would administer the first dose of the COVID-19 vaccine to their parents.

Harpell says when her pharmacy began giving COVID-19 vaccinations in April there was a celebratory atmosphere as clients came through the door and rolled up their sleeves. "It was much more exciting than flu season," she says with a chuckle. When her parents' day arrived, her mother showed up with cake for her daughters and the staff.

Diane Harpell (far left) and Tiffany Savary (far right) stand with their parents, Arthur and Sharon Hodder, at The Medicine Shoppe on Baker Drive in Dartmouth. Harpell, a pharmacist who owns the shop, was happy to have the opportunity to vaccinate her own parents.

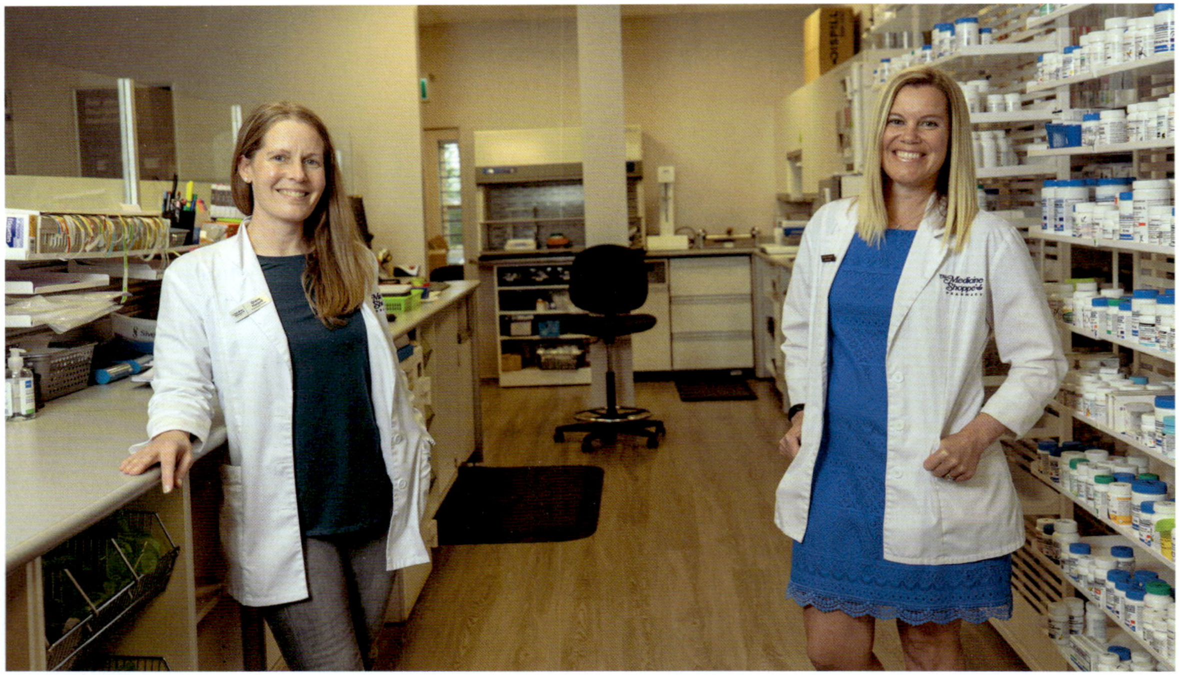

| *Pharmacists and sisters Tiffany Savary (left) and Diane Harpell.*

Harpell's pharmacy is just one of the hundreds that stepped up to play a critical role in Nova Scotia's vaccine rollout. Nearly three hundred pharmacies ran their own vaccination clinics, and by early July 2021, Nova Scotia had administered more than five hundred thousand COVID vaccine doses through those pharmacies.

The sisters feel COVID has highlighted the important role pharmacists can play in Nova Scotians' overall health care. "It's not just injections; it's prescribing, renewing emergency prescriptions, treating minor ailments, anything you can think of. Right now in New Glasgow there's a pharmacist-run walk-in clinic, so instead of seeing a doctor you see a pharmacist," Savary points out. "We've been able to do these things for a few years, but now we're getting a little bit more recognition, which is nice."

The pandemic has also showcased the potential for pharmacists to do even more.

"If you look at health care in Nova Scotia and the problems that we're facing with not enough doctors, not enough access—we've got three hundred pharmacies sitting here that can basically be three hundred walk-in clinics going forward," says Harpell. "I think it's finally the opportunity, now that the public and the government have seen that this is what pharmacies can do."

Sharon and Arthur Hodder are particularly proud that their daughters have been able to play such an important part in the pandemic response; they're also very happy they've been vaccinated. "It was a relief, really, when we got the first dose, and even more so with the second dose," says Arthur Hodder.

Tiffany Savary is relieved as well. "It's incredible to... see all the things that have played out for pharmacy," she says with a smile. "We are essentially a big part of saving the world right now."

NO PLACE LIKE HOME

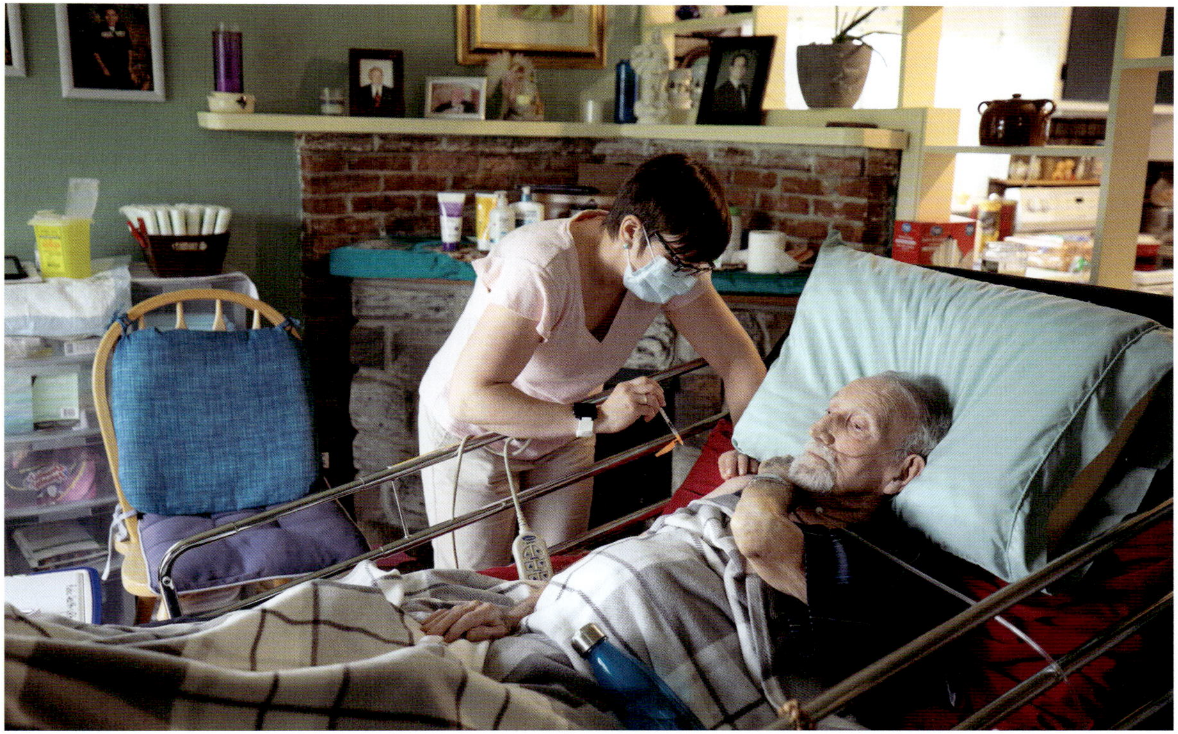

THIS PAGE: *Sarah Fells (in pink T-shirt) is a care co-*ordinator in Yarmouth who, along with Jennifer Hayes, RN, (in purple flowered top) is able to bring the COVID-19 vaccine to people who are unable to leave their homes to get immunized.

She is shown here delivering a vaccination to Kenneth Doucette, a continuing care client in Hebron, Yarmouth County. "A lot of these clients have been really worried about how they're going to get vaccinated because it's just really hard for them to get out," says Fells. "So being able to actually go into people's homes and give it has been great. They're usually very, very thankful that someone's doing this. It gives them a sense of comfort and safety knowing that they can protect others, too."

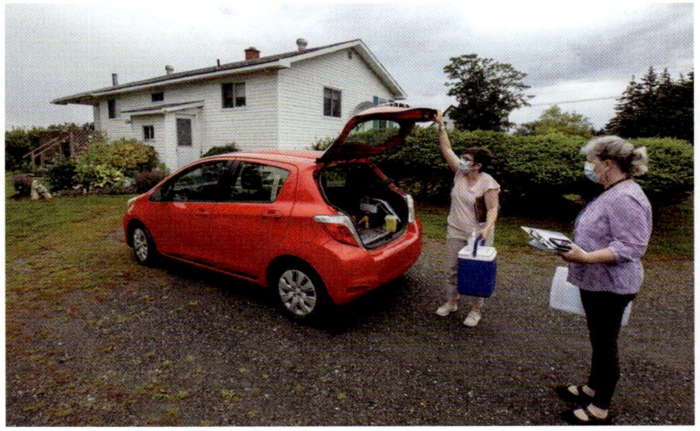

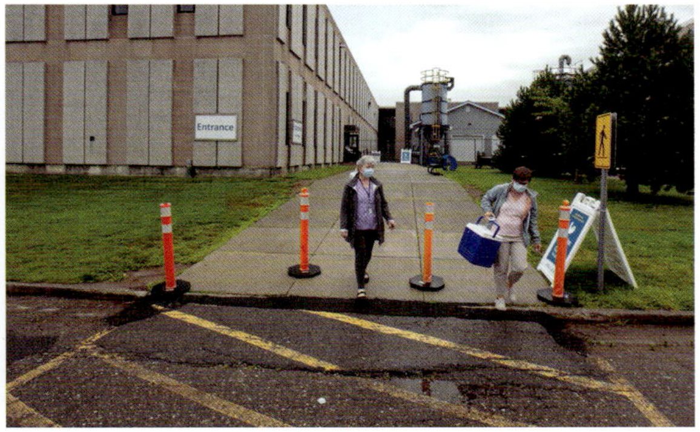

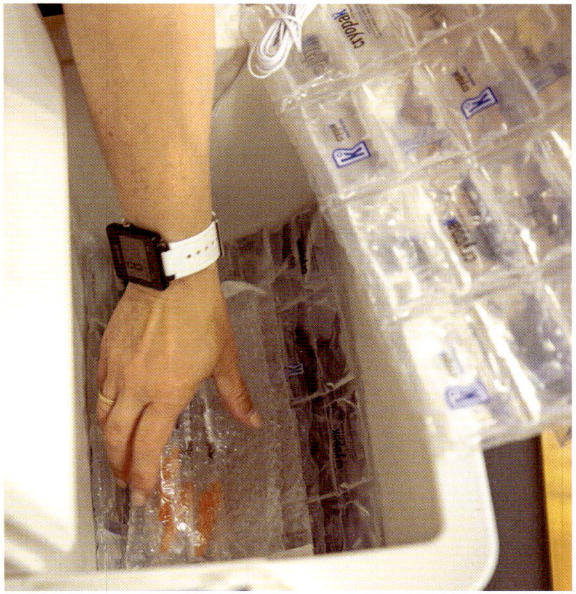

FACES OF HOPE

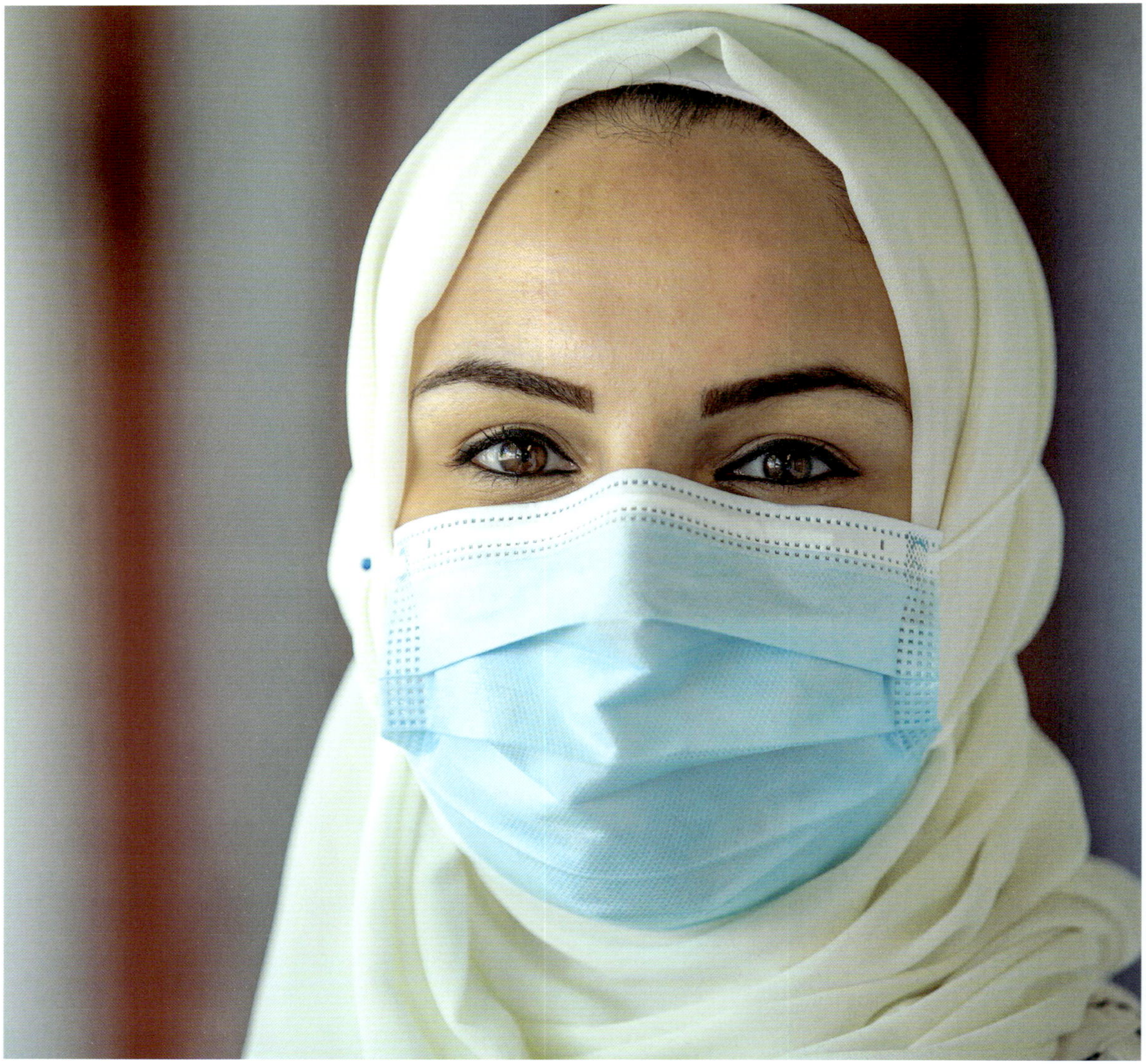

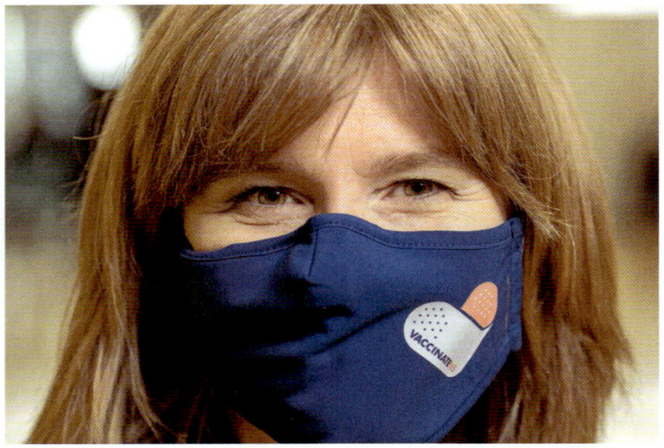

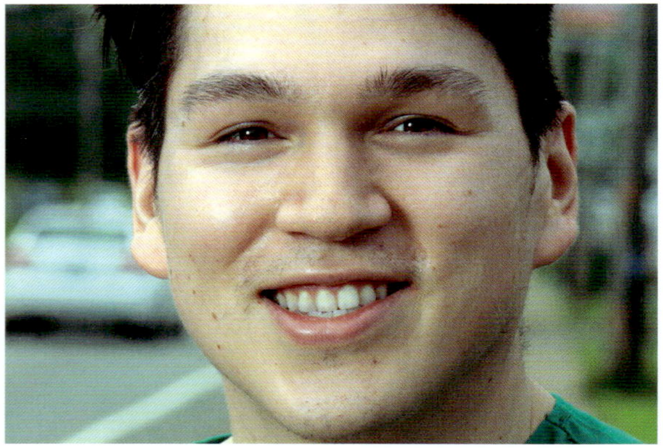

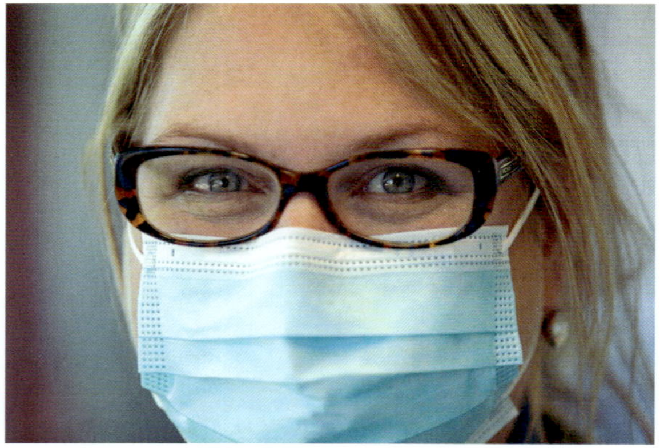

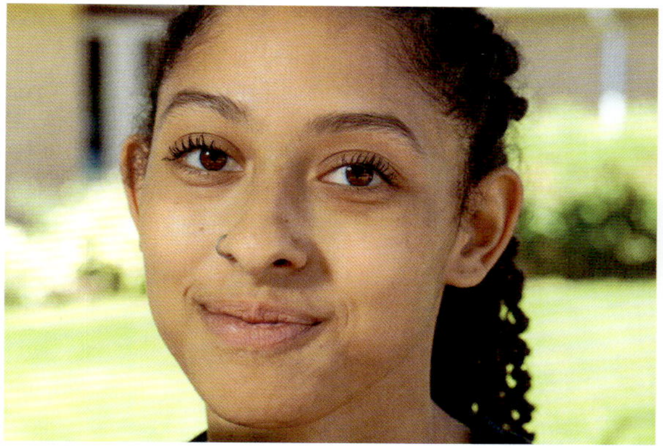
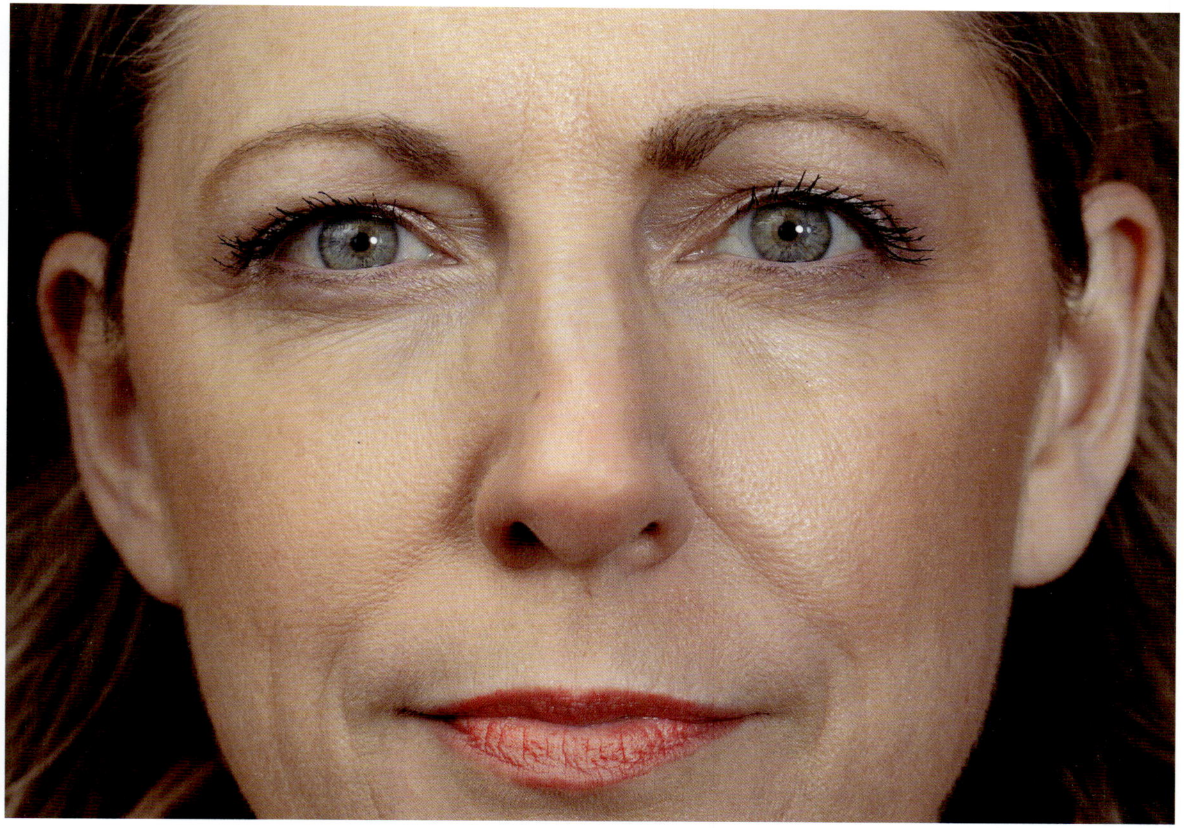
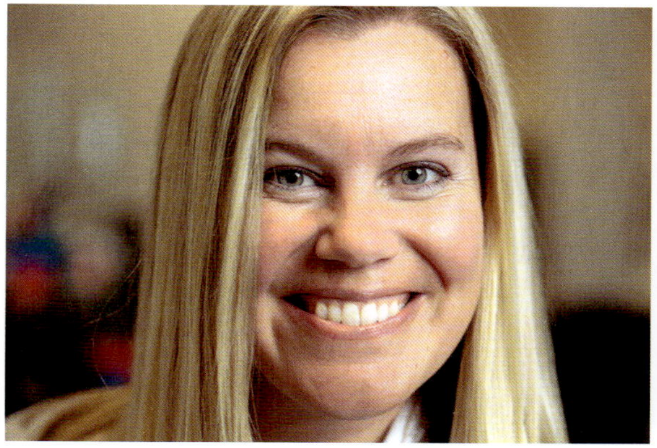
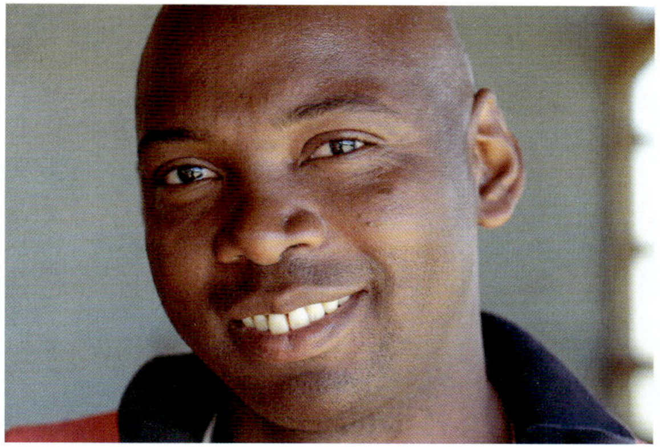
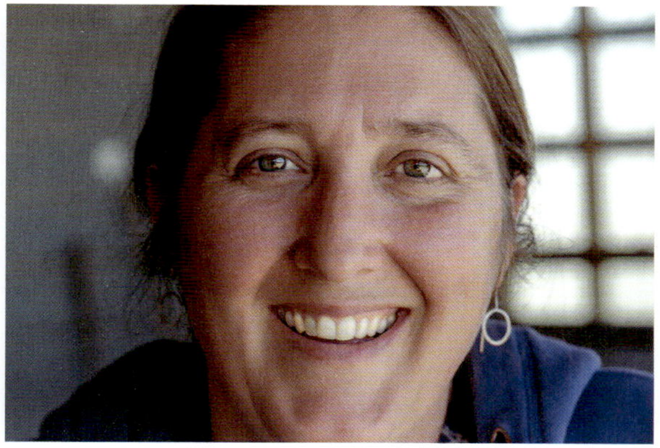
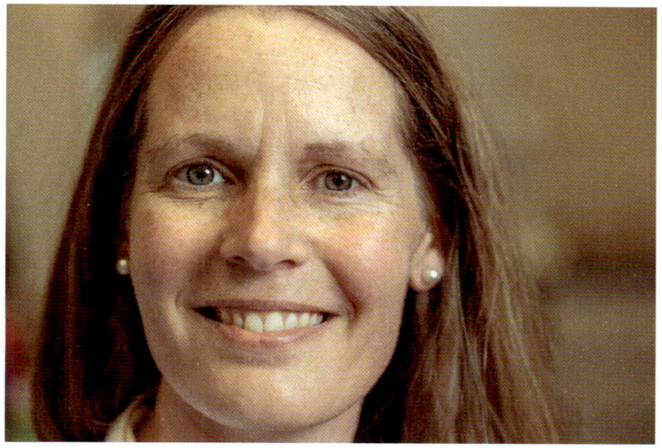

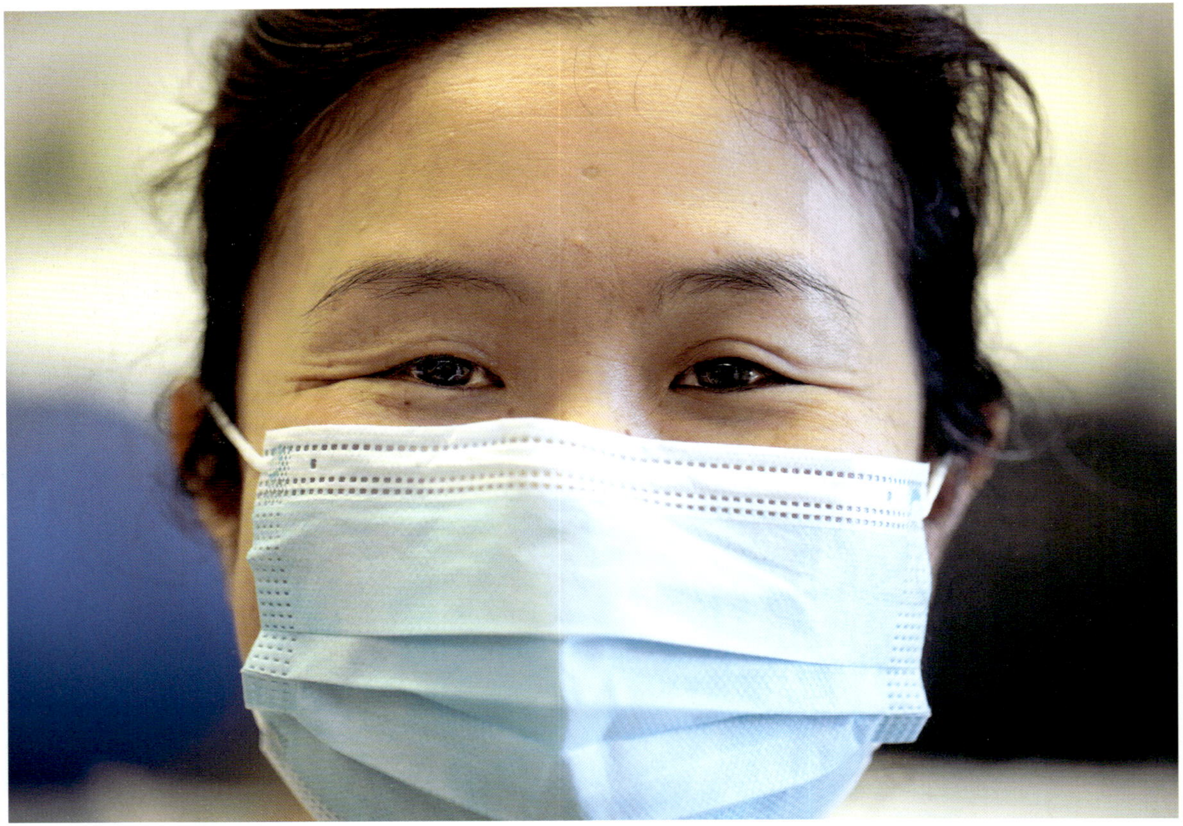

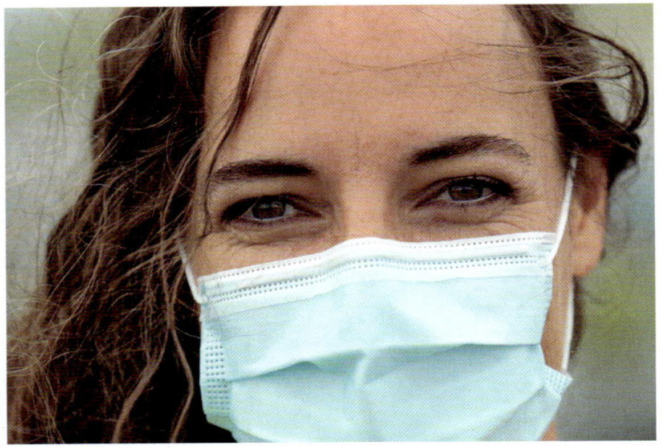

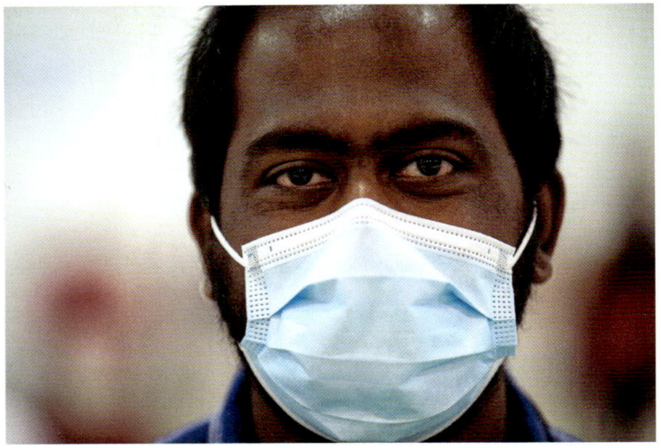

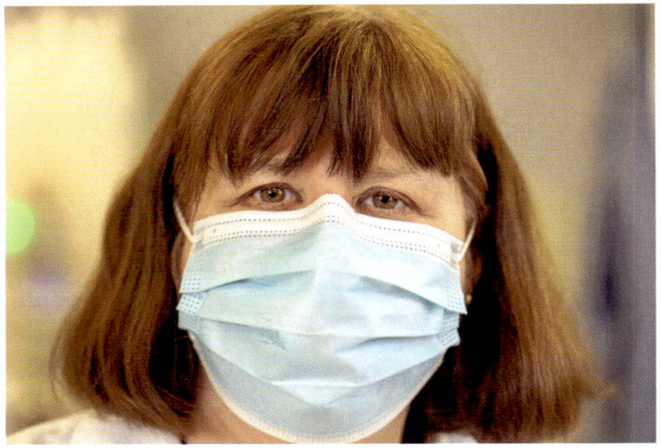

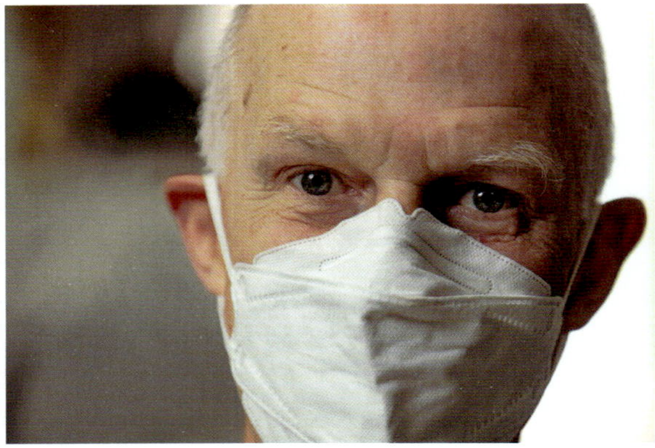

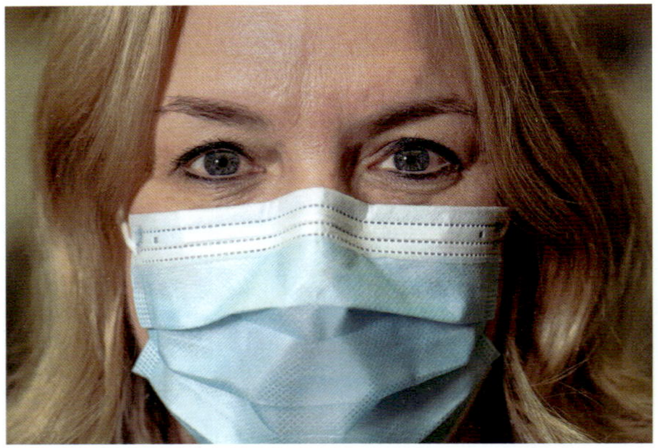

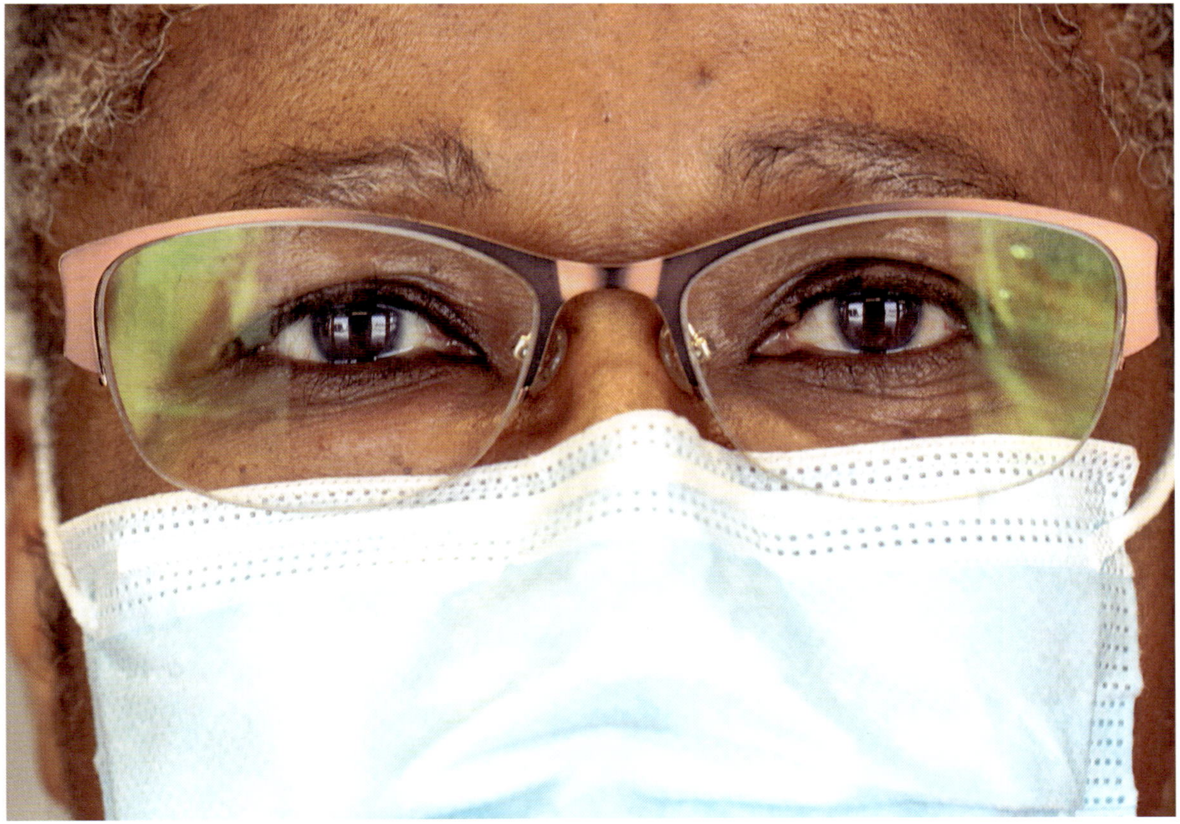
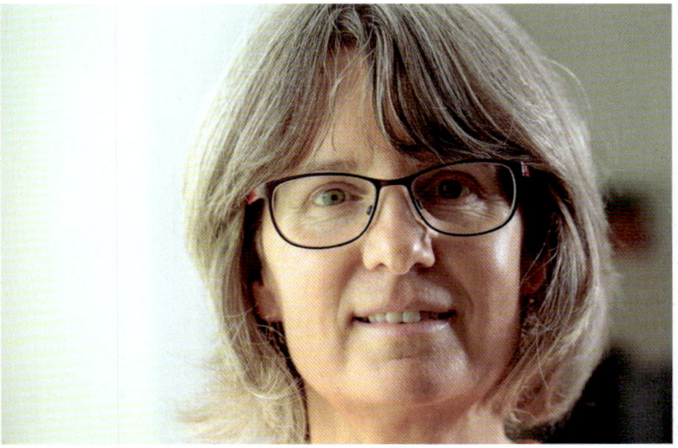
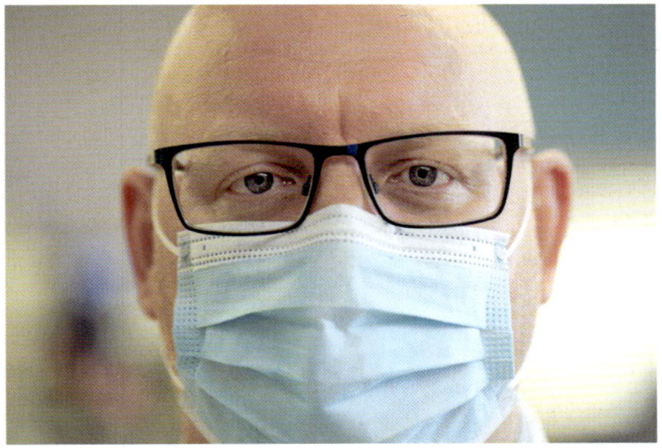
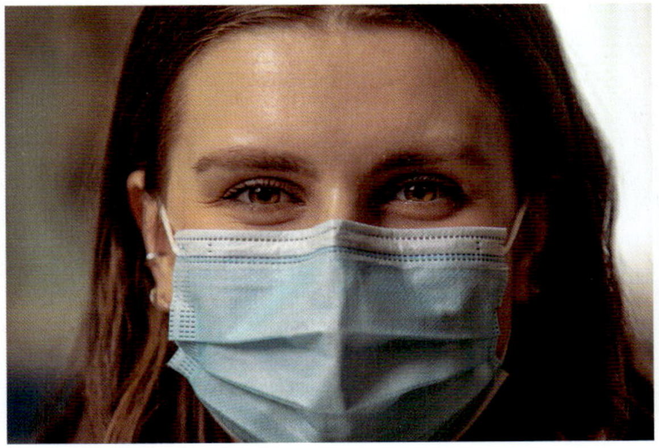
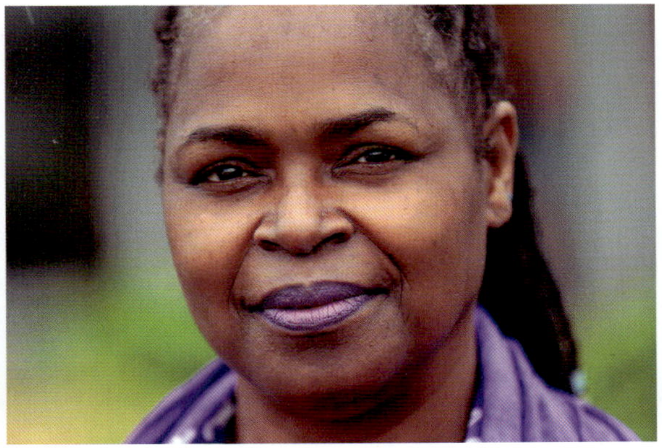
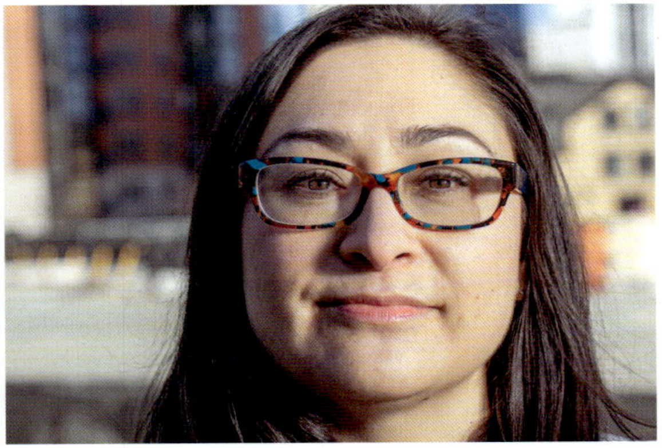

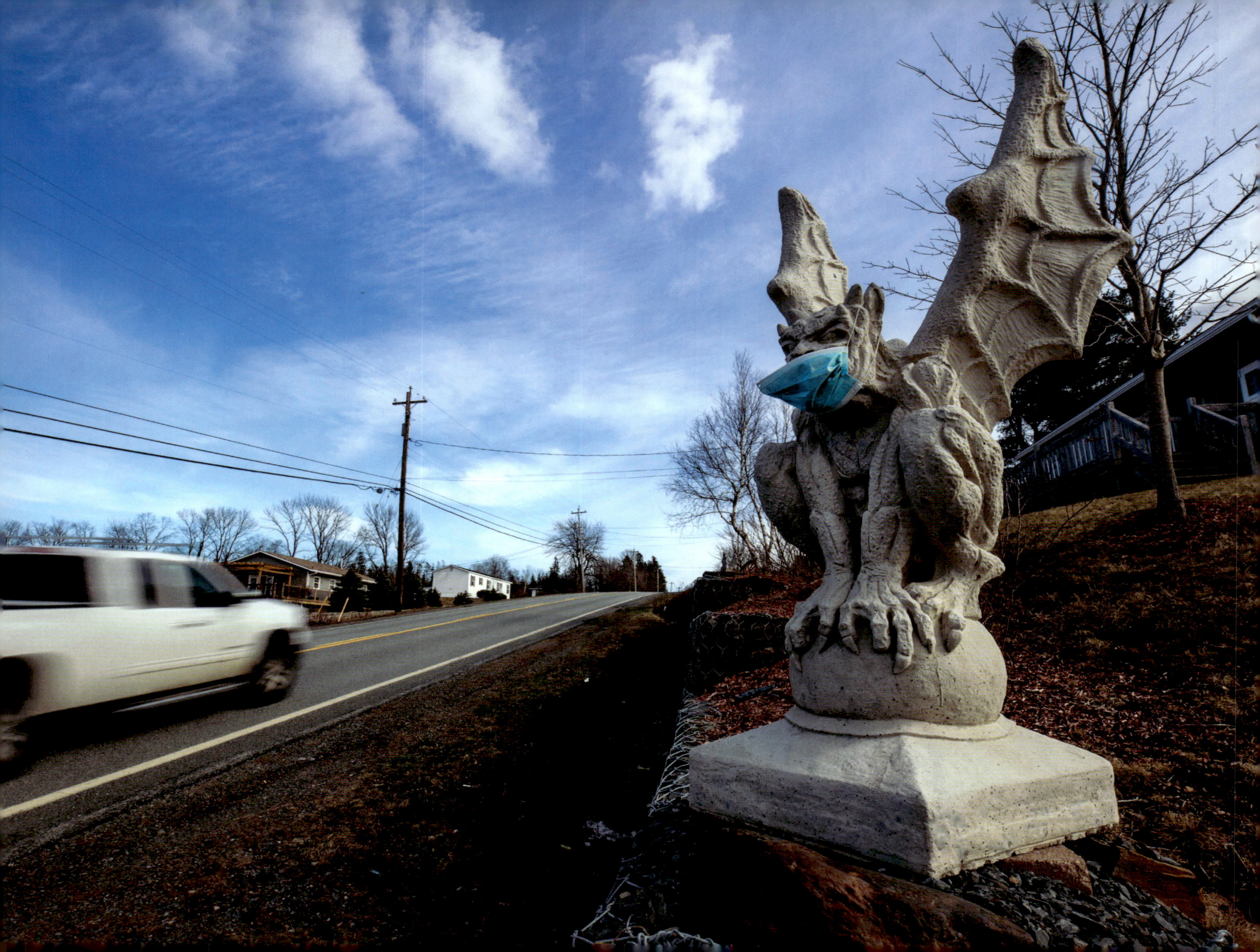

PART THREE: BEARING THE WEIGHT

A GUIDING LIGHT: *Dr. Robert Strang*

The Peggys Cove lighthouse looms large as Dr. Robert Strang, Nova Scotia's chief medical officer of health, stands tall on the granite rocks, amicably adjusting his stance as photographer Len Wagg captures yet another iconic image. To Strang's left, the sky glows orange, then red, as the sun slowly sets. To his right, a small crowd of onlookers has gathered, waiting for an opportunity to ask for a selfie with the man they all know and admire for the calm, cool guidance he's provided throughout the COVID-19 pandemic.

Despite the admiration and the rock-star treatment, Dr. Strang is very humble about the role he's played as the key figure behind Nova Scotia's pandemic strategy, and he's a little uncomfortable about taking the credit.

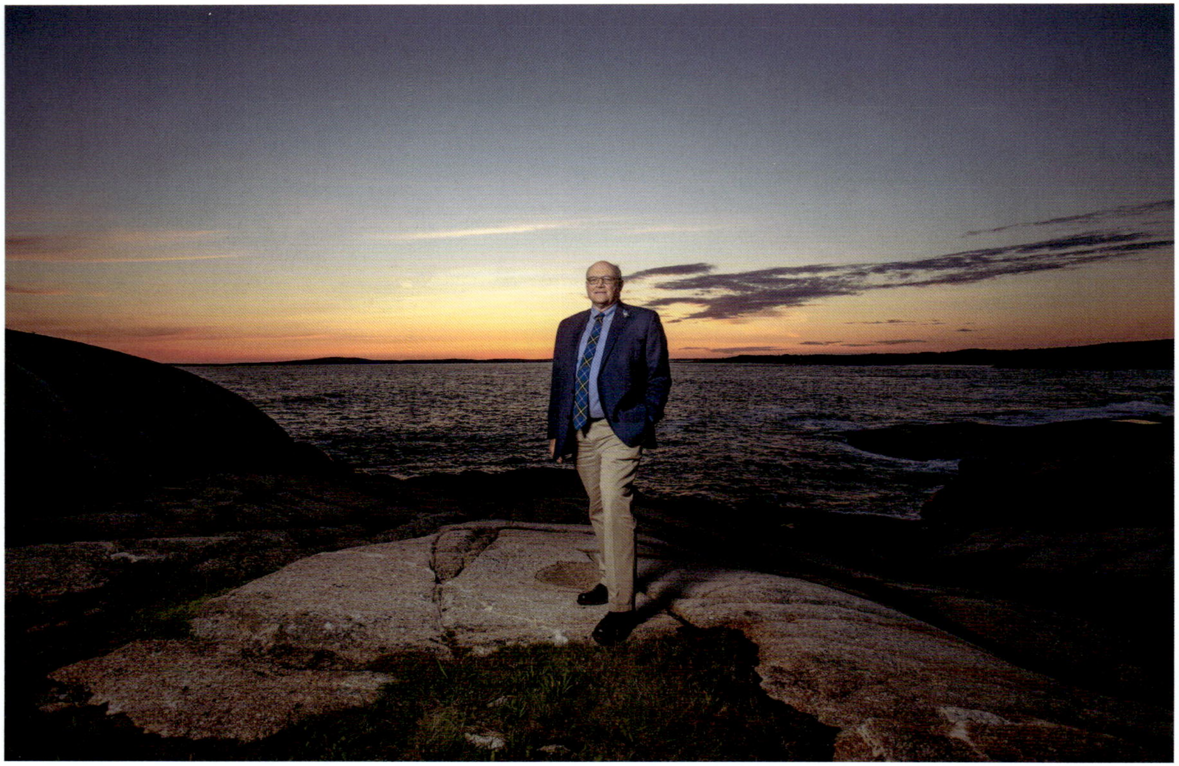

"I'm just one person; I know that I represent hundreds and hundreds of others," he says. "There are so many people that have worked day and night for the last year and a half, so it's not all about me; I'm fortunate enough to represent all of them."

There's no denying his even-tempered demeanour has inspired the kind of trust among Nova Scotians that has been essential to weathering the COVID storm, and he applauds Nova Scotians for cooperating with the public health guidance.

"You can never police and enforce your way through a situation like this," he says. "I give Nova Scotians lots of credit because they have heard and answered the message that the way we get through this is to care more about others than ourselves; to put community and others first."

It hasn't been easy, of course. As the science has evolved, and as the world's understanding of the virus has changed, so has the messaging around how to prevent transmission and how to approach vaccination. That changing guidance can lead to confusion and a lack of trust in public health measures, says Dr. Strang, adding that he works hard never to box himself in with his language and his approach.

Dr. Robert Strang, Nova Scotia's chief medical officer of health, acknowledges it's been difficult to bear the weight of the responsibility for keeping Nova Scotians safe, but he says the keys to getting through the third wave have been caring and kindness.

"We are doing things based on the best available evidence, and as that evidence changes, we will potentially change," he says. "It's hard. I know it's hard for people, because there are some people who just want certainty. But when you're going through a pandemic, certainty is the last thing you can have."

Dr. Strang says he has a few guiding philosophies when it comes to making the tough calls. One, he says, is, "What is the evidence telling me? I've got good people around me. We talk things through; I've got colleagues around the country, so when we finally come to a decision, I'm comfortable that I've gotten the advice that I need."

Another, he says, is focusing on what's best for people. "It's about making the best decision to minimize the impacts on individuals."

And finally, he says, "I'm a person of faith. I believe in God and that there's a higher power that actually is ultimately in charge of all this. Some people don't like to hear that, but at the end of the day, I don't feel I have to carry all of this on my own shoulders. I can go home and I can go, 'I've done the best I can.'"

His best has been very good for Nova Scotians. Nevertheless, the burden of the pandemic has been a lot to carry. As of late August, ninety-four Nova Scotians had died since the start of the pandemic, twenty-eight of them during the third wave that began around March 2021. The impact of public health measures on businesses, large and small, has been significant, and the sacrifices required of individual Nova Scotians has left them exhausted and worried about the future.

"The biggest challenge for me," says Dr. Strang, "is the weight of the responsibility. People have had to do a lot of really hard things and there have been a lot of really substantive and profound impacts on people."

But despite always being the picture of cool reassurance, he admits there was a moment during the third wave when he was more than a little concerned.

"Those days when we got a hundred, then over two hundred cases, I was very nervous and anxious, but I knew that we'd acted quickly and that we had the right things in place. It was going to take a little bit of time for them to show their impact," he says. "But there were a few nervous days going, 'If we don't start to turn the corner pretty quickly, I don't know what comes next.' Fortunately, we did."

He says the key to his approach is always to find the balance. "How much do we need to do in terms of restrictions without going too far? If you don't get it right, if you don't have enough restrictions, then you're not going to get the control you need. Our hospitals were stretched to the breaking point, and it could have gotten worse if we hadn't had been as successful as we were."

As the summer of 2021 progressed, infection numbers were coming down and the number of Nova Scotians vaccinated was going up—allowing a glint of hope that a "new normal" was on the horizon. But Dr. Strang admits his hope is that, as the restrictions loosen, not everything goes back to the way it was in the days before COVID-19.

"Normally in government and health care we're pretty bureaucratic and we can be very siloed—and it takes forever to get something done because of some of those silos," he says. "We've had to be very different. People have come around the table, very solution-oriented, saying, 'How do I help?'"

He also hopes—without it being mandated—that people will be a little more cautious about spreading viruses and other infectious diseases, particularly during the winter months. "Maybe we all should be more careful about wearing masks, especially in crowded indoor public places, washing our hands more, staying home if we're sick," he says, then adds, "But that's a good example of something—how do we support people whose jobs don't allow them to stay at home if they are sick? How do we build those kinds of supports and build a society and workplaces that are more respectful of infectious diseases?"

As the setting sun turns the sky a brilliant purple behind him, Dr. Strang is cautiously optimistic about the future. "We're going to be different, but we can be better while we're being different," he says.

"I've heard so many stories of families and communities caring for each other, it brings me to tears.... It's been really hard, but let's continue to be really caring and loving and kind to each other. That's what's gotten us through."

LIFE IN INTENSIVE CARE:
Dr. Sarah McMullen

In March 2020, the world watched as images from intensive care units around the world began to flash across our screens—images of patients on ventilators, of doctors and nurses with bruised and chafed faces from hours spent wearing tight masks, and of exhausted health-care workers.

Dr. Sarah McMullen, a critical care physician in Halifax, knew then it was only a matter of time before the virus made its way here—and that it would mean developing a whole new way to practice medicine in her intensive care unit (ICU).

"This was on a scale that we hadn't really seen, and that was ... pretty terrifying and daunting. You want to make sure that you're doing your best for the patients while keeping your colleagues and your family safe."

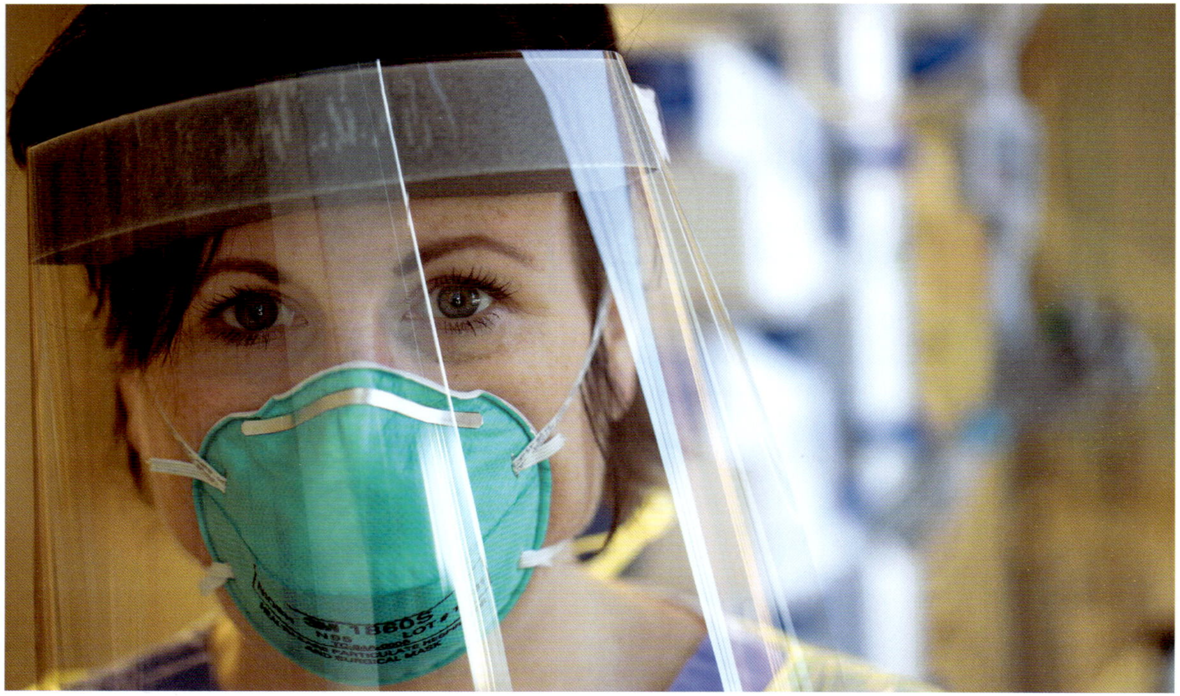

Even before COVID, McMullen says, the ICU was a fast-paced, technology-heavy environment. "There's always lots of noise. There's always lots of light. It's machines, it's monitoring vital signs, it's the ventilator alarm setting going off and on, it's medications running out and needing to be replenished. It's a sensory-overload kind of environment."

The COVID unit at the QEII Health Sciences Centre in Halifax is a sealed-off room. To avoid needless travel in and out, nurses use two-way radios to stay in contact with the rest of the unit. Providing care in that kind of environment requires a special kind of team bond.

"I'm ten years into critical care. My job actually felt relevant for the first time in a long time; I felt a renewed sense of purpose in my career. I was extremely proud of how the team functioned together, and it felt collegial on so many levels."

McMullen credits Nova Scotia's chief medical officer of health, Dr. Robert Strang, with helping Nova Scotians avoid the worst of the pandemic. "I can't say enough about Dr. Strang. He's really been such a kind and level-headed voice throughout. If

Dr. Sarah McMullen is a critical care physician in Halifax who worked in the intensive care COVID unit at the QEII Health Sciences Centre in Halifax through the pandemic.

there was that sort of leadership in other places, they would probably be in a different boat," she says. "I've got colleagues in other parts of the country who have been looking after sick COVID patients for an entire year, and they're exhausted. They're fed up and they're exhausted."

Still, the physical and mental toll of working for a year and a half during a pandemic has led to a wave of people leaving the profession.

"We had huge attrition in terms of nursing after the first wave. I personally felt very buoyed and carried by the nurses—their strength and their 'we're going to do it; we'll get done' attitude."

And through it all, McMullen says she has learned a lot about herself.

"I'm fairly resilient, and I've learned that you can help people just by trying to be positive and collegial. I've also learned that life is incredibly fragile, and that just because we want things to go back to normal, we can't necessarily expect things to go that way."

THIRD WAVE THOUGHTS FROM THE ICU *by Dr. Sarah M. McMullen*

The third wave was a tsunami—of COVID cases, hospitalizations, deaths; it was also a tsunami of emotion. We had done so well, for so long, I think most of us were shocked and disappointed to find ourselves crushed under the weight of this advancing tide when we were so close to the finish line.

I was angry—angry at the careless folks who visited Nova Scotia and didn't isolate upon arrival, angry at the family members here who didn't follow the rules either.

I was also frustrated. But I wasn't scared the way I had been in wave one. We now knew what we were dealing with, and most of us on the front lines were, thankfully, vaccinated. We knew what to do and how to do it.

Even though we had not had it nearly as tough as the rest of the country (in particular, Ontario, Quebec, Alberta...), we were all tired of COVID and ready for it to be over. That said, we laced up the bootstraps and got to work. It was brutal in the hospital for a few weeks, and we quickly ramped up to almost a hundred hospitalized patients, with thirty patients requiring critical care—dramatically outpacing what we had seen in waves one and two.

People worked together like I'd never seen before. It was remarkable. I unfortunately suffered a COVID exposure at work, and despite being fully vaccinated, had to self-isolate for two weeks in the middle of the crush of the third wave. I was angry—I wanted to be at work, pulling my weight and helping the team. I was not worried about getting sick, but about letting the team down.

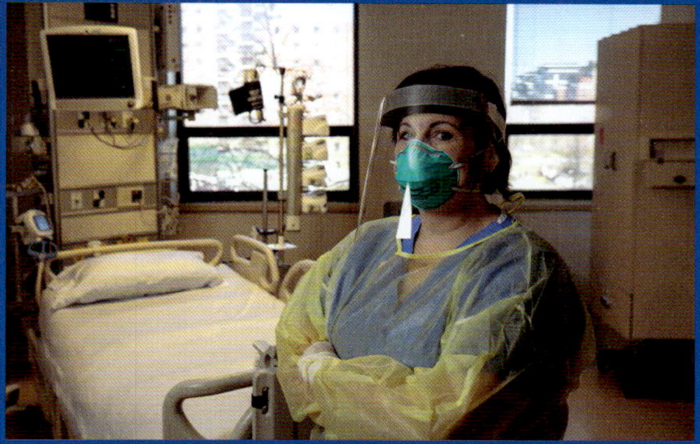

Once I got back to work, COVID was ramping down, but the ICU was still hopping; so many sick patients. The ICU is an emotionally wrought place at the best of times, but was particularly so during the pandemic.

The hardest part was being unable to allow family members to be with their sick and dying loved ones. It was terrible to only be able to let families in during palliative times...normally they're at the bedside in our units, taking part in rounds and care plans. Having them grieve from afar was heartbreaking.

So there you go…the tsunami of emotions: anger, frustration, worry, heartbreak. But also a sense of teamwork, of working together, and ultimately, of hope—hope for the end of the pandemic and for brighter days ahead. And thanks that ultimately, our third wave was relatively brief—thanks once again to strong leadership and the actions of Nova Scotians who banded together to get tested, follow the rules, and "stay the blazes home" when it counted most.

THE CAVEMAN BRAIN AND THE MENTAL HEALTH STORM:

Dr. Dayna Lee-Baggley

"If this was World War Three, we would have gotten rid of all kinds of expectations and just focused on the war effort," says Dr. Dayna Lee-Baggley. "But in this pandemic, we've just added the stresses of the pandemic onto the stresses of everyday life."

She makes a good point, but then, she knows what she's talking about. Lee-Baggley is a registered psychologist with a PhD in clinical psychology; she has worked for more than fifteen years with the medical, surgical, and cancer-care units at the QEII Health Sciences Centre in Halifax. Most recently, she began providing mental health training and workshops for clinicians and health-care providers around the world—both in person and through her virtual clinics.

"We run groups on helping people charge their batteries to help cope with the stress of COVID," she says, noting that the pandemic has hit many people hard. "It's a real challenge to live through, as it should be. I don't think we should have an expectation that we can all cope with this as normal. We probably all need some support to get through it."

She says statistics show that depression and anxiety have gone up, but that everyone's stressors are different, depending upon their circumstances. "If you have children at home, we know that's an incredibly stressful situation—to be trying to work from home," she says. "If you lost your job, that's a different circumstance. If you're a frontline provider, that's a different circumstance. If you get locked down by yourself... that's a real challenge."

One of the greatest challenges stems from the limits that have been placed, by necessity, on personal contact.

"We know that social connection is good for well-being. I like to say it takes a village to be well, and that's part of what's hard about the pandemic. To follow the public health guidelines, we often are disconnected from our social networks. There is certainly a benefit of those in-person interactions that we're missing," she says.

"I like to say that our caveman brains are on fire and our frontal lobe batteries are incredibly spent," she says, explaining that the "caveman brain" functions automatically and unconsciously, regulating things like emotions, memory, learning, and appetite. "You can't turn it on and you can't turn it off. It gives great advice for things like a bear attack.... It's slightly less effective for a pandemic that goes on for over a year, but we don't have a choice about that system activating."

She says the other relevant part of our brain is the prefrontal cortex, which controls behaviour. "That's where our self-control comes from. That's where willpower comes from. That's about starting and stopping behaviour. And unlike our caveman brain, it's like a battery"—meaning that, because of the demands of COVID, it gets run down, and there often isn't enough battery power to get through the days. That's when things like anxiety, depression, and eating disorders can kick in, she says, because there's just not enough frontal lobe capacity available to help us make good choices.

Front-line workers, from health-care workers to police to teachers to grocery store employees, are particularly susceptible to these brain challenges. "You're in an environment where there is a threat and other people that you can't control, which activates that caveman brain that says, 'Danger! Threat! Do something!'"

But she notes that, despite the threat, health-care workers are consistently diligent, perhaps to their own detriment. "They're going to keep things going as much as possible during the crisis. It's really after the crisis ends that we're going to see some of the after-effects of that." She predicts that things like turnover, early retirements, and disability claims will rise when the pandemic is over because health-care workers are already so exhausted and burnt out.

"There have really been no breaks in health care. In wave one we were all at very high levels of threat

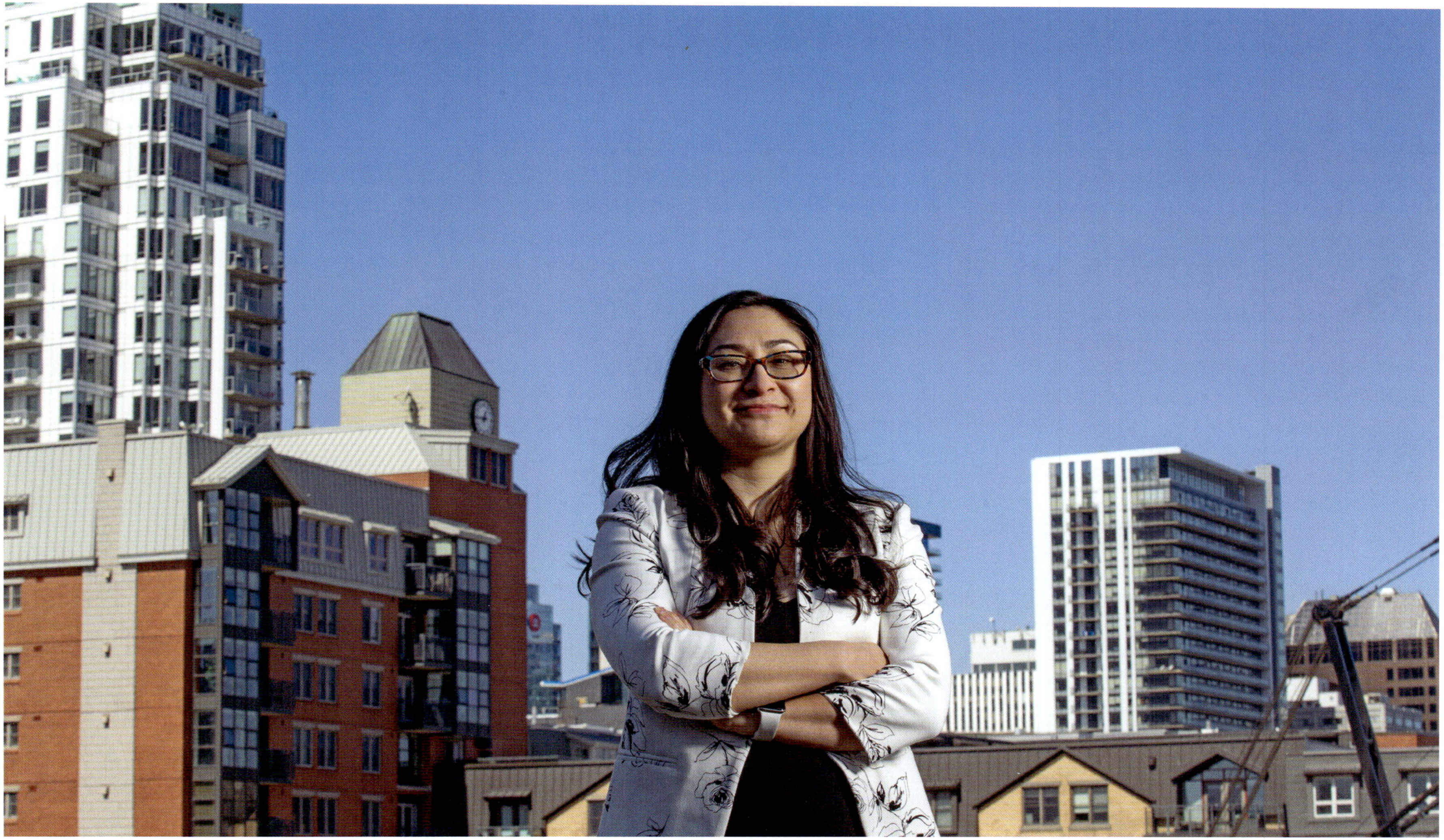

Dr. Dayna Lee-Baggley is a registered psychologist with a PhD in clinical psychology who recently began providing mental health training and workshops for clinicians and health-care providers around the world—both in person and online.

in terms of waiting for the surge and not knowing whether it was going to come or not. That anticipatory anxiety is sometimes worse than the actual event."

And even after the first wave was over, health-care workers had to deal with a huge backlog of patients—people who had delayed testing and interventions for chronic diseases. "So we still have the burnout ... plus kind of traumatic experiences."

She says it's important that people find ways to manage those stresses. "Going to the office and having a chat with someone at the coffee station is probably a bit of a recharging activity, but some of those things are not available to us in the pandemic, so we have to be more deliberate," says Lee-Baggley. "A recharging activity is something that makes you feel more energetic at the end than when you start." She says for some people that might mean a nap or a walk in the park, while for others it might be spending time with friends.

But whatever an individual's stressors are, she adds, it's always better to talk about them.

"Other people are likely experiencing the same thing," she says, "so bringing it out, talking about it, that's absolutely one of the best ways to deal with it. If you don't have someone in your network who is kind and compassionate about that, then it's about finding people who respond compassionately, even if that's a therapist or a psychologist."

Lee-Baggley says she hopes the social awareness around mental wellness carries on after the pandemic and that people continue to reach out for help. "No one can get through this by themselves. The best version of a human is not someone who's isolated and independent and doing it on their own; the best version of a human is someone who's connected to safe, trusting people. That's when we're our bravest. That's when we're our most courageous. That's when we have the most resiliency—when we have that village."

She says it's also important to acknowledge that we have a right to feel drained.

"In Atlantic Canada, clearly we've done exceptionally well relative to many other places," she says. "[But] I also like to say that we haven't been spared the burden of the pandemic. Some people in Atlantic Canada feel like, 'Well, I shouldn't feel tired because we didn't have the outbreaks the same way other places did.' But we've been doing the public health regulations arguably for longer and more consistently than other places. We have not been spared the burden of those frontal lobe battery expenditures on changing every aspect of our lives."

And despite the challenges, there may be an upside. Lee-Baggley says the pandemic may have taught us to focus on what really matters. "Partly what the pandemic may have highlighted is that life is fragile," she says, "so [it's important] to spend our time in the most meaningful way."

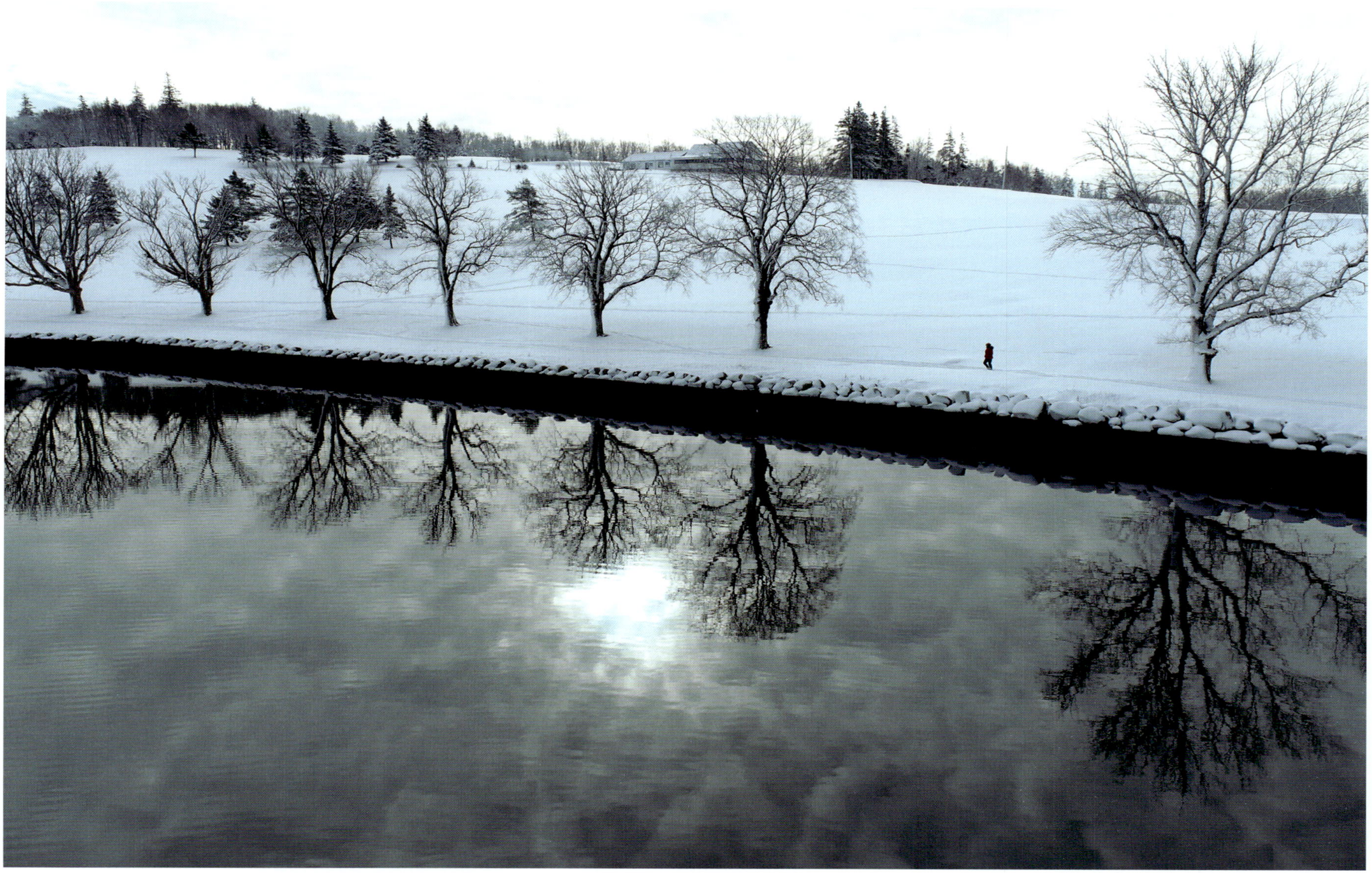

In early 2021, Nova Scotians were keeping to their "bubbles" and socially distancing—but we could still walk to maintain our physical and mental health. Here, a lone person goes for a stroll in Lunenburg.

FIRST PERSON—COVID AND COMPASSION:
Paul Brothers

COVID AT THE DOORSTEP

On the evening of Friday, April 23, we were in what I assume was the same boat as a lot of Nova Scotians—getting supper ready but also trying to digest the news from earlier that day that the province would be going into another lockdown amidst a third wave of COVID-19.

Then the phone rang and our story took a turn.

It was my two-year-old daughter's daycare calling to inform us that one of her teachers had tested positive for COVID-19; the teacher had been at work that week and had not worn a mask (Public Health made masks mandatory in all daycares four days later). We were told to get Andie tested as soon as possible and she was to self-isolate until we got results back.

Our initial reaction was one of shock. We had followed all the public health guidelines, kept our social circles tight, and still COVID-19 was on our doorstep. (On a side note, my wife even went to Calgary to compete in the Scotties Tournament of Hearts curling competition—in a bubble—and still did not come home with the virus, yet here it was, just around the corner at our daycare.)

The next day at 9:00 AM Andie was tested for COVID-19 and we started playing the waiting game, hoping for that email telling us she'd tested negative, but also leery of the phone call that would confirm she'd tested positive. What followed felt like the longest wait of our lives. Little did we know at that time that Public Health would be dealing with a backlog of some seventy thousand tests, so the waiting game would last over eighty hours until we finally got the bad news. In that eighty-hour span we all developed symptoms, and in the week that followed we all ended up testing positive for COVID-19.

As the news reports will tell you, COVID-19 affects everyone differently, and that was true for our family.

Our daughter had a bad cough similar to croup, but only for a couple days. Then it was my wife's turn and she went through days of extreme fatigue, coughing, and loss of taste and smell. Then it was my turn and I went through feverish chills nearly every night for a week, a very bad hacking cough, headaches, and weird pain around my eye sockets (a symptom Public Health would tell me was cropping up more during the third wave.) As for my son, by the time he started showing symptoms, the rest of us had COVID-19 and could not leave the house, so Public Health actually sent an EHS team to our front door to give him a swab, which eventually came back positive. He went through a cough and runny nose, and a fever that luckily was controlled by hourly rounds of Tylenol and Advil, both day and night.

After a week and a half of symptoms, and the anxiety that goes along with them, we felt I was well enough to appear on *Global News Morning* with my co-host Alyse Hand to tell concerned viewers where I had been. I did the interview from our rec room in the basement; I talked about how the whole family caught COVID-19, and about how, despite the fact that we were on the mend, it was something that nobody should want to go through—echoing the call to stay safe and follow public health guidelines.

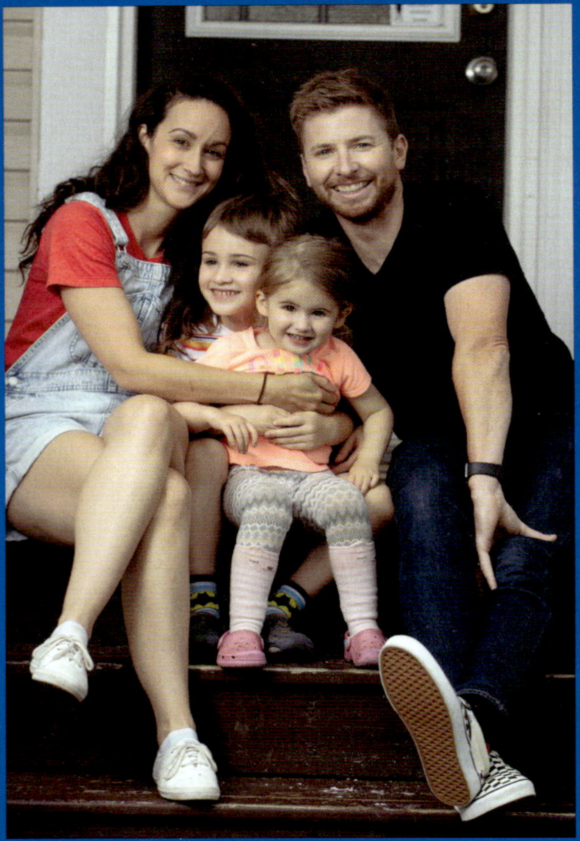

Global News Morning *anchor Paul Brothers and his entire family were diagnosed with COVID in April 2021. He is shown here with his wife, Jill, and their children, Casey and Andie.*

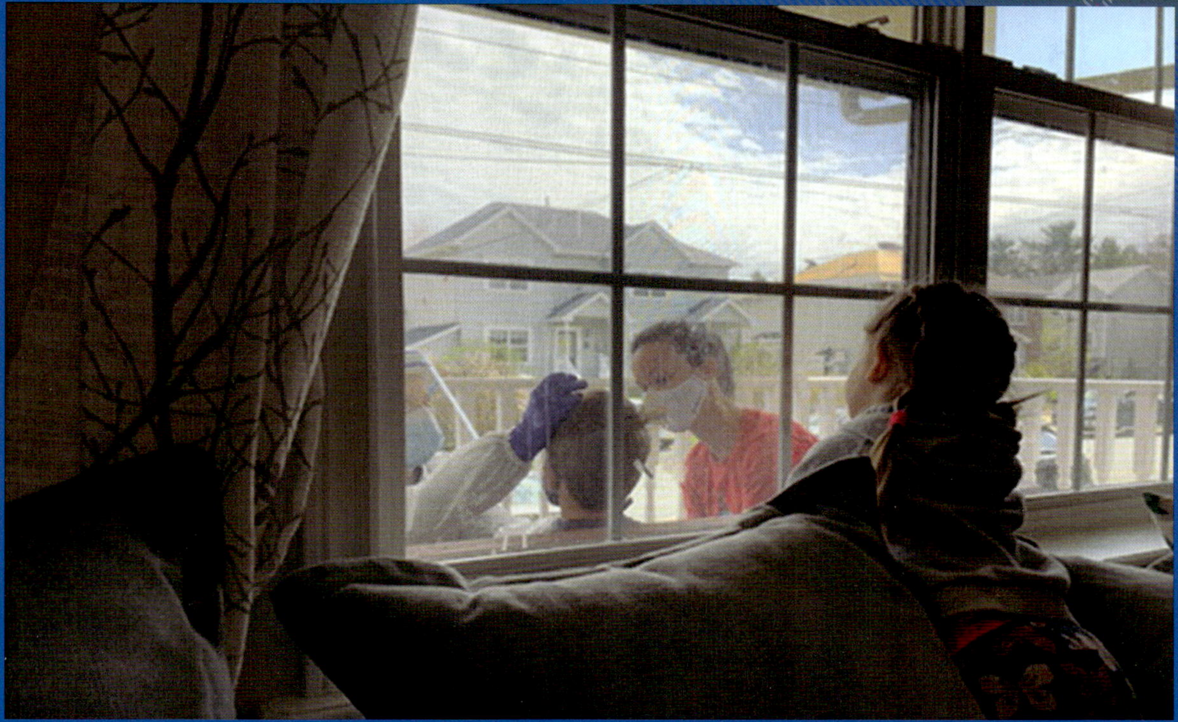

COMPASSION AT THE DOORSTEP

During the pandemic, Dr. Robert Strang spoke of the three C's—caring, compassion, and community—and after my brief appearance on *Global News Morning*, the outpouring of those three C's was overwhelming.

Friends, family, and strangers all began sending "get well soon" messages virtually; some sent care packages or home remedies to our doorstep. It felt like every hour there was someone reaching out or someone tapping on the door and giving a wave down the driveway (behind a mask, of course) after delivering a parcel.

There were gift baskets from Sweet Jane's, containers of homemade chicken soup, naturally sourced honey, bottles of fermented coconut juice, and enough craft beer to start our own taproom. (One neighbour even duct-taped a lime to a bottle of Corona beer and called it the "Newfoundland Survival Kit" for COVID-19.) An entire street around the corner banded together to drop off toys and gift cards for food from Kitchen Door Catering. Neighbours celebrating Eid al-Fitr (the end of Ramadan) actually dropped off food and sweets for us after going without every day from dawn to dusk for over a month!

If it wasn't food, it was creative ways to boost our spirits in the absence of a hug or a hand. My best pals got together and sent us a personal get-well wish from Toronto Blue Jays play-by-play man Buck Martinez; local councillor Tony Mancini organized a fire truck to swing by to entertain the kids; even the folks at LEGO Canada somehow saw my my son's LEGO collection in the background of my interviews and sent him a LEGO City set. We even got a phone call from Halifax mayor Mike Savage, who echoed a lot of people's messages when he said I and my family had put a face on COVID-19, and it woke a lot of people up to the fact that COVID is a real and potentially deadly virus, and that even if you are healthy it can certainly knock you down a few pegs.

Needless to say, the tears from not knowing what COVID-19 would bring turned to tears of being overwhelmed at how caring and kind people could be (I'm tearing up just writing this).

In the end we all came through it without any hospital stays, so we consider ourselves lucky, as the third wave was exceptionally brutal for younger, healthier, Nova Scotian families. Our kids are kind of sad all the care packages have stopped arriving, but they will get through it. My wife and I are back to work, slowly getting back into physical activity, and have been vaccinated, but there is always the anxiety of the long-term effects and the many unknowns of a COVID-19 diagnosis.

It is true the third wave hit us hard, but the tidal wave of caring, compassion, and community will have ripple effects on our family for years to come.

Thank you.

Paul Brothers is co-host of Global News Morning *on Global Halifax. He lives with his wife, Jill, and children, Casey and Andie, in Bedford, Nova Scotia.*

IN IT FOR THE LONG HAUL:
Jennifer Mont

On Thursday, April 23, 2020, Jennifer Mont woke up with a bit of cough and a sore throat. The twenty-eight-year-old wasn't overly concerned—she often had allergy-like symptoms due to non-allergic rhinitis. But that Saturday, she woke up, she says, "feeling awful." A friend advised her to contact public health, who sent her immediately for COVID testing.

"The next day they called and said I was positive. I was like, 'You're kidding me.'"

They weren't.

"I hadn't been anywhere," she says, adding she struggled to figure out how she'd contracted the virus. "I was doing the proper things that they were telling us to do, like keeping your distance, washing your hands. I had not been around anyone who had travelled, and I was doing the whole, you know—only go out once a week to grab what you need, kind of thing."

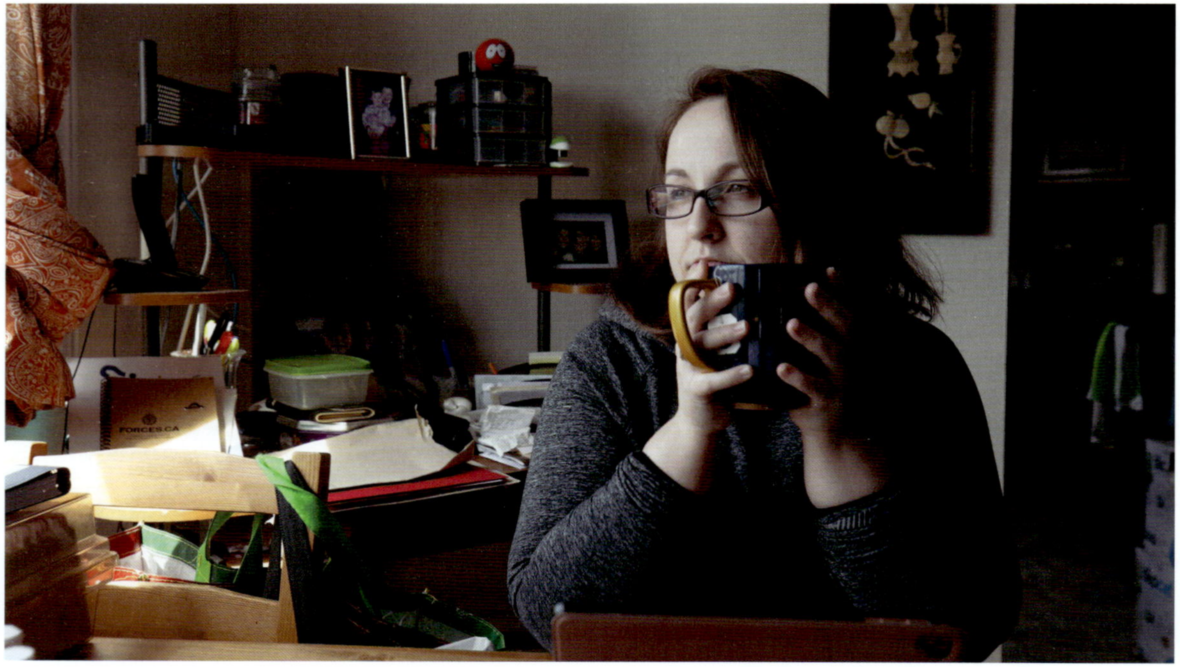

She isolated herself and waited for the symptoms to pass. And then she waited some more.

"I just never got better," she says. On May 6, thirteen days after her first symptoms, she was experiencing such severe shortness of breath her doctor advised her to go to the hospital. Doctors ordered a chest x-ray and sent her home with a puffer. Two days later, she was back at the hospital again. The doctor in the acute care ward who treated her told her, "Looks like you're going to be in this for the long haul." It was the first time she'd heard that phrase in relation to COVID.

The Public Health Agency of Canada is working to understand the condition commonly referred to as "long COVID." The range of symptoms is broad, and can vary from mild to severe; it can affect both young and old regardless of the severity of their COVID-19 symptoms in the acute stage, and can last weeks or months after a person has been infected with the coronavirus. The condition has been recognized by the World Health Organization as "Post-COVID-19 condition," but people experiencing long COVID are sometimes colloquially referred to as "long-haulers." The numbers of Canadians experiencing

Jennifer Mont was diagnosed with COVID in April 2020 and has never really gotten over it. She's one of an increasing number of people known as "COVID long-haulers."

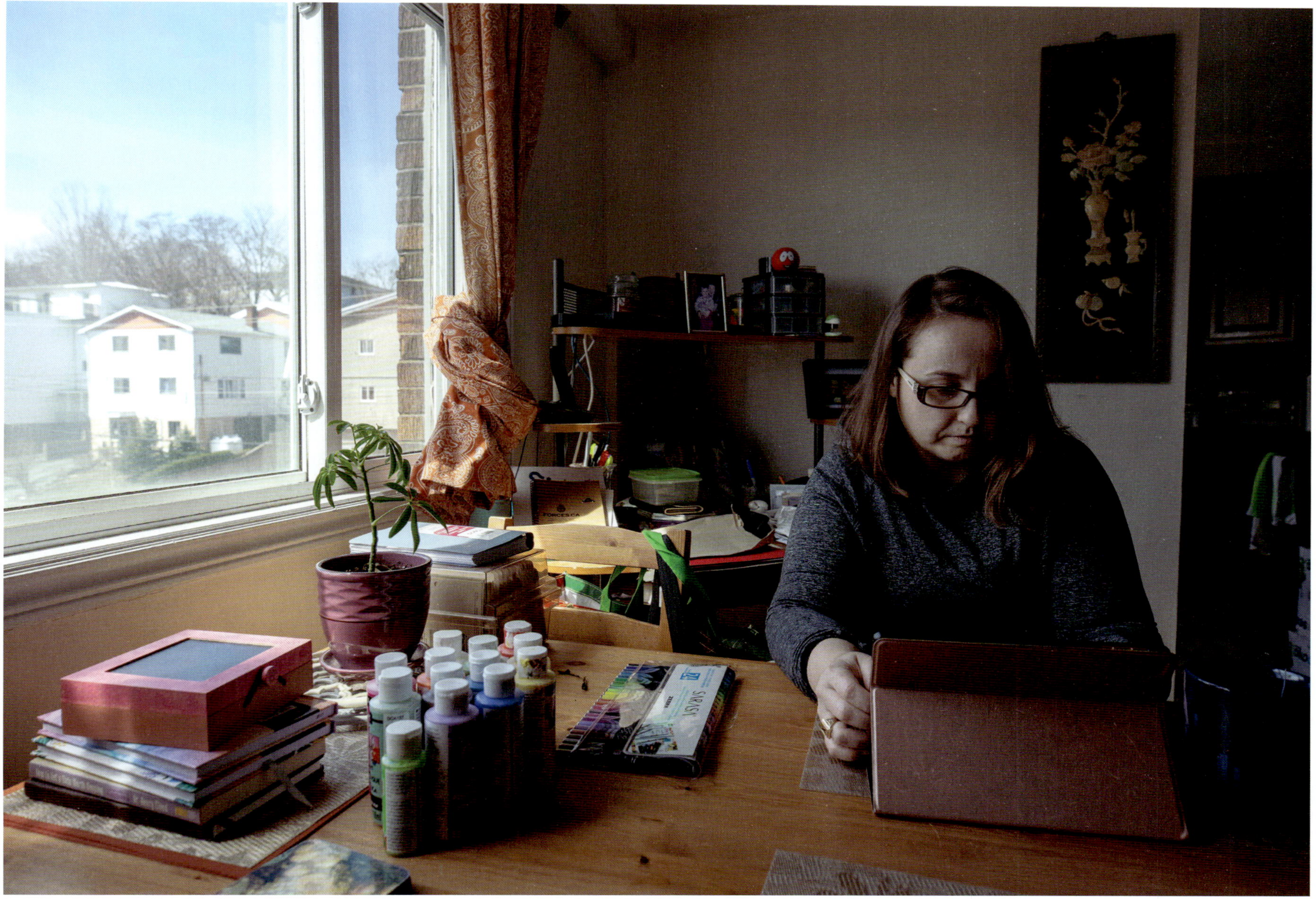

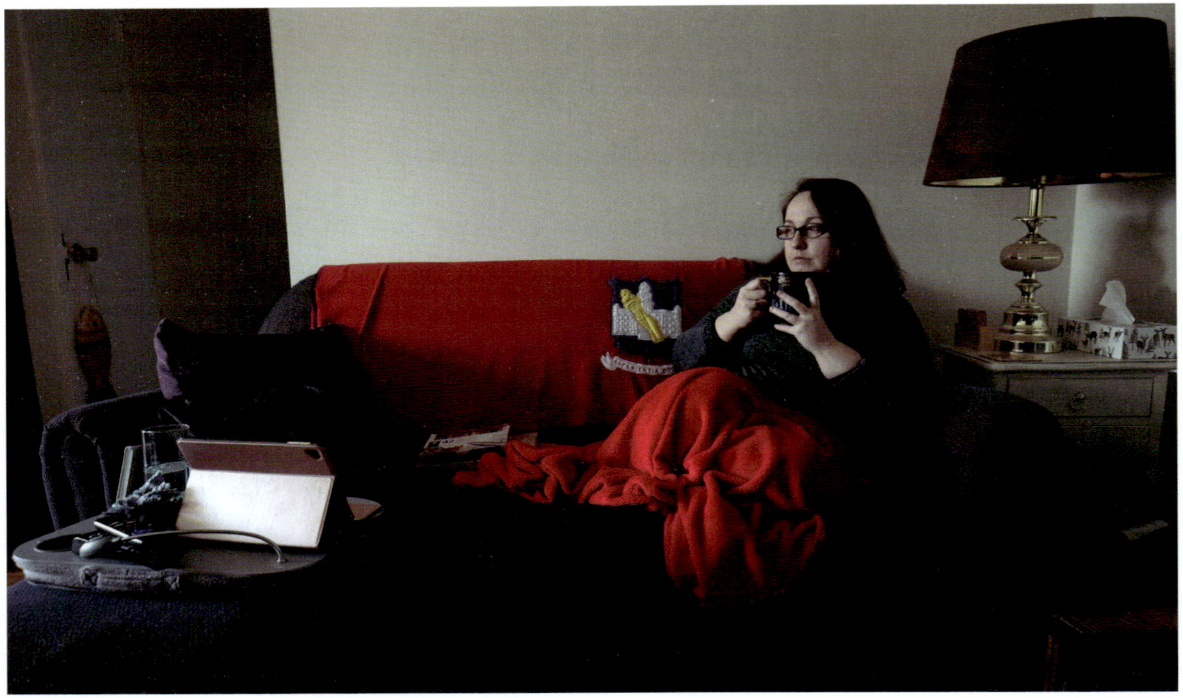

Jennifer Mont is living with what the World Health Organization calls "Post-COVID-19 condition."

long COVID aren't clear, but a Facebook group called "COVID Long-Haulers Support Group Canada" has more than fourteen thousand members—and is continually growing.

By mid-May 2020, despite the fact that she was still experiencing fatigue and shortness of breath, Mont was no longer considered infectious, and she was cleared to return to work as a part-time personal support worker. In early July, about two weeks after starting back to work, she says, she hit a wall.

"I was sitting there and all of a sudden this huge wave of fatigue hit me and I could not even understand it," she says. "It wasn't like I was doing anything too strenuous; I was just doing assisted daily living tasks with a client."

Her body pain returned. The chest pain came back. "It was just like I regressed," she says.

Her family doctor recognized that Mont was experiencing post-COVID-19 symptoms, but was at a loss as to how to treat her. Eventually, Mont was referred to Integrated Chronic Care Service (ICCS) a unit of Nova Scotia Health that provides comprehensive assessments and care planning for individuals with complex chronic conditions.

When we spoke, Mont was anxiously awaiting the appointment. "It's going to be a team of professionals who try and figure out a way to help me manage what I have, so hopefully I can move a little bit forward," she says.

Meanwhile, her ongoing symptoms have made it difficult for her to work. But her challenges have given her a new perspective.

"Yes, I'm going through some shitty stuff, but I'm also learning a lot about myself. I'm becoming more authentic with myself and able to set boundaries, able to figure out how to bring some more calmness into my life, even though things are very uncertain. And I'm learning the stuff that I love again because, you know, life is stressful and you get away from that."

Her hope for the future is simple. "Honestly, I just want to be able to get to a level where it doesn't hurt anymore so I can try to move forward and help people again."

KEEPING THE VULNERABLE SAFE:

Life and Work in Long-term Care

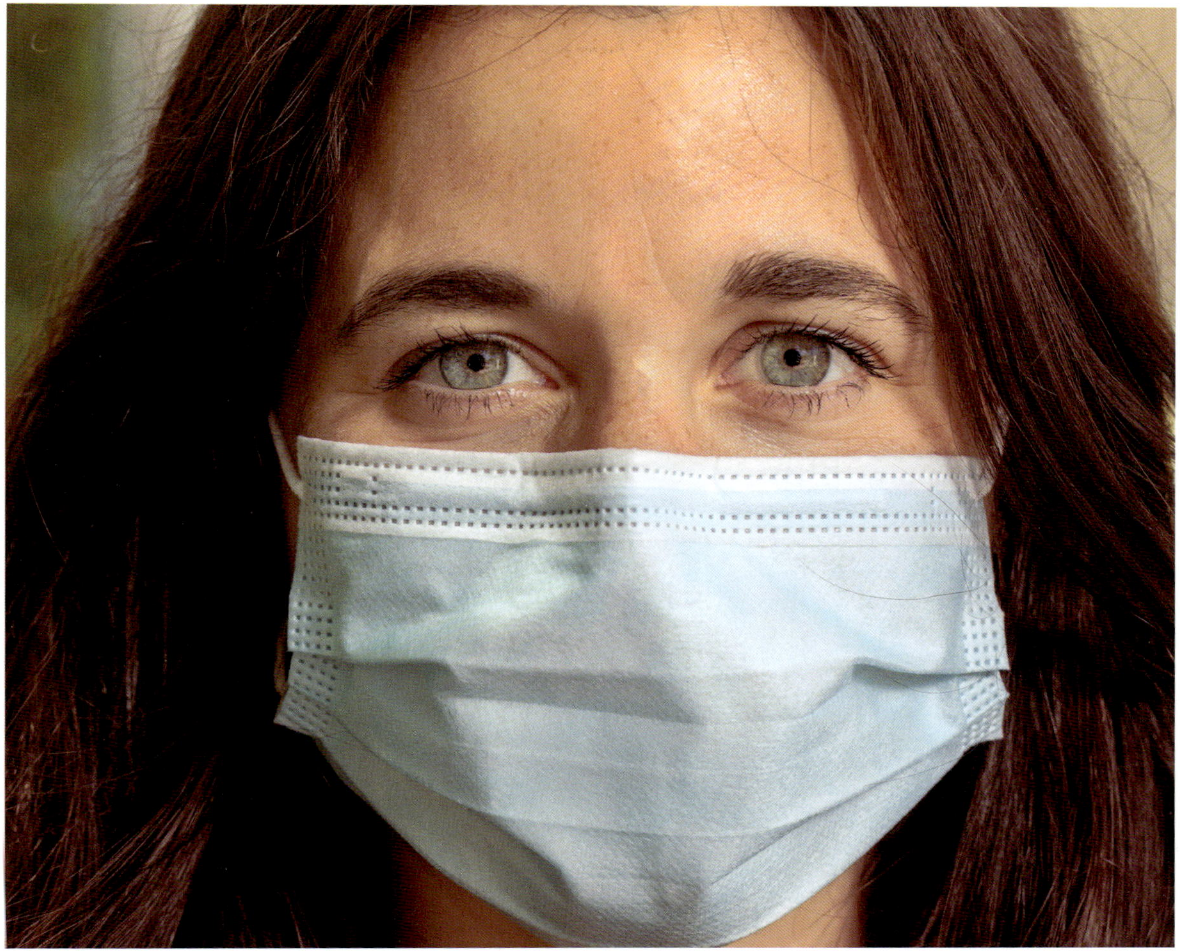

Shelby Davis is health-care supervisor at Dykeland Lodge nursing home in Windsor.

The COVID-19 pandemic has been hard on everyone, but it's been particularly hard for the thousands of people living and working in long-term care in Nova Scotia. Lockdowns and restrictions have meant residents have endured months without visitors, and the evolving science around transmission and infection control has created challenges for the people working with a population very much at risk.

Jennifer Tempro, a recreation programmer who works at Dykeland Lodge, a long-term care home in Windsor, admits that the early days of the pandemic were challenging.

"Working here at the beginning of the pandemic was kind of scary, just because we were working with the most vulnerable population," she says. "There were new changes every day, and everyone was doing their best to figure out what was the right thing to do to keep everyone safe.... It took us a while to get on our feet, but once we did, I think we did a great job keeping everything together."

With a little more than a hundred residents and two hundred staff, safety was a big concern. For Tempro, that meant essentially isolating with her family outside work, with the exception of gas and grocery runs. And although she missed circulating out in the community, she says all the residents and staff at Dykeland became very close.

"There were times through the pandemic where all visits were off; we were doing FaceTime and Skype phone calls," she says, pointing out that many of the

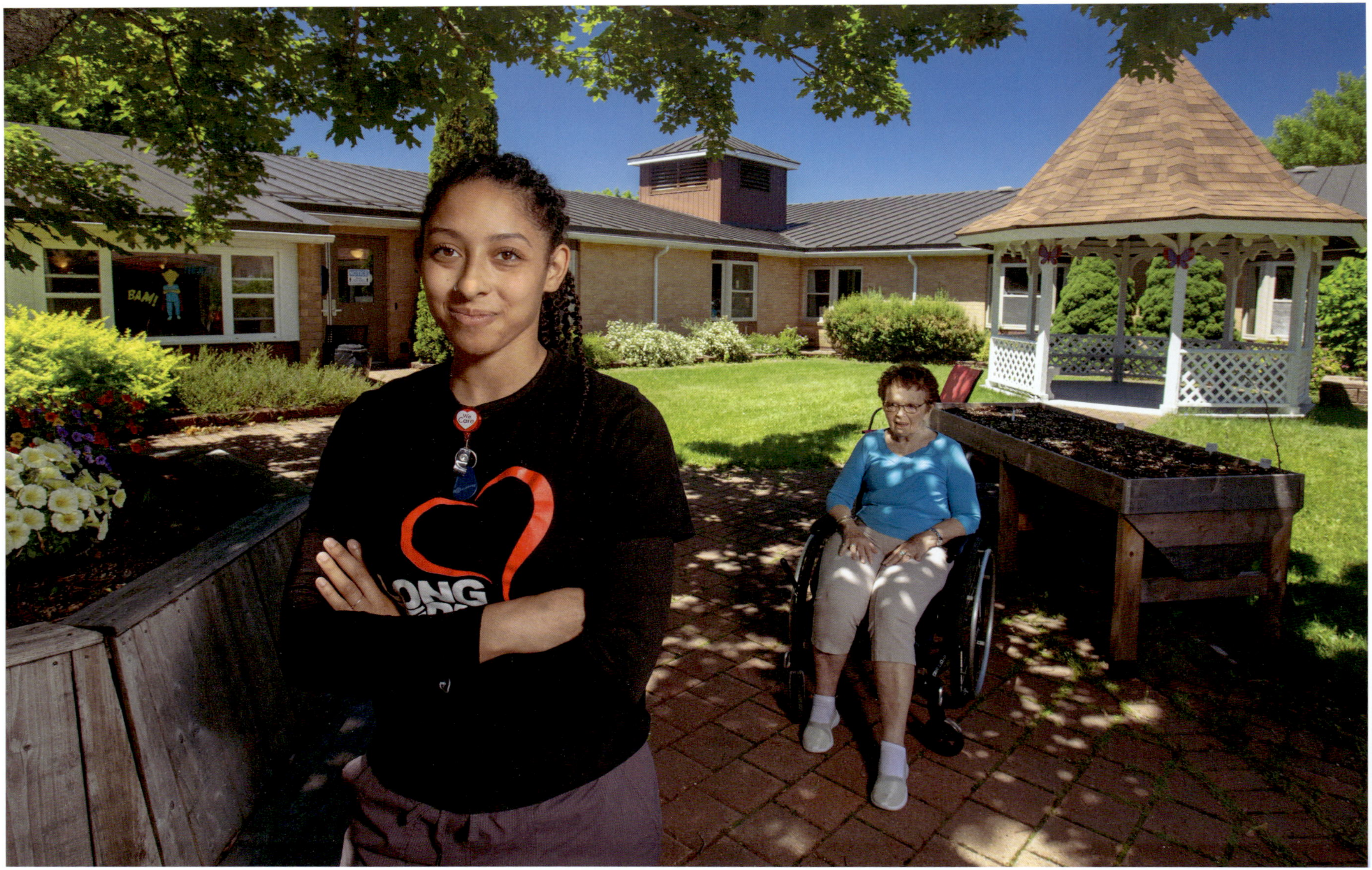

Jilisa Tempro (left) is a support aide at Dykeland Lodge. She is shown here with resident Arlene Jean Lane.

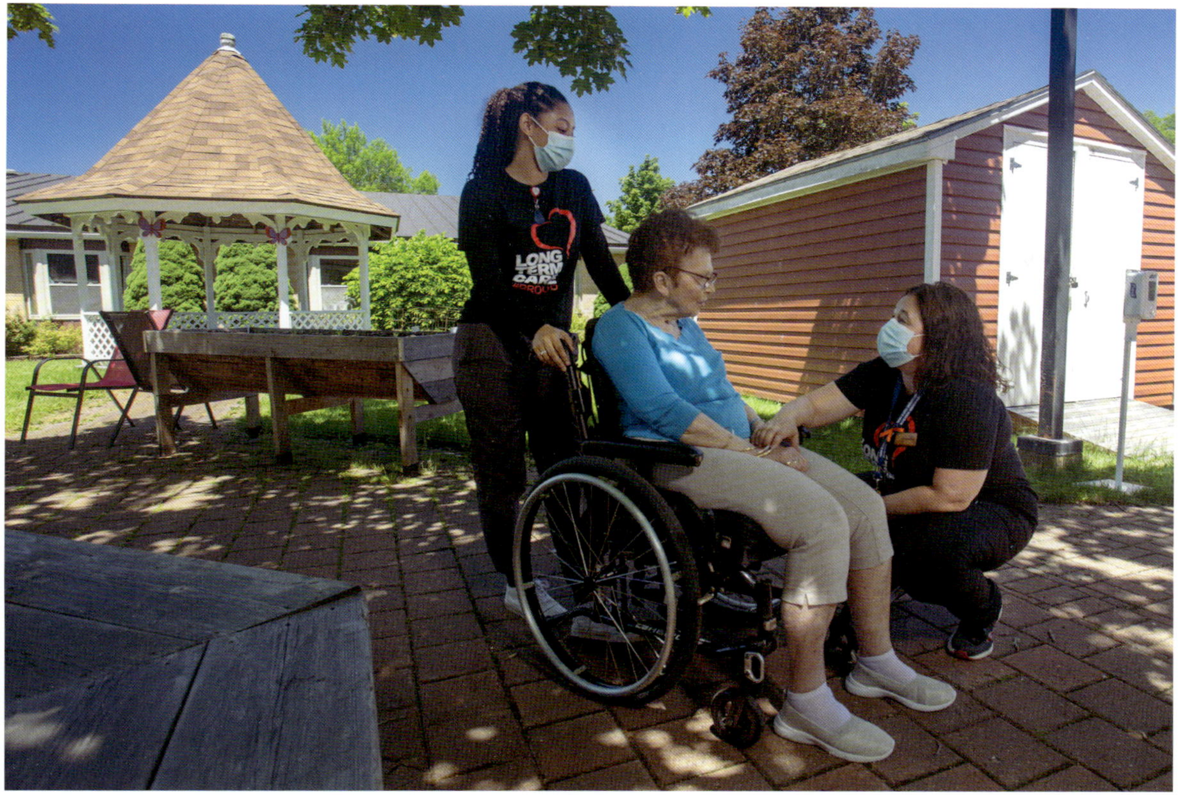

(left to right) Jilisa Tempro, Arlene Jean Lane, and recreation aide (and Jilisa's mom) Jennifer Tempro at Dykeland Lodge.

residents didn't even have access to those kinds of technology. "So there was a long time where it just felt like it was us. Like this was our family.... It gave us a real feeling of closeness with them because we were their everything."

Dykeland CEO Krista Beeler agrees. "We became the hands, we became the hugs. We became the people who wrapped our arms around the residents," says Beeler. "I think a piece of the success was staying so close to the families and the residents. Taking the time to hear the tears, taking the time to talk to families, taking the time to message them. I would text families who would say, 'I don't know if I can do this, Krista.' And if it meant I had to run down the hallway and snap a picture of their mother and text it to them, then I would."

Arlene Jean Lane has lived at Dykeland Lodge for close to two years. She says she missed being with her daughters and her grandchildren, who live in Halifax, through most of the pandemic. For a period she was allowed only to see one visitor from behind glass. "I missed the social interaction with people and being able to go where I wanted when I wanted," she says. "But [the staff here] looked after me and put up with all our whims and wants and all that, and they tried to do that for each and every one of us, and that felt good."

Shelby Davis is a nurse and the health services supervisor at Dykeland. Part of her job is to make sure the Lodge's employees understand the ever-changing policies, procedures, and safety protocols issued by the provincial government.

"For the first little bit it was very daunting, because everything just happened so quickly," says Davis. "Now that everything seems to be slowing down a little bit and I have some time to reflect... I definitely have a sense of pride. I feel like I was able to do something that really matters."

She says it's a huge responsibility to care for so many people who have "done so much in this world," a sentiment echoed by Jennifer Tempro, who adds, "I am honoured to be given the opportunity to be here and spend the last days, weeks, and months with somebody that has lived their life giving to this community; giving to this world."

Jilisa Tempro, a support aide at the home, says working with seniors through the pandemic has given her a renewed perspective on aging. "The thought of aging as a young adult is terrifying, but when you come into a place like this and you see like how life can still be great and how people are still forming new bonds and still learning new things—that really changes the way you look at things."

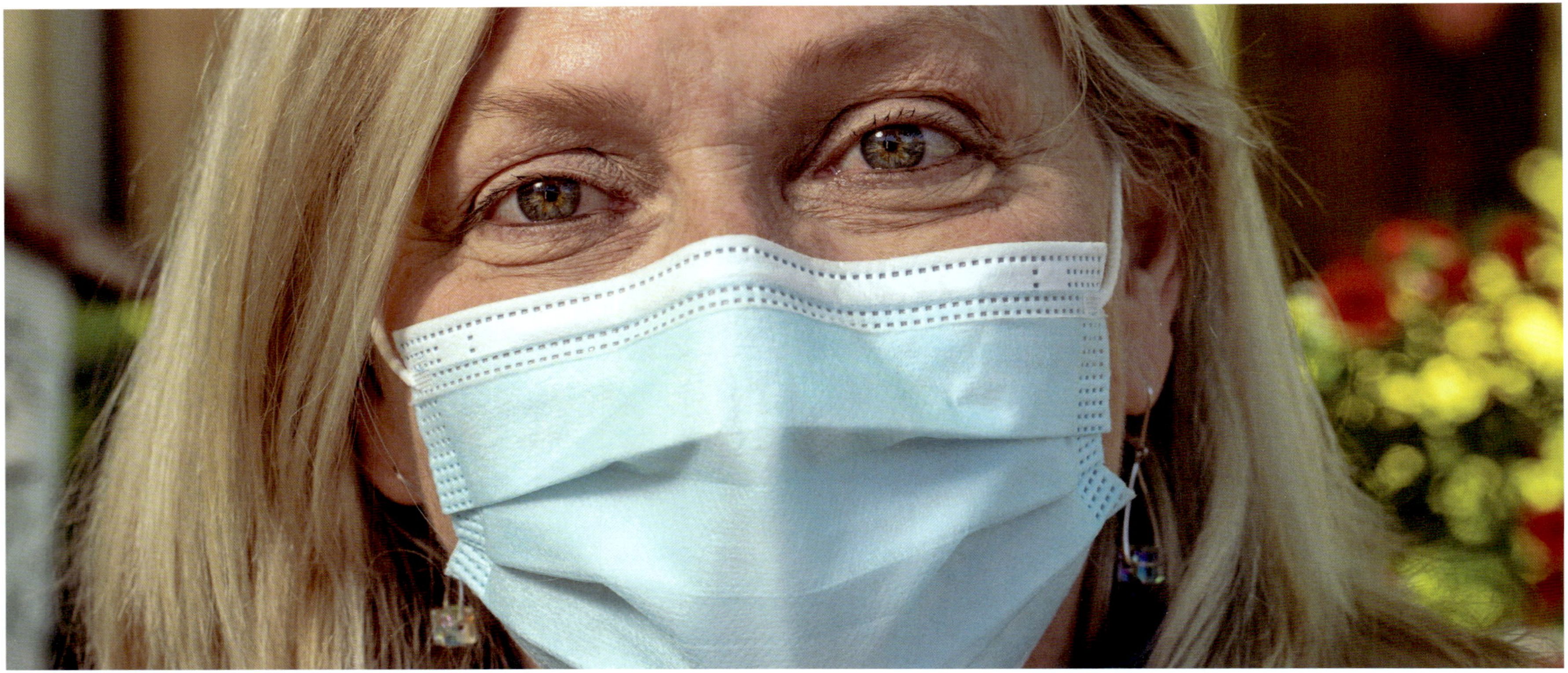

Krista Beeler is the administrator at Dykeland Lodge.

Krista Beeler says making it through the entire pandemic with no recorded cases of COVID-19 was a daunting task.

"I had an underlying goal at the very beginning of COVID, and that was: we've got to make it to the vaccine. We have to make it to a double vaccine. And we looked ahead to prepare for that—and we made it."

Vaccination day, says Beeler, was an emotional one. "The residents were rolling their sleeves up because they knew that in the end they were going to get a hug—that this meant it was going to get them closer to their family.... It was a day filled with tears when, as an administrator, I was able to take a deep breath and go—wow, I think we're gonna make it through this. I think we're gonna be okay."

When families were finally allowed in to visit again, she says, there wasn't a dry eye in the house. "We had families who had not hugged their mothers in seventeen months and they held onto them for five minutes. It was beautiful."

Beeler says the staffers at Dykeland have become "a real live group of superheroes" in her eyes.

"It almost brings tears to my eyes to think about it," she says. "I will be forever proud of this team. I will never work with a team that gave so selflessly ever again. I can't imagine it."

VIRTUAL CARE: *Dr. Amy Hendricks*

One big change in the lives of many Nova Scotians during the pandemic was the switch to "virtual" patient care by their family doctors and specialists. In some cases, that meant physicians used audiovisual technology to connect with their patients, in others, it meant communicating by phone.

For Dr. Amy Hendricks, a general internist who works out of St Martha's Regional Hospital in Antigonish, the switch to virtual patient care was easier than it might have been for many physicians—because it had already been a part of her practice for most of her career.

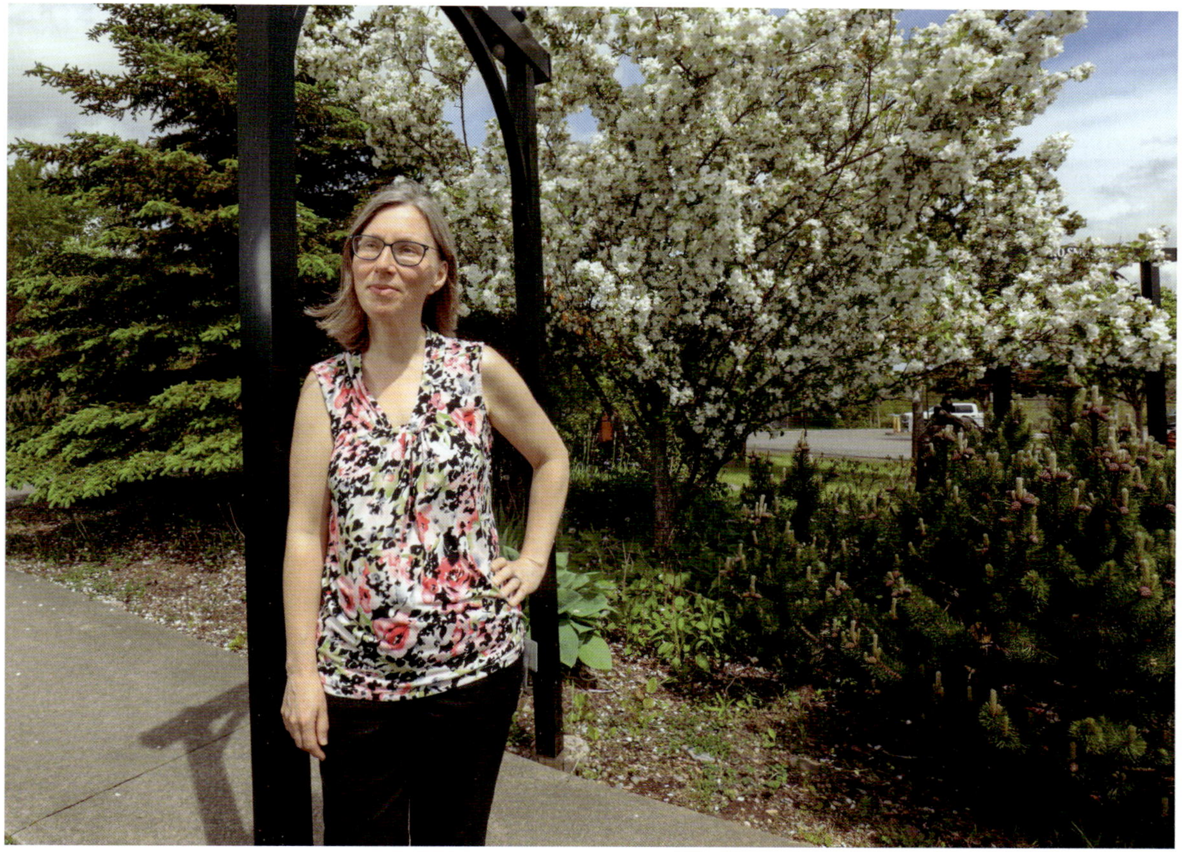

Dr. Amy Hendricks, a general internist who works out of St. Martha's Regional Hospital in Antigonish, says the switch to virtual patient care was easier than it might have been for many physicians—because it had already been a part of her practice for much of her career.

"I have always done a lot of travelling to remote or rural areas, and I've also conducted a lot of my appointments by phone with my patients," she says. In fact, virtual care and telemedicine were central to the way she practiced medicine while working in Canada's north for fifteen years.

When she moved to Nova Scotia in 2016, she discovered that there was no billing code for virtual appointments, meaning she could not get paid for providing that type of care. She and her secretary, Kai-Lee Walsh, didn't let that stop them.

"I said, we can't bill for it, but this is what we're going to be doing because a lot of people have to choose between gas to go see the specialist and money for rent. And we are not going to put our population in that situation. If I can do it by phone, I'll do it by phone."

Nova Scotia did bring in a billing code for follow-up appointments by both family physicians and specialists before the pandemic—in May 2018—but it was largely underutilized and not really announced or promoted, says Hendricks.

"I was probably billing more phone calls than anybody else in the province [at that point] because

I had always done it. So by the time the pandemic started, I was doing twenty phone follow-ups a week," she says. Before the pandemic she would do the initial consult in person and give her patients the option to have the follow-up by phone or in person. During the peak of the second wave, she did the initial consultations by phone as well.

"The relationship is the same," she says. "You're just doing things in a slightly different way."

Hendricks says it all comes down to each patient's needs. "If the purpose of an appointment is to see how you're tolerating these pills, what your blood pressure is, and what your bloodwork shows, we can do that on the phone," she says. "If the pieces are in place, why would you bring in the patient? Why would you force them to come? If you think about it, our system has always been extremely provider-centric: 'You will come to my office when I tell you to come. I can run late, but you'd better not be late for that appointment.'"

Her point is a good one: "That has been the model for care, particularly specialist care. And I think we can do better."

During the third wave of COVID-19, Hendricks was particularly concerned about her patients travelling from Cape Breton to the clinic. "I did not want my waiting room to become a place where someone who would turn out to have COVID had been in contact with other people, because that wreaks havoc with people's lives," she says. "So I used that standard to decide who was going to be seen in person." She also didn't see the sense in having people drive in dangerous winter conditions to come to a ten-minute specialist appointment.

In the spring of 2021 Nova Scotia extended the temporary billing code for virtual care to March 2022. "I think we are at a point of trying to figure this out as a health-care profession. And I think within every specialty there are important conversations happening about 'What is the right place for this? Where does it belong?' And I think a lot of that depends not just on the kind of medicine you do, but on the individual physician and the individual patient," she says.

"I think the one thing that we've finally done is we have started to ask the question, 'How should this person's medical care be delivered?' instead of assuming that it will be delivered in the way that's most convenient for the care provider," says Hendricks. "I think this experience will allow us to consider models of care that we were too afraid to consider before."

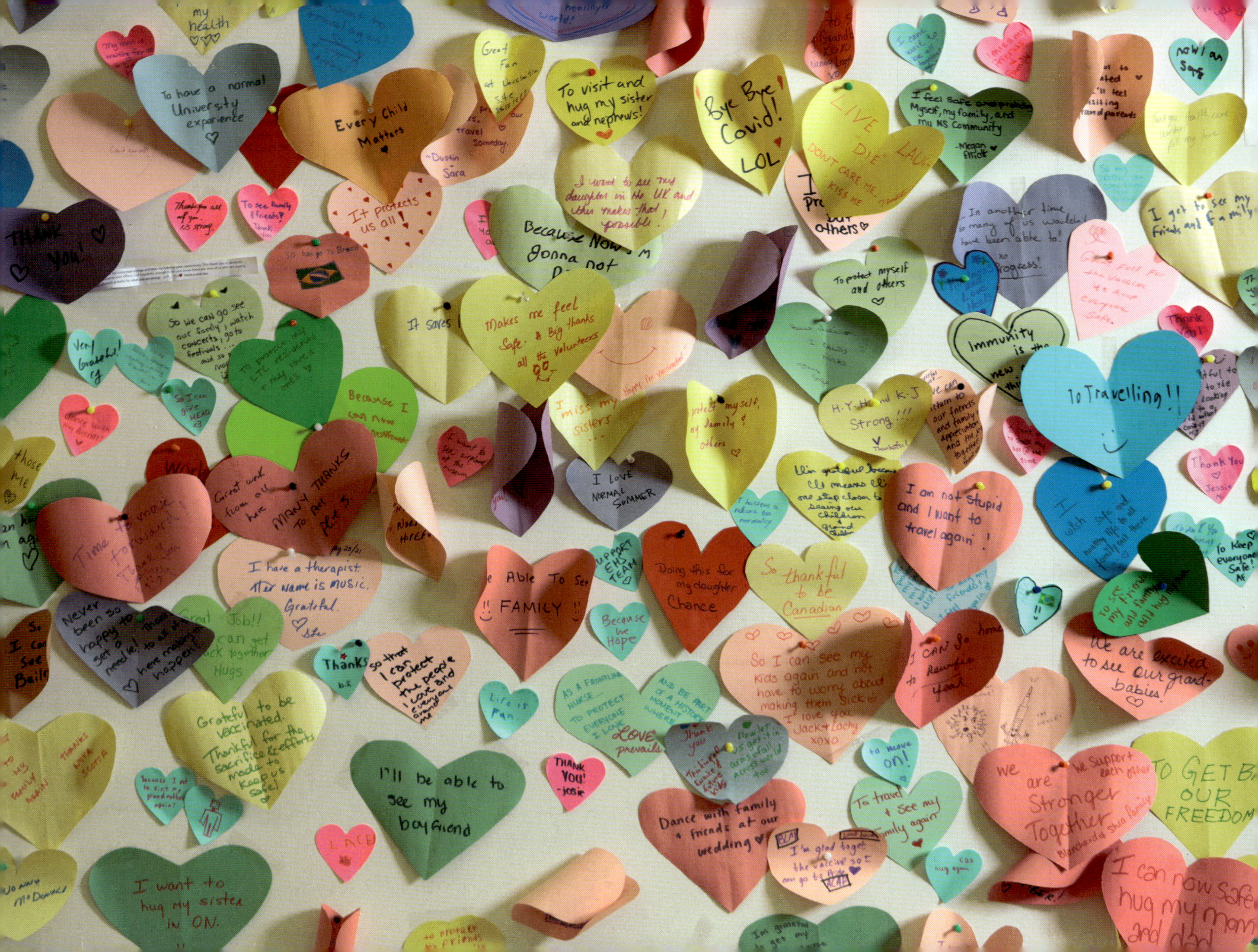

To have a normal University experience
Every Child Matters
To visit and hug my sister and nephews!
Bye Bye Covid! LOL
I feel safe and protect Myself, my family, and my NS Community
I want to see my daughter in the UK and other makes that possible
It protects us all!
Because Now I'm gonna not
To protect myself and others
In another time so many of us wouldn't have been able to!
I get to see my friends and family
So we can go see our family, watch concerts, go to festivals
It saves
Makes me feel Safe. A Big thanks all the Volunteers
Immunity is the new
To Travelling!!
Very Grateful!
Because I can now
I miss my sisters
protect myself, my family & others
H.Y. and K-J Strong!!!
I LOVE NORMAL SUMMER
Great work from all here
MANY THANKS To All
Time to move forward
I am not stupid and I want to travel again!
I wish safe and healthy life to all
Thank You
I have a therapist Her name is Music. Grateful
Able To See FAMILY
Doing this for my daughter Chance
So thankful to be Canadian
Never been so happy to see a needle!
Great Job!! Can get back together Hugs
Thanks
So that I can protect the people I love and everyone
Because we Hope
Life is Fun
As a Frontline Nurse, to protect everyone I love
LOVE prevails
So I can see my kids again and not have to worry about making them sick. I love you Jack + Lachy xoxo
I CAN go home
We are excited to see our grand-babies
Grateful to be vaccinated. Thankful for the sacrifice & efforts made to keep us safe!
I'll be able to see my boyfriend
THANK YOU! -Josie
Dance with family & friends at our wedding
I'm glad to get the vaccine so I can go to
To travel & see my family again
We are Stronger Together
TO GET BACK OUR FREEDOM
I want to hug my sister in ON.
I can now safely hug my mom and dad

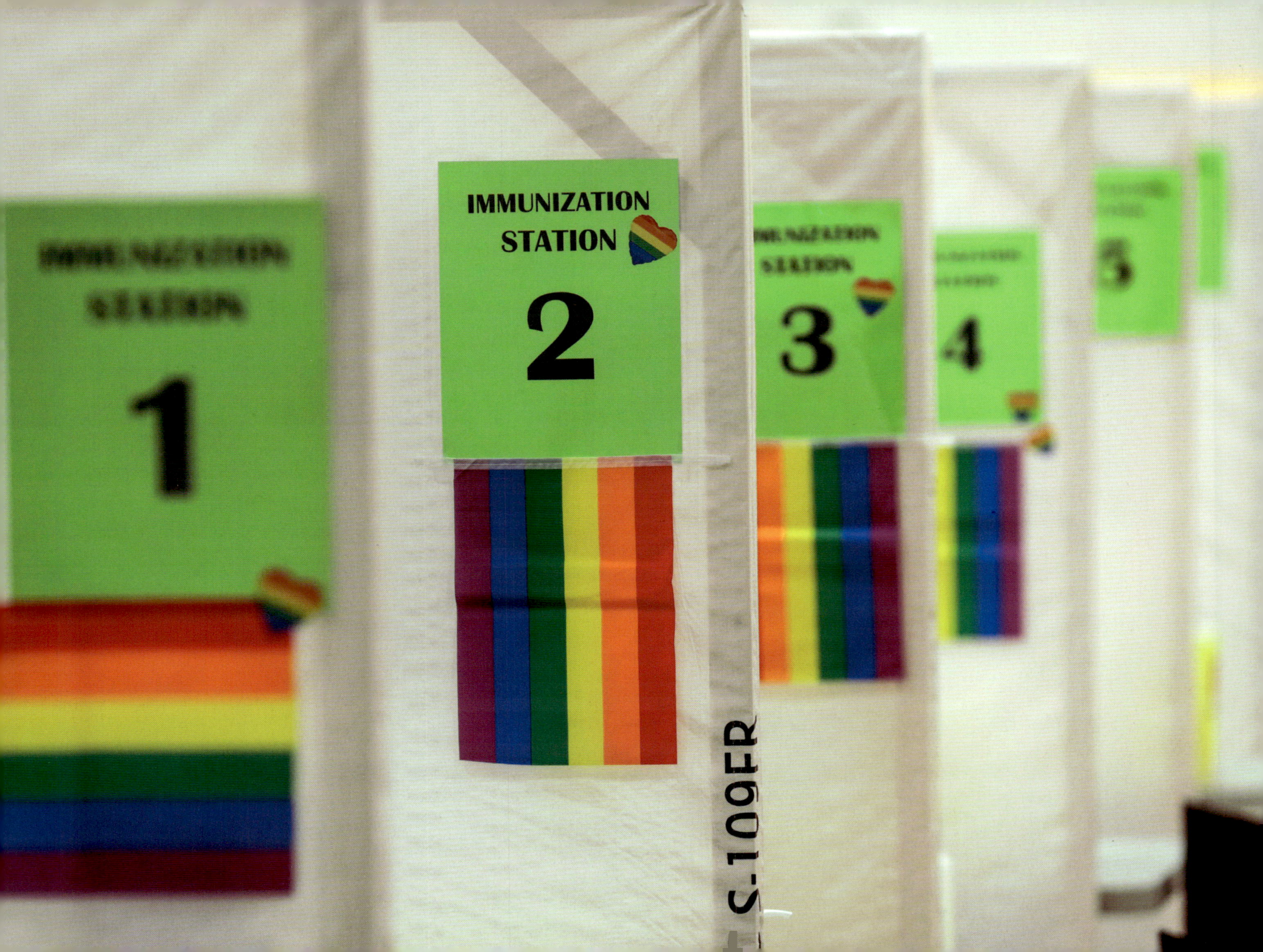
1
IMMUNIZATION
STATION
2
3
4
5
S-109FR

Part Four: LIFE GOES ON

SIGNS OF HOPE:
Richard Martell and Debbie Johnson-Powell

Week in and week out, since the start of the pandemic, many Nova Scotians have dutifully tuned in to provincial government briefings to get the latest information about COVID numbers, travel and gathering restrictions, vaccinations, and testing, first from Premier Stephen McNeil, then from Premier Iain Rankin, then from Premier Tim Houston, together with Chief Medical Officer of Health Dr. Robert Strang.

But—and let's be honest, here—many of us spend most of the briefings watching the box in the lower left corner of our screens in which Richard Martell, a sign language interpreter, is animatedly translating the proceedings for the benefit of Deaf and hard of hearing Nova Scotians.

Martell, who is a Deaf sign language consultant, is just one half of the interpretation equation. His off-screen counterpart is Debbie Johnson-Powell, a

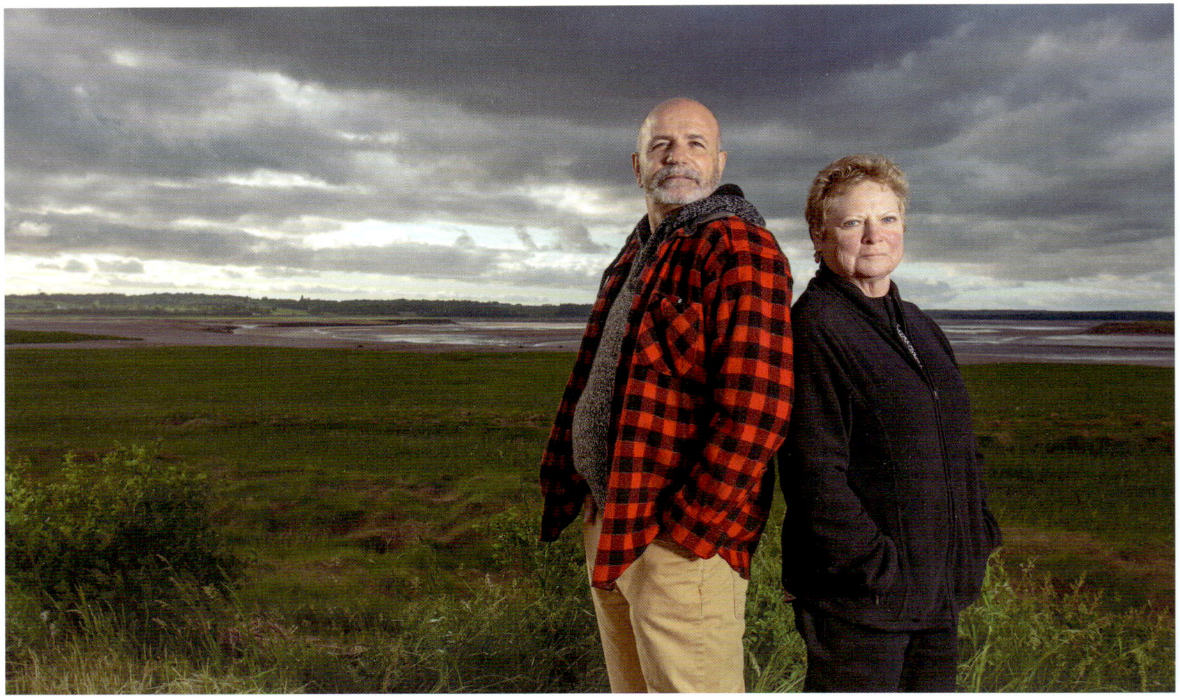

Richard Martell and Debbie Johnson-Powell teamed up to provide sign-language interpretation of Nova Scotia's COVID briefings for Deaf and hard of hearing audiences.

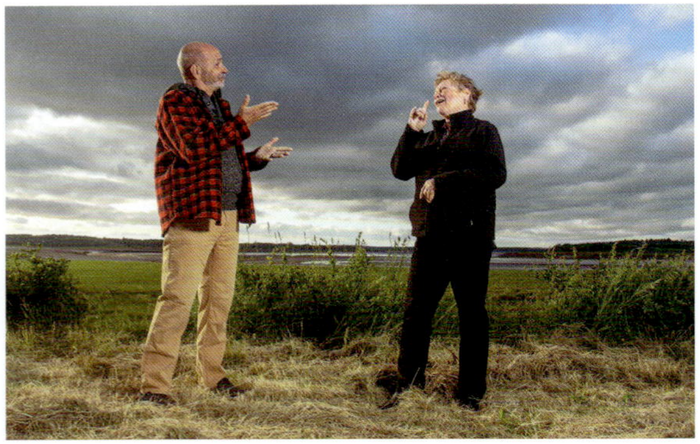

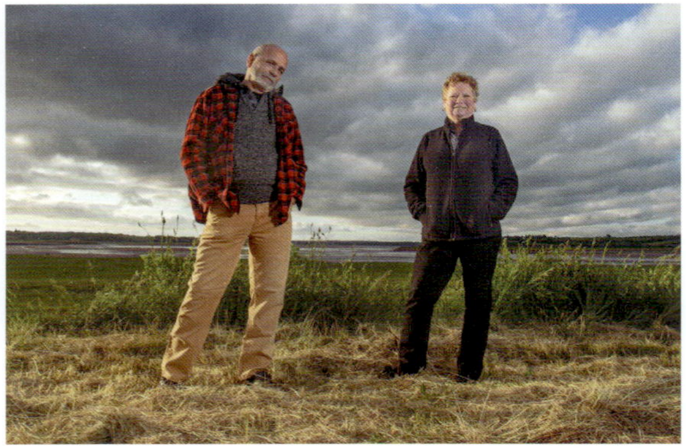

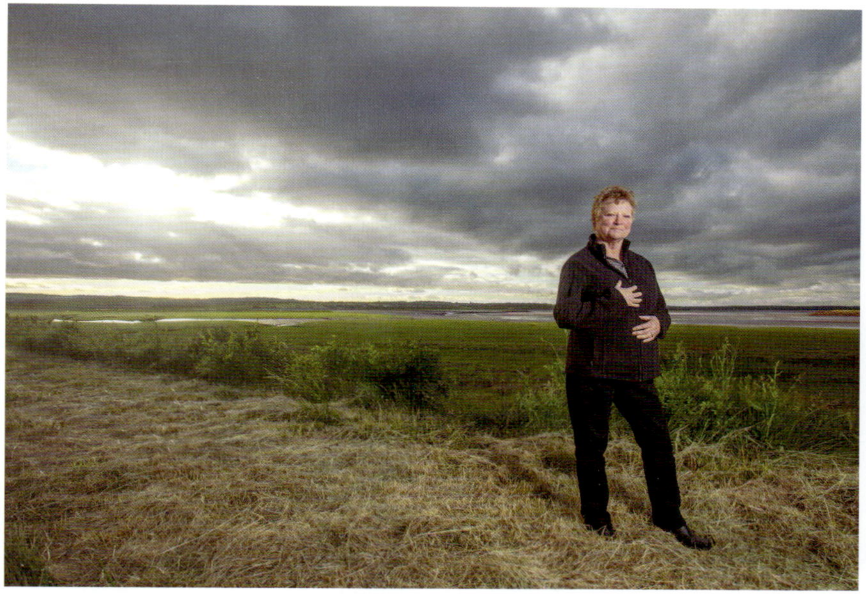

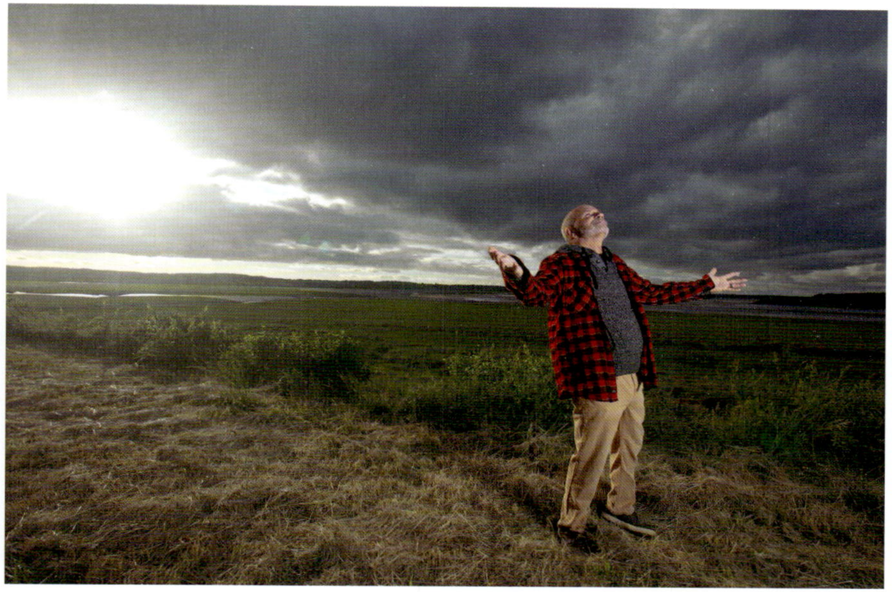

hearing sign language interpreter who conveys what she hears to Martell, who then signs the information to the camera.

For both Martell and Johnson-Powell, their first language is American Sign Language (ASL); Martell also uses Maritime Sign Language, an offshoot of British Sign Language which was used primarily at the Halifax and Amherst Schools for the Deaf, and which places a lot of emphasis on the use of facial expressions.

Martell was born Deaf, while Johnson-Powell grew up in a household in which both her parents and her brother were Deaf. According to the Society of Deaf and Hard of Hearing Nova Scotians (SDHHNS), there are approximately 58,000 Deaf, hard of hearing, Deaf-blind, and late-Deafened people in the province of Nova Scotia.

Before the pandemic, the two knew one another as acquaintances but had never worked together. "I'm proud to work with Debbie," says Martell as Johnson-Powell translates. "I have deep respect for her." Now, they are an indispensible team—and they have captured a following among Nova Scotians from all walks of life.

"The year's been stressful, but interpreting the COVID briefings has been a pleasure," says Johnson-Powell. As testing and vaccination have ramped up in 2021, they have both felt the importance of their roles. "We have to educate people," says Martell.

Martell's very visible role has put a spotlight on the importance of sign language interpreters, and the two acknowledge they have helped elevate awareness of ASL in Nova Scotia. Martell's calm, professional approach, even when conveying bad news, has captured a following.

"People who don't know sign language watch me," says Martell. "The feedback I've been getting is amazing. A lot of people have contacted me wanting to learn ... sign language, so they've started booking the classes with me."

And every once in a while, despite the seriousness of the subject matter, they make a mistake during a live broadcast that causes them both to chuckle. "We have to keep our composure and try to continue interpreting," laughs Martell. "It's all her fault when she starts laughing."

He looks over at Johnson-Powell. "When I first met Debbie to start working together I thought, 'I don't know how this is going to work,'" admits Martell, "but Debbie and I just connected and now it's like we're a perfect team."

FAMILY TIME: *COVID Babies, Kittens, and Puppies*

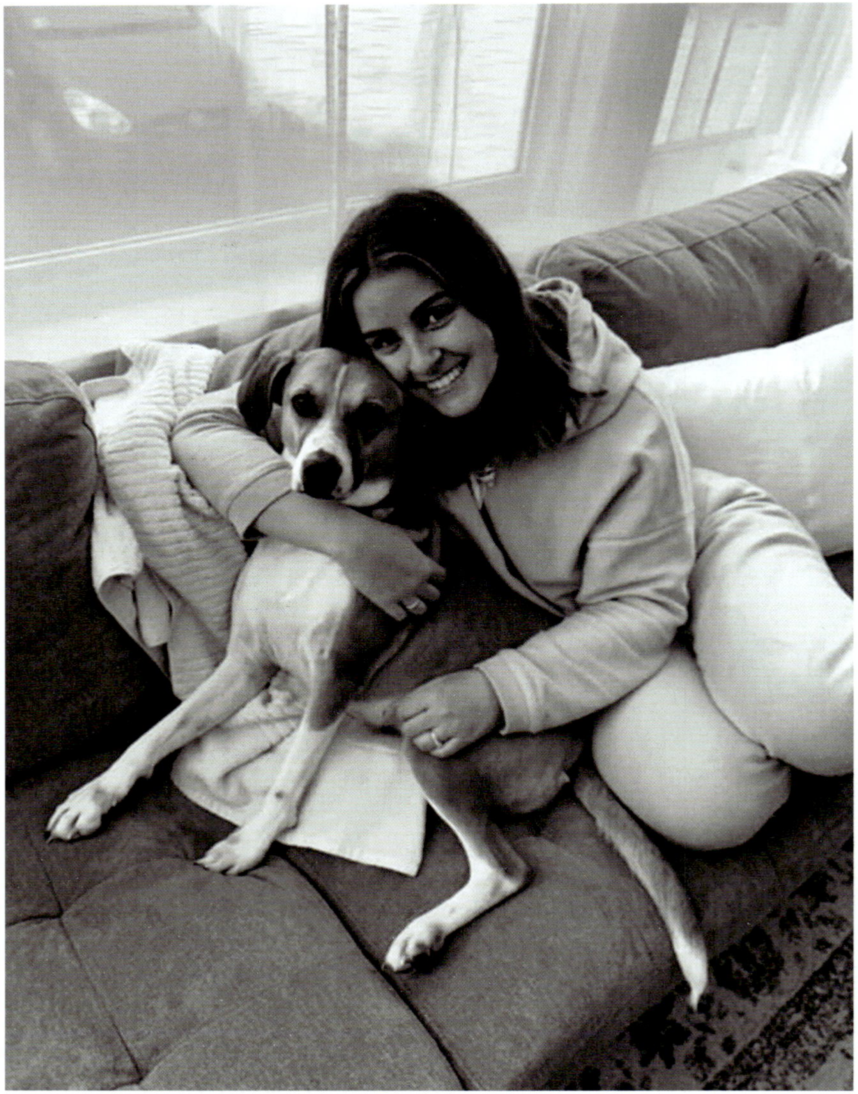

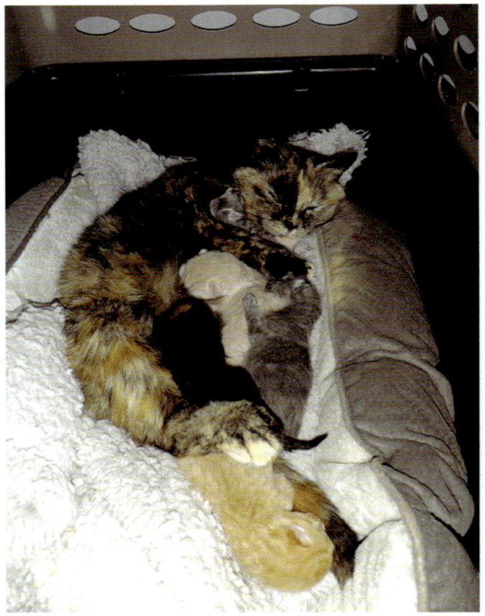

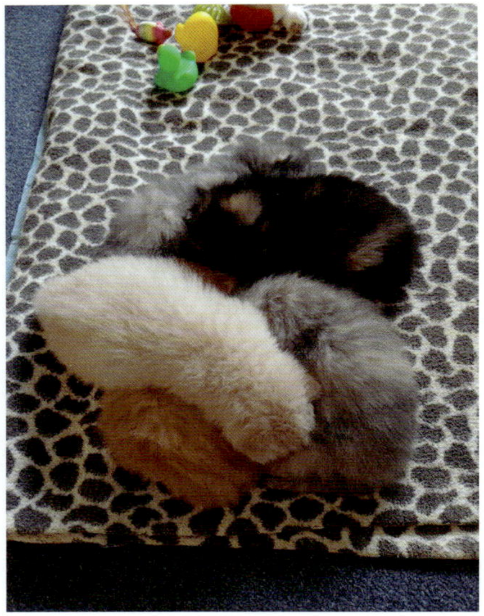

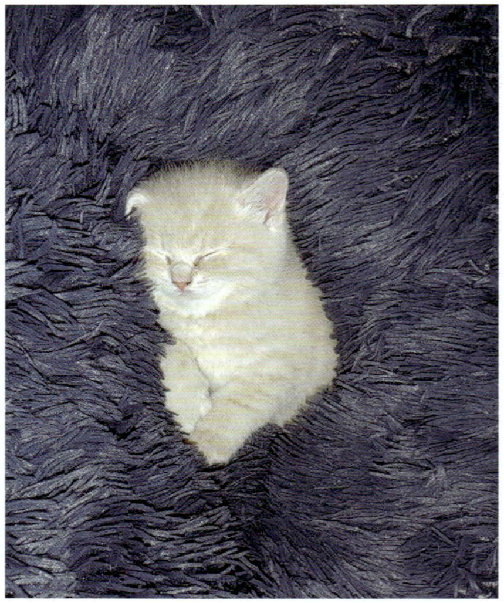

FAR LEFT: *Stephanie Watson of Cole Harbour writes, "[My husband and I] adopted a rescue dog during the pandemic and we love her to bits!"* (**STEPHANIE WATSON**)

TOP AND BOTTOM CENTRE AND ABOVE: *Corinna Penney of Yarmouth writes, "During this lockdown I decided to become a foster momma for our local SPCA shelter. I love animals and they help me cope with anxiety and depression. These five babies and their mom provided me with joy and happiness. Along with these six, I have two cats and a dog of my own."* (**CORINNA PENNEY**)

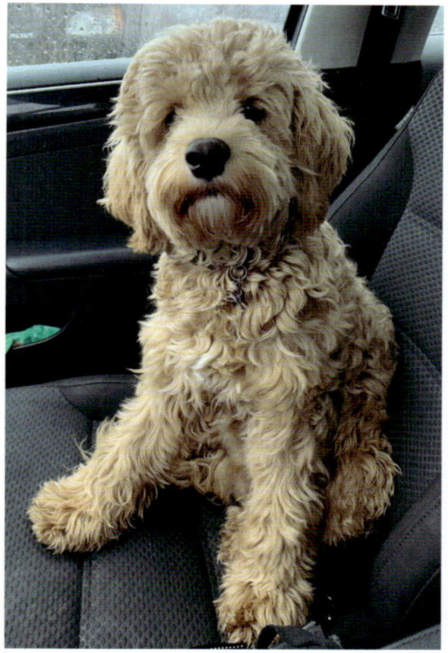

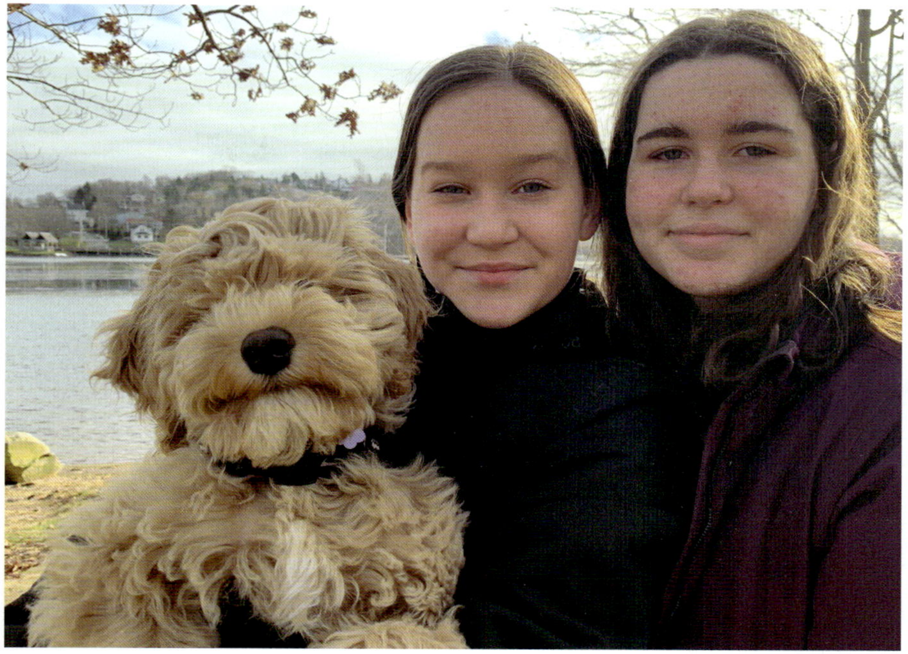

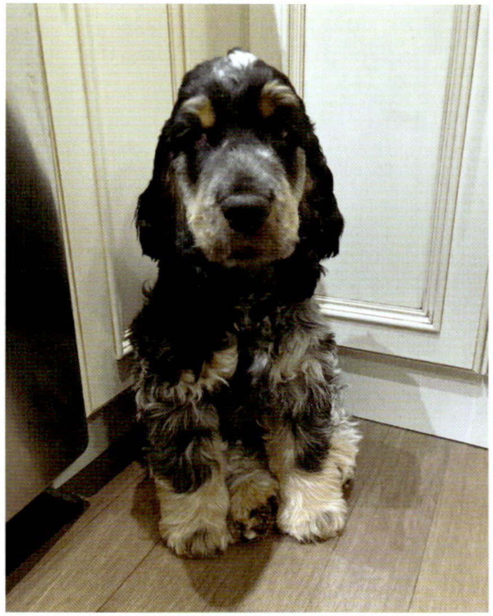

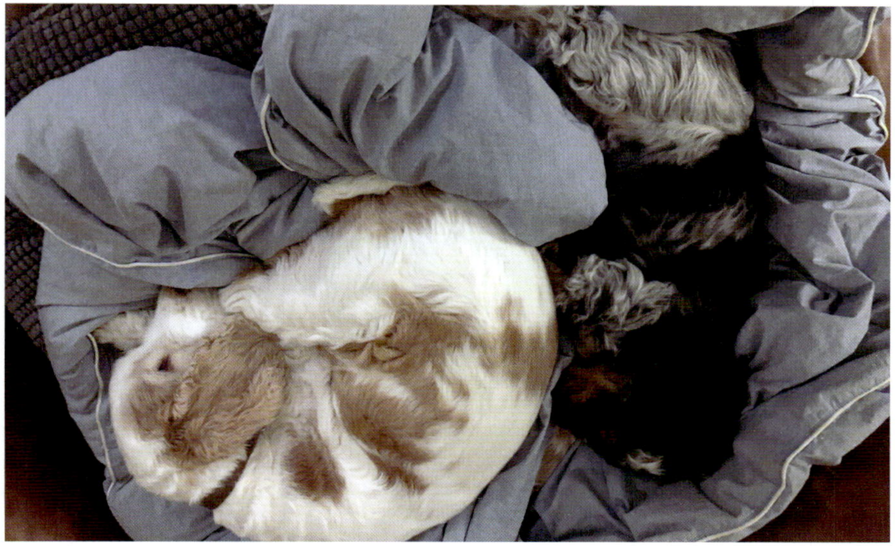

TOP LEFT AND RIGHT: *Colleen Goggin of Dartmouth writes, "We would never have adopted Auggie, our now 7.5-month-old cockapoo, had it not been for the pandemic. I was never home during the day so it was not an option for my family. We love him! Those are my daughters, Rachel Coady (fifteen) and Jane Coady (thirteen) with Auggie at Birch Cove on Lake Banook, Dartmouth, in December 2020. Rachel is holding Auggie."* (**COLLEEN GOGGIN**)

BOTTOM LEFT AND RIGHT: *Jennifer Church of Dartmouth writes, "Before Christmas we had no intention of getting a puppy. In January, after many family conversations and figuring out logistical issues and the current realities of live cargo air travel, Sprocket arrived in Nova Scotia. He's a four-month-old English cocker spaniel. Also pictured is his older brother, Flynn."* (**JENNIFER CHURCH**)

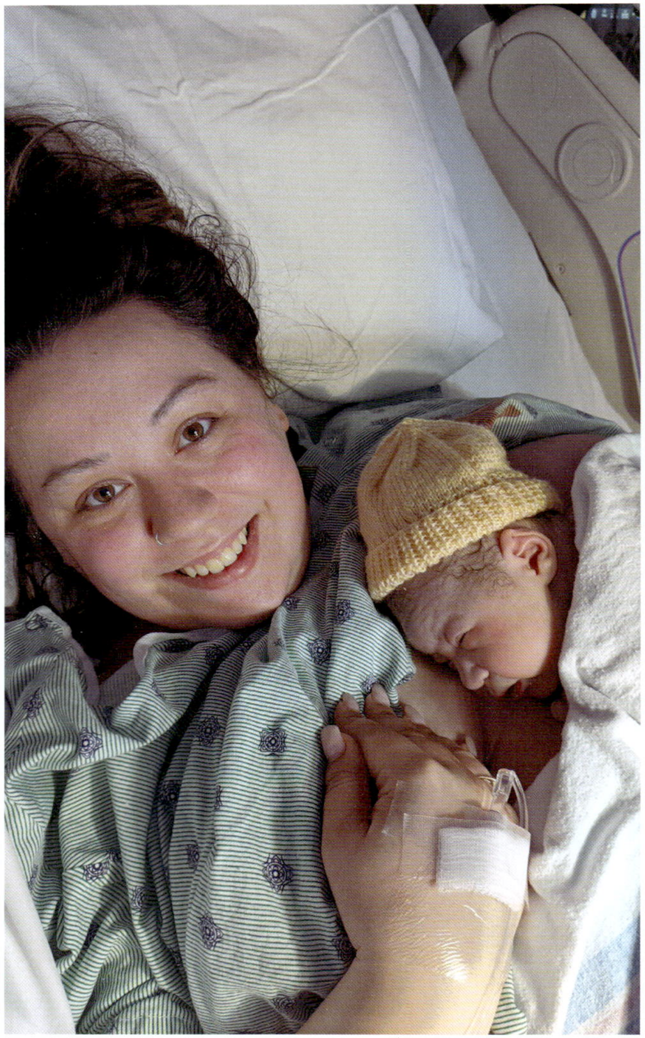

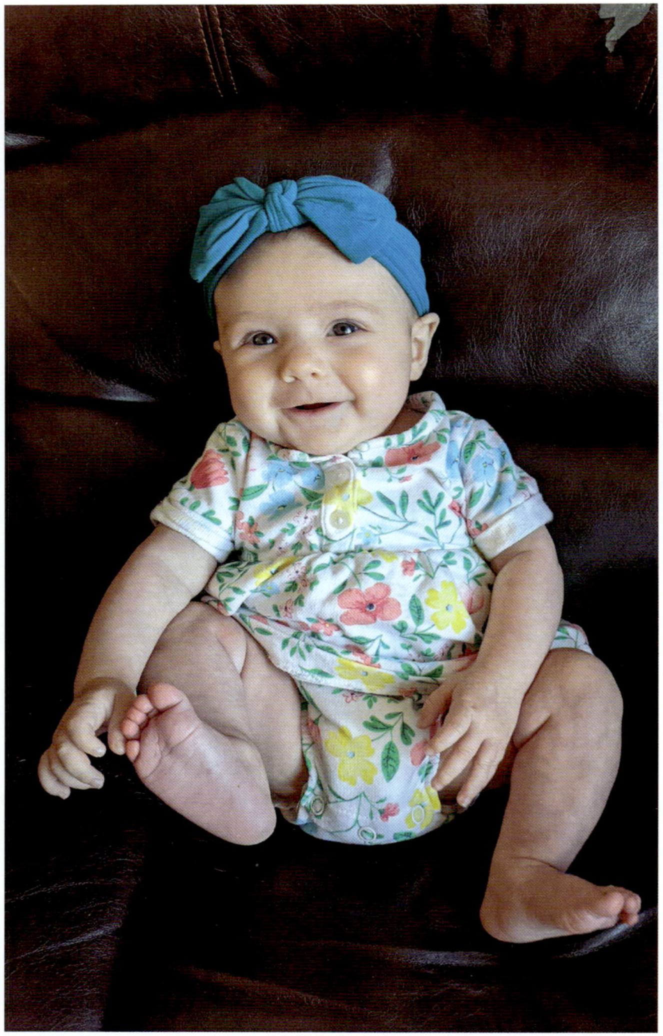

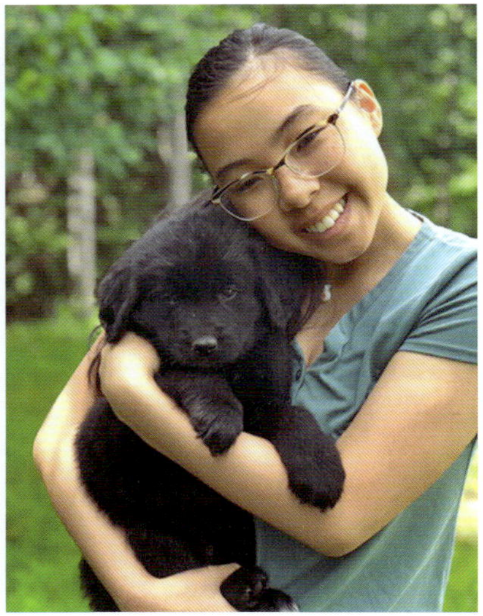

Kate Whalley of Tantallon is shown here with her retriever-mix puppy, Mo. Kate's mom, Sandra Clark, writes: "Mo was born May 11, 2020, and came to her new home on July 1. A great puppy and a great time to get a puppy—a real positive of the pandemic." (**SANDRA CLARK**)

Alexandra Lajeunesse of Dartmouth writes, "Although 2021 may not have been the best for everyone, it was the best for us! After many years of trying, we joined the cool club they call parenthood—DURING A PANDEMIC! It was not easy, as two weeks after Lillian's birth Nova Scotia went into its third lockdown, preventing our little one from meeting any of her Cape Breton family. Since restrictions have eased we've been able to visit and not only introduce Lillian to her family, but show her why we love Cape Breton so much." (**ALEXANDRA LAJEUNESSE**)

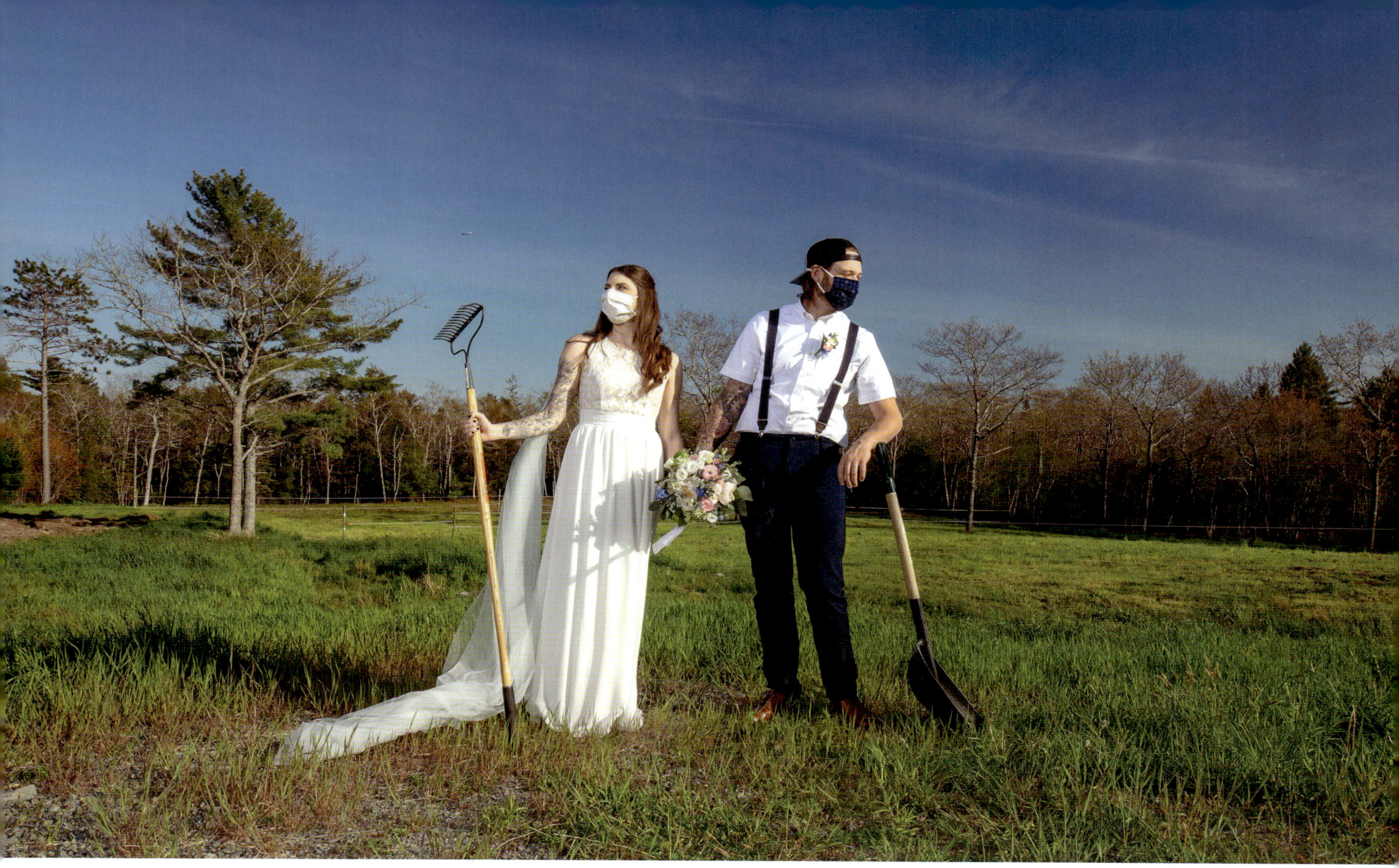

After seeing many friends and family members postpone, rebook, or cancel their weddings over the past two years, Jodi Wagg (left) and Brett Byng decided to seize the moment. Despite the lockdown that limited the size of their gathering to five plus the officiant, they were married in an intimate ceremony on a beautiful afternoon in May 2021. "We missed having the rest of our family there but it worked out well with just our parents," says Wagg. "Friends let us get married in their barn and it was us, the donkeys and horses, and our dog, Gauge—who played the roles of maid of honour, best man, flower girl, and ring bearer."

THE TEACHER BECOMES THE STUDENT: *Susan Campbell*

It hasn't been easy to be a student—or a teacher— through the COVID-19 pandemic.

Veteran teacher Susan Campbell, who teaches French and English to students in grades nine through twelve at Dalbrae Academy in Mabou, says she remembers the day in March 2020 when the kids were supposed to return to school after the March break. Unfortunately, the first lockdown meant they would not return to the classroom for the rest of the school year.

"I think the hardest part was probably engaging the kids in home learning and knowing how to navigate that," Campbell says. "That was a very challenging time."

When the students returned to Dalbrae in September for the 2021 school year, they found that everything had changed since they'd left the year before.

Masks were required, hallways had been altered to accommodate one-way traffic, and the collaborative classroom setups they were used to had been replaced by widely separated rows of desks, as they would have been decades before.

"I was impressed with how the kids adapted," says Campbell. "They're so resilient, and they just realized that this was a new reality and they accepted it.... I was very impressed with that. And then something would change—we'd get a new directive—and we'd tell them and they'd accept it."

But then, of course, came the second lockdown. In late April 2021, a rising tide of COVID-19 infections in the province meant that schools had to once again revert to at-home learning. Campbell says the challenge with that was recognizing that every home is different and learning how to adapt to the different learning needs of each student.

"Most students learn better in person, while other students adapted really well to home learning," she says. "So we tried to focus on supporting the individual needs of students while trying to be culturally responsive to where they were at home."

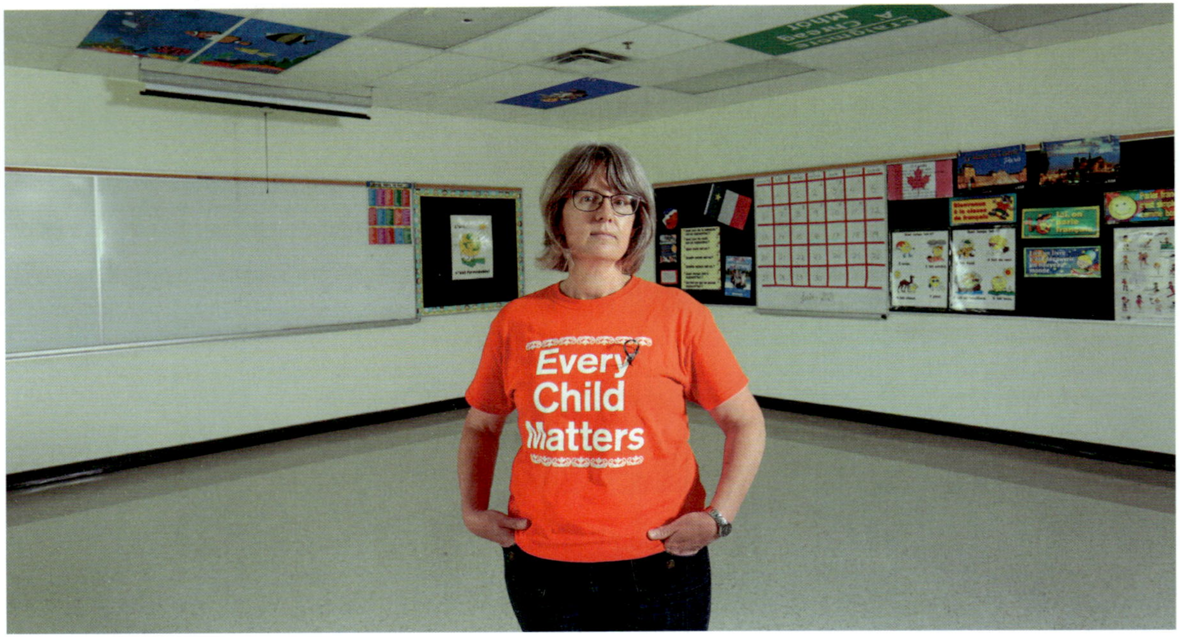

Susan Campbell, who teaches French and English to students in grades nine through twelve at Dalbrae Academy in Mabou, had to learn to adapt as Nova Scotia's schools switched to virtual learning and back again to in-class learning through the course of the pandemic.

Campbell says it was a good reminder that she is as much a student as her pupils are. "We've just had to do so much learning and revamping of everything," she says. "And we told them: we're just figuring this out ourselves."

Many of her students expressed concern about how much time they were spending on electronics at home, but Campbell also noticed that the extra time at home wasn't necessarily a bad thing for some of her students. "A lot of them started to find new pastimes—that was really neat to see," she says. "A lot of students started working on four-wheelers and their bikes, taking on little projects. Some kids took up running and some got a dog or a cat—so then all of a sudden they're out walking the dog more often, and one kid was telling me that they were biking forty kilometres a day."

Perhaps most gratifying, because she teaches English language arts, was discovering that some of her kids were enjoying writing poetry and short stories. "I think it was kind of an escape for them, and many of their stories were great—fantastic! So that was very rewarding."

When school once again resumed in June, Campbell says some of the students were nervous, but many of them were happy to be back—and she was, too. "It was great to be able to tie up some loose ends and get the kids that had some difficulty with the home learning caught up before the summer—and make them feel good about the school year."

Her hope for next year is that there's minimal disruption. But either way, she says, "I'm just glad that we succeeded in getting through it. We're proud of the kids."

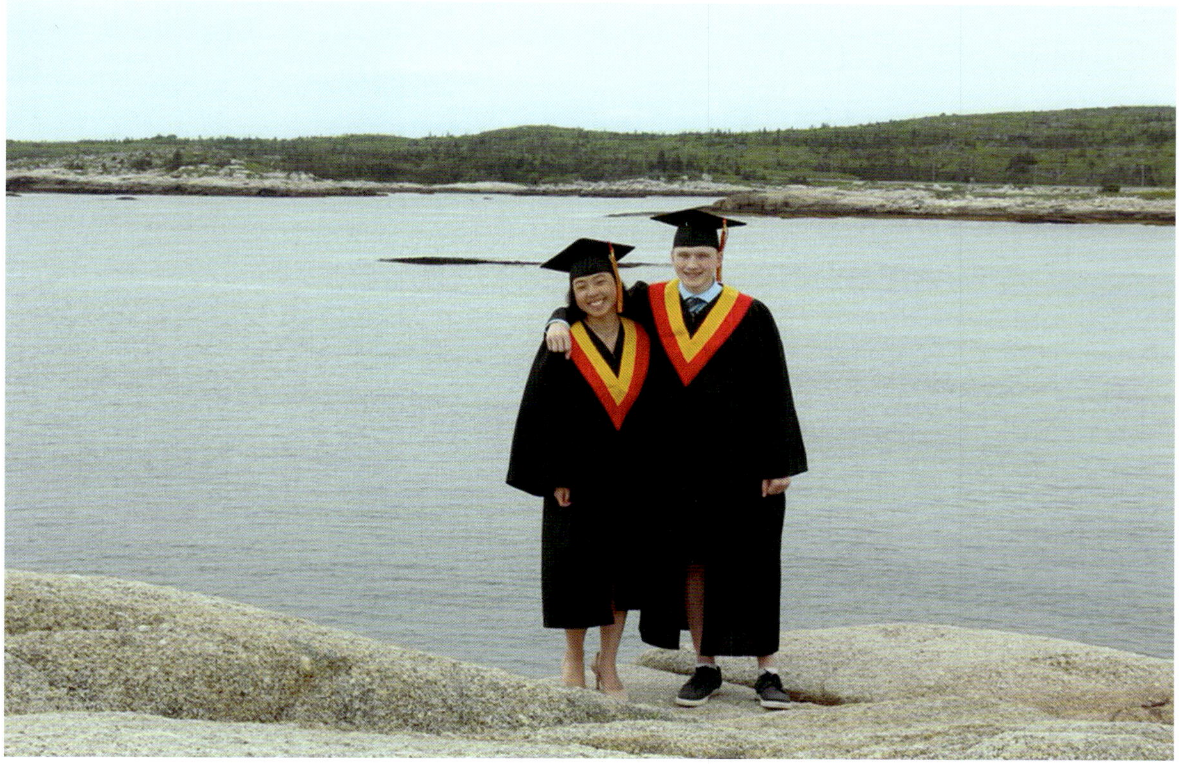

Kate Whalley (left), was a graduating student at Sir John A. Macdonald High School (now Bayview High) in Tantallon. "In 2020 we all thought there'd be, at most, two extra weeks of March Break before everything settled down, she says. "Two weeks turned into a full-scale pandemic that lasted throughout our final year of high school. After ten months of masks, misery, and ever-changing restrictions, our teachers and parents were able to put together a graduation and prom for us. Though they might not have been enough to completely reframe the year as a joyous one, it was almost cathartic to finally end it with tassel throws and expensive formal wear."

Jack Goulden (right) was her classmate. "Because of the pandemic, I found school to be extra difficult," says Goulden. "The constantly shifting regulations played heavily into this. However, despite this, my classmates and I have graduated. And despite the restrictions on large social gatherings, it's still a momentous occasion for us all."

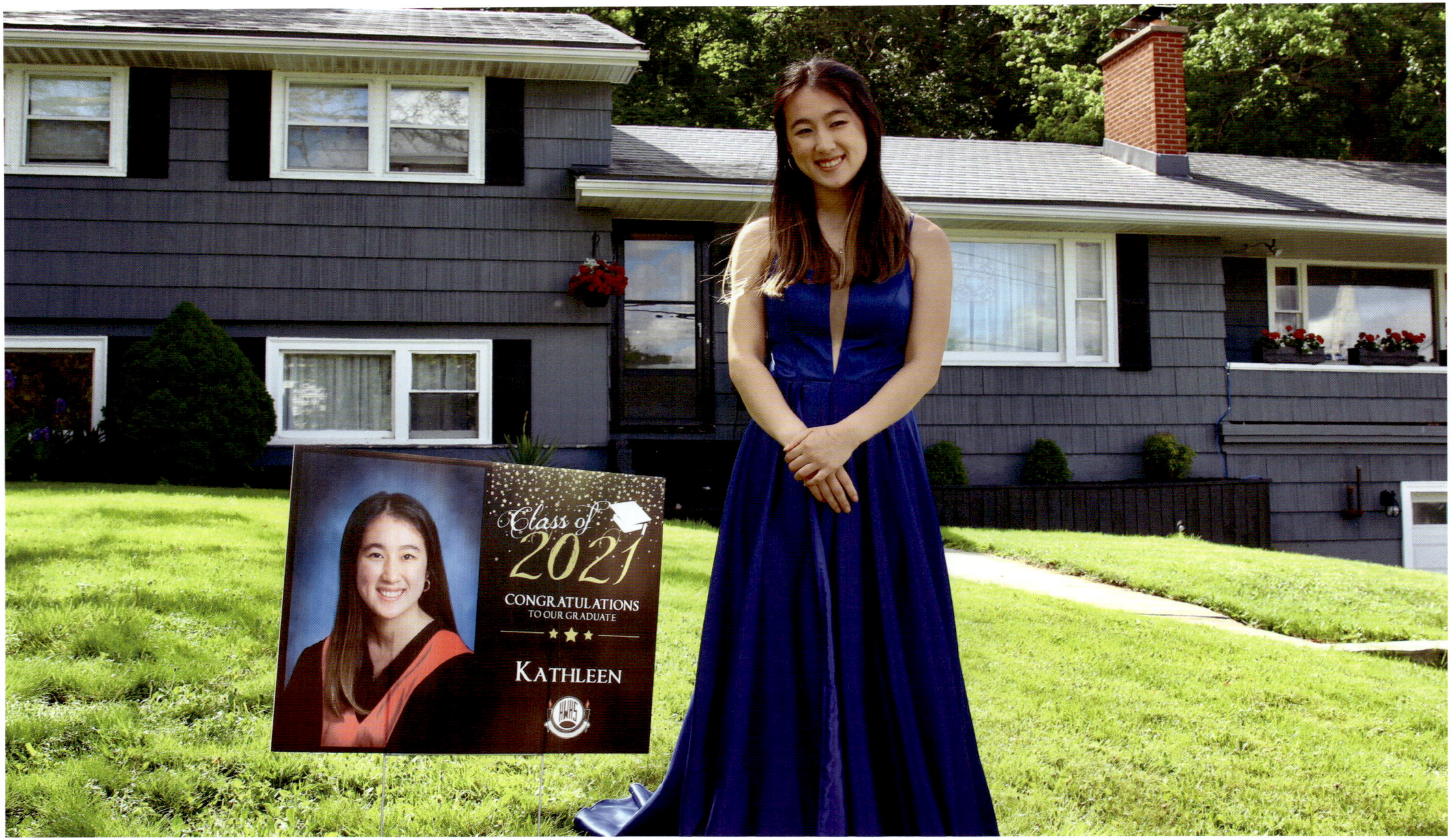

Katie Murray was a grade twelve student at Halifax West High School who graduated in 2021. "Grade twelve was very different from how I thought it would be," she says. "When we finally got back in the classroom I was identified as a close contact of someone with COVID-19—twice! Four weeks of quarantine gave me a lot of time to practice guitar and to FaceTime with friends, but we got through it. I graduated with Honours and was able to celebrate graduation with my friends. I'm looking forward to the summer, and in the fall it's off to Saint Mary's University. I'll never forget my grade twelve year!"

THE STAYCATION SOLUTION

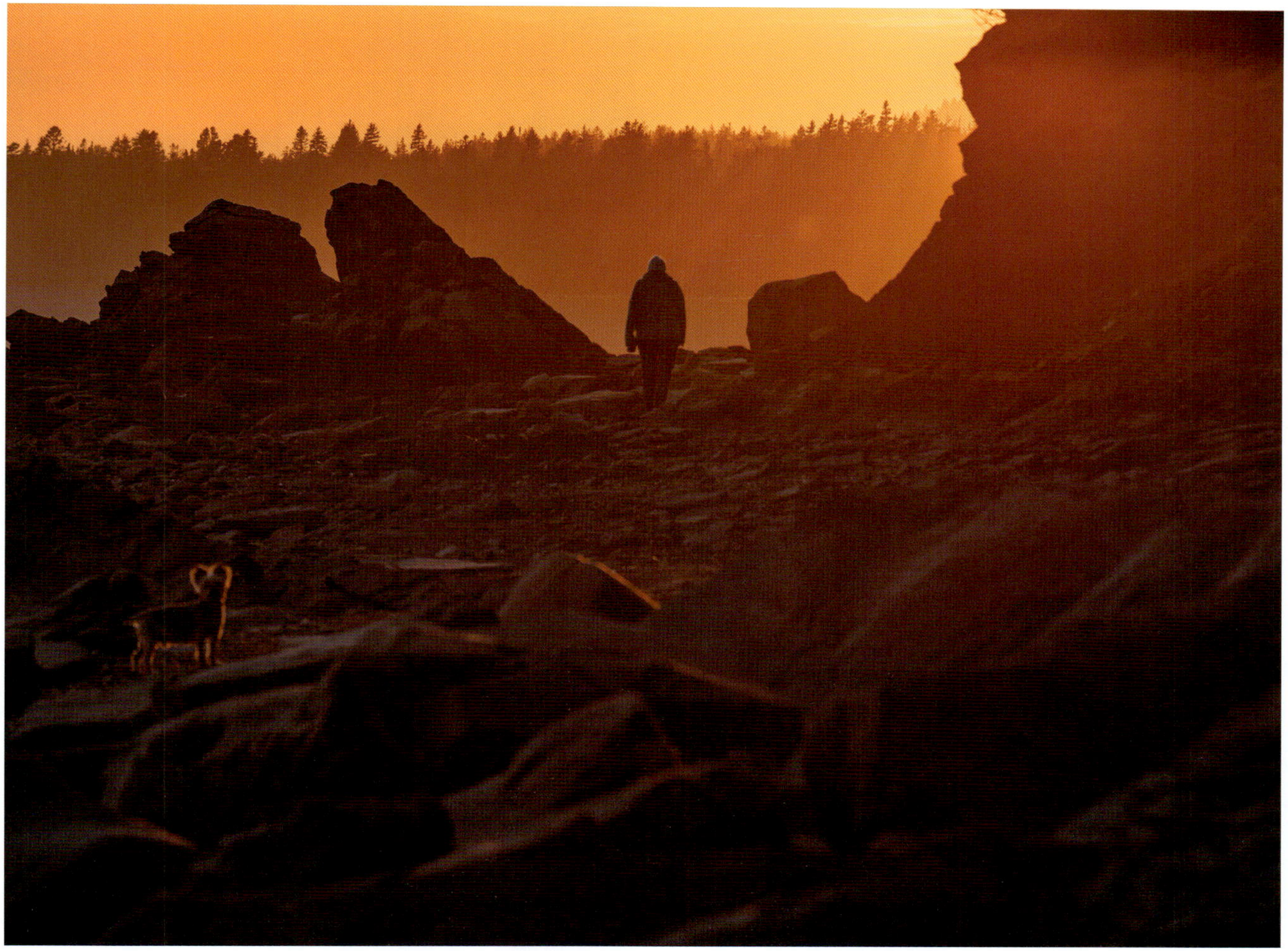

LEFT: *Kyle Hebb of Diligent River writes, "This photo was taken at sunset on one of our recent beach walks (May 26, 2021) in search of continued health, local beauty, and the tranquility of the ocean. In the photo is my wife, Lynne Hebb, as she walks between the rocks to get a better look around the corner as the sun dips below the horizon, while our Yorkshire Terrier, Buddy, stops and looks straight at me as if to ask if I am coming or not!*

"If there is anything that these COVID times has taught us, it is without question to appreciate the simple things all around us, and to never miss an opportunity for a great sunset. We feel so fortunate to live overlooking these ever-changing tides of the Bay of Fundy, but we often experience a sense of guilt for enjoying our lives so much through these difficult pandemic times while so many others struggle in so many ways—health-wise, personally, mentally, and financially. We so miss being able to spend precious time with our families and friends, but we remain confident that better days are soon to return, leaving us with a deep and lasting appreciation for those things we maybe took for granted pre-pandemic." (**KYLE HEBB**)

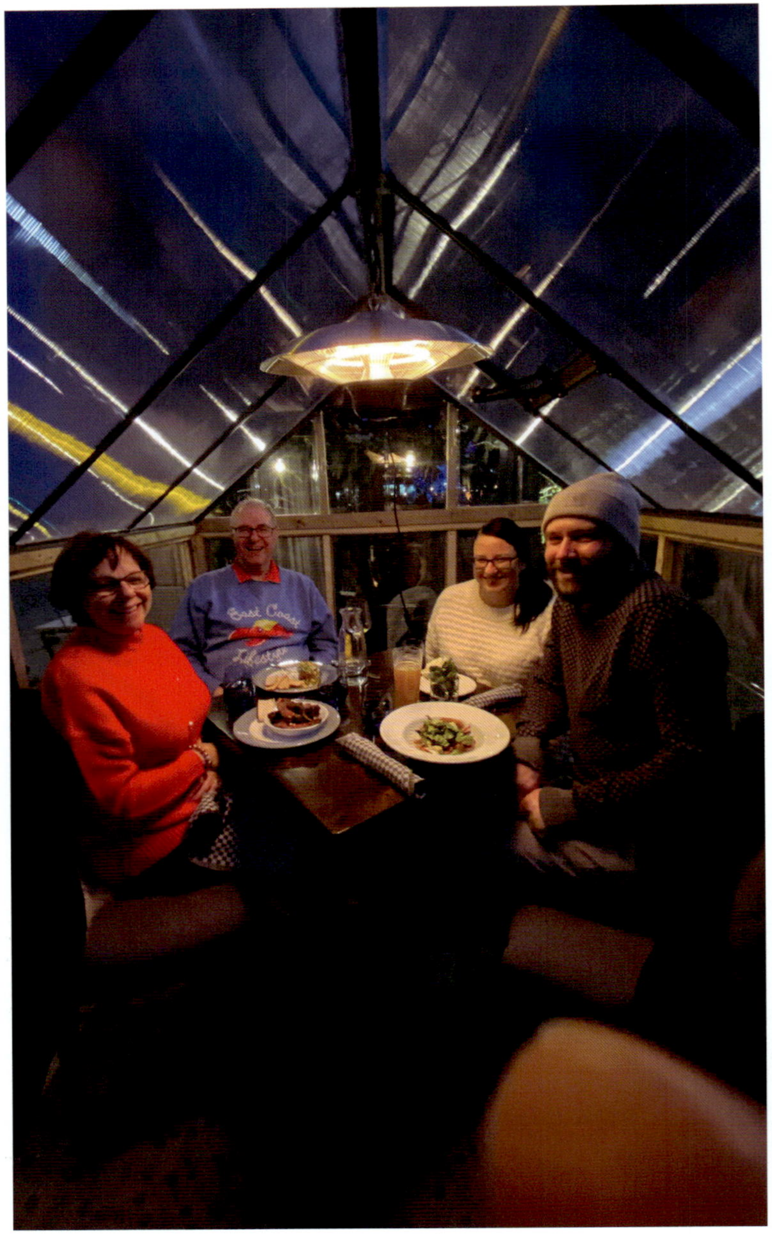

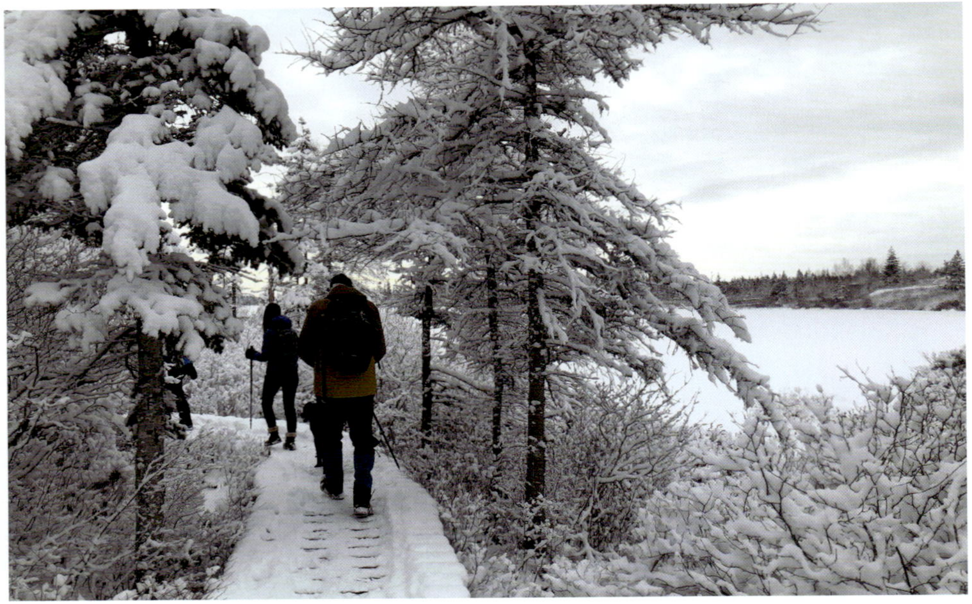

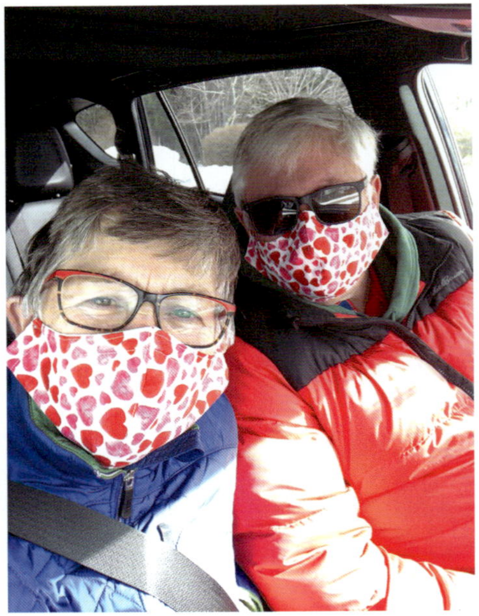

FAR LEFT: *(left to right) Andra Abraham, Jim Abraham, Holly MacKay, and Jamie Abraham enjoy dinner in one of the outdoor huts at The Bicycle Thief restaurant in downtown Halifax.* (**ANDRA ABRAHAM**)

ABOVE AND BOTTOM RIGHT: *Pam Johnson of Cole Harbour writes, "My husband Mike and I celebrated our fortieth wedding anniversary on February 14, 2021. What was supposed to be a European vacation turned into an overnight stay in Halifax followed by two nights at Oceanstone Resort. We had a wonderful time enjoying the pubs and food of Halifax, then hiking the rugged areas of High Head, Polly Cove, and Peggys Cove, and enjoying more good food and celebratory drinks."* (**PAM JOHNSON**)

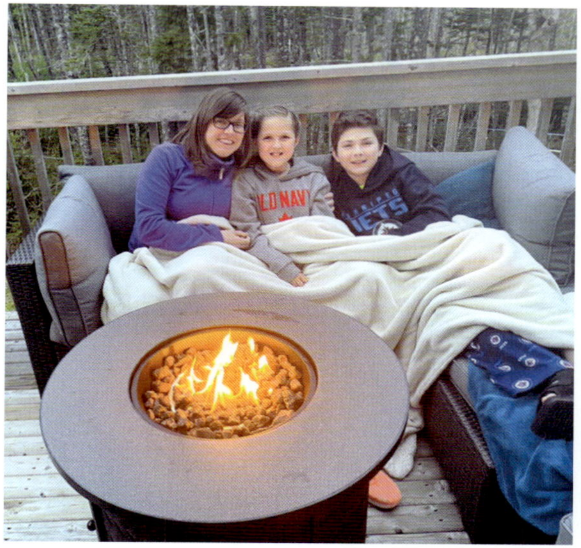

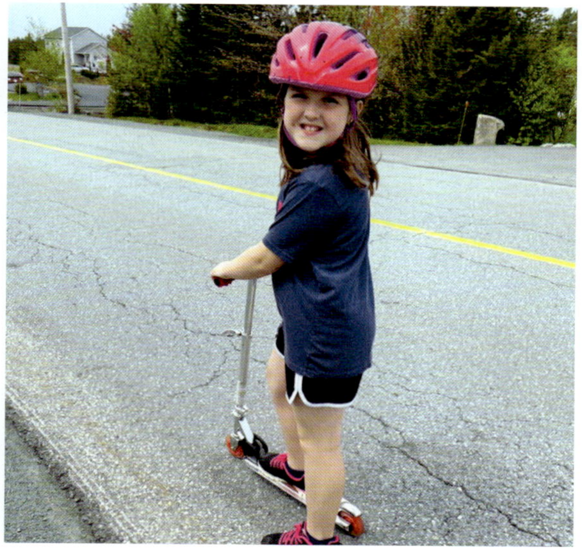

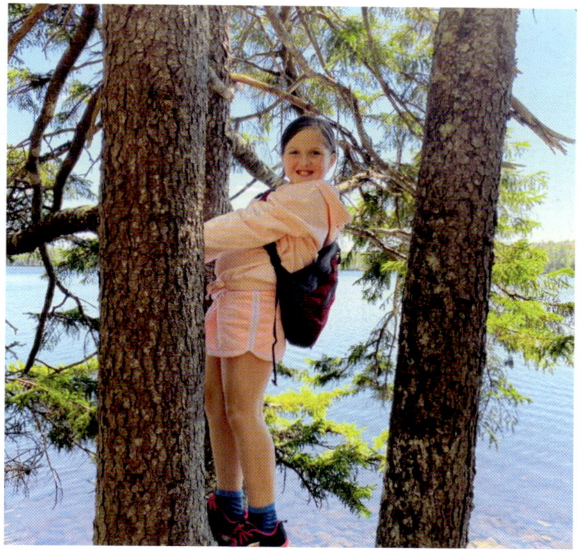

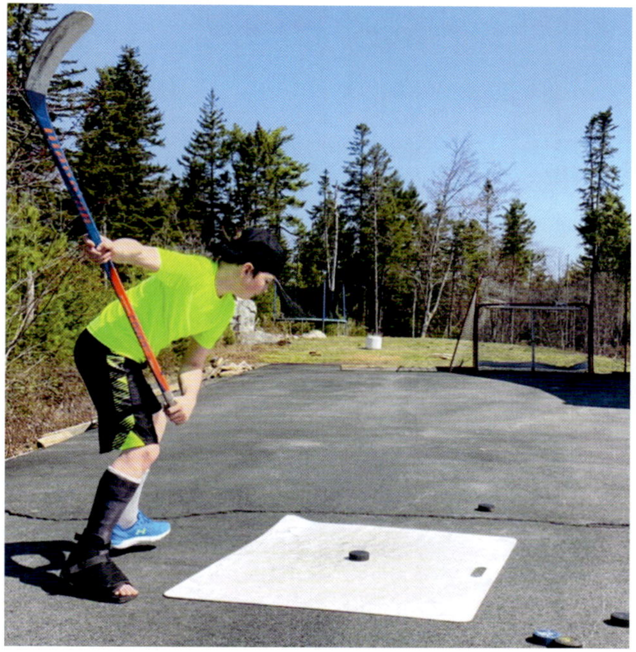

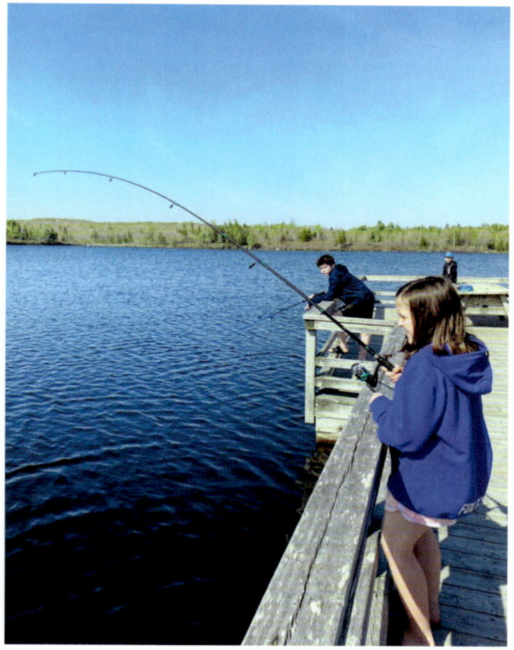

THIS PAGE: *Tina Thibeau of Tantallon writes, "This lockdown has been tough for the kids. It's been important to us to get them out of the house so they can enjoy the outdoors when online school and work from home is done. We've gone for walks, scooter rides, bike rides, and bikes in our neighbourhood. We've climbed trees, gone fishing, practiced our hockey shots, and had lots of family outdoor fires to pass the time. We will get through this as family." Pictured are Annik Foley, Tyson Foley, and Tina Thibeau.* (**TINA THIBEAU**)

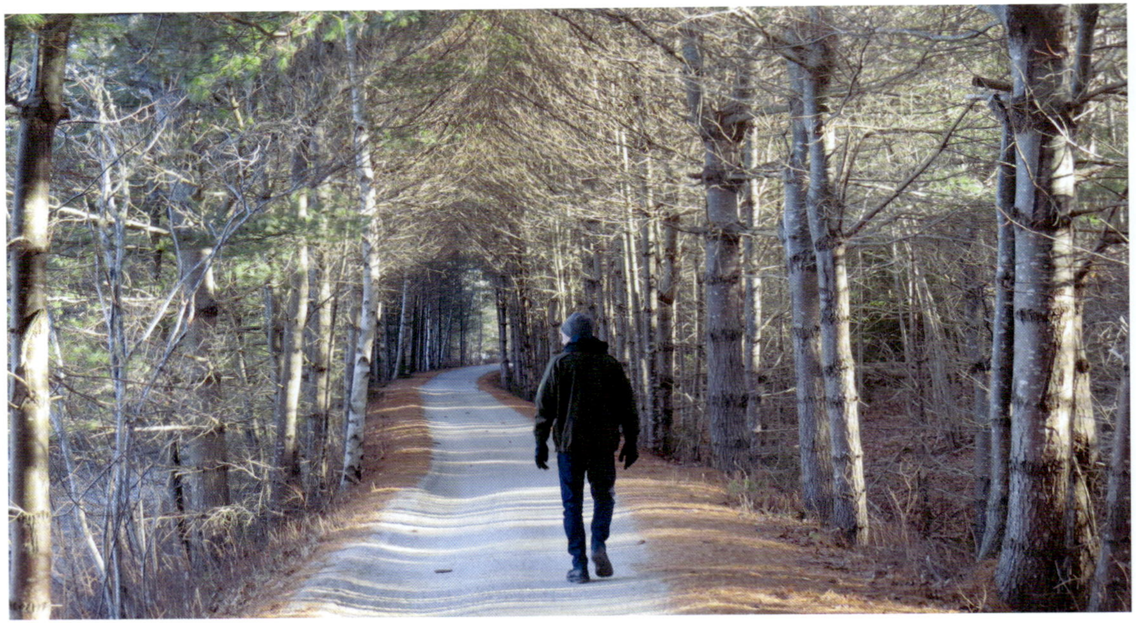

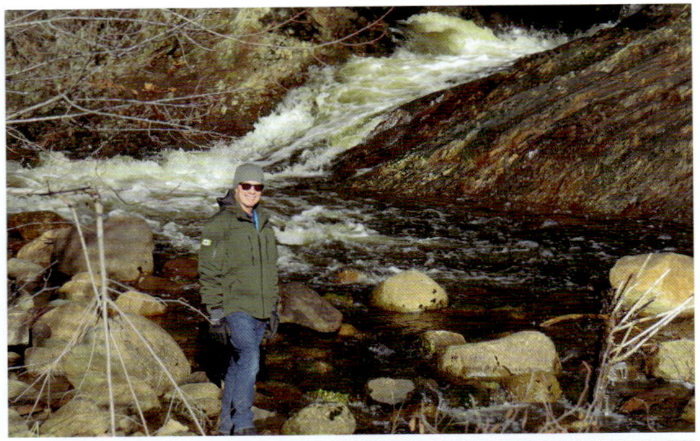

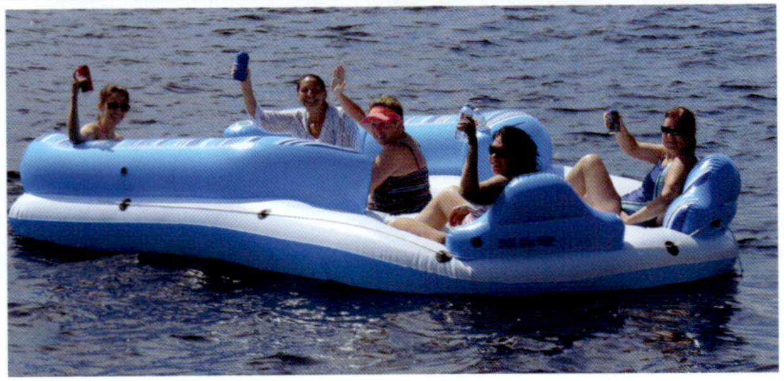

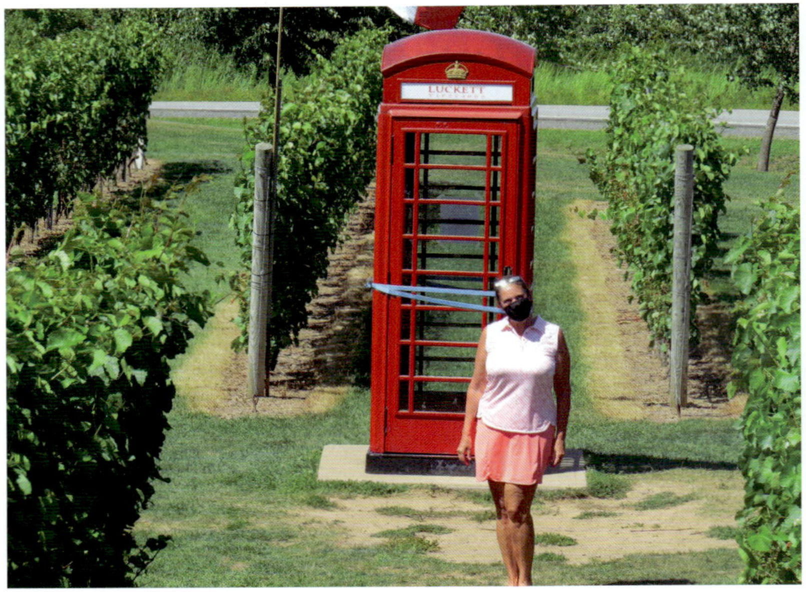

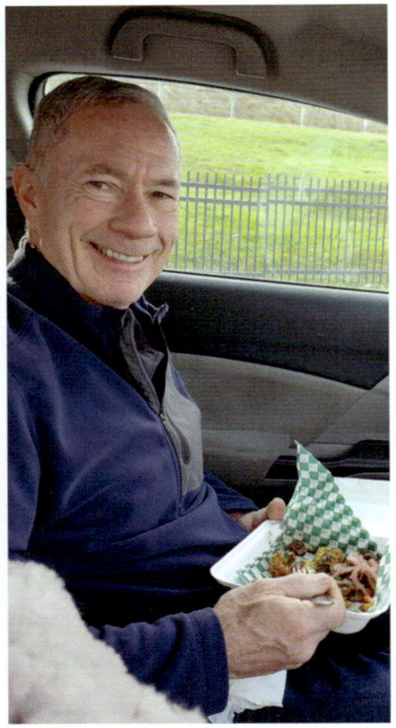

THIS PAGE: *Stephanie Watson of Cole Harbour writes, "This past winter with not as much snow and some warmer days was a great time to get out and hike Nova Scotia's beautiful trails.*

"...Last summer my husband and I continued to visit local businesses and restaurants and support Nova Scotia with our staycations. We stopped at Luckett's where...the famous red phone box was closed. It did not take away from the experience.

"...I love to 'dashboard dine.' My husband and I do curbside pickup and eat on Citadel Hill to enjoy the view and support local.

"...[And] my yearly Running Girls Weekend was downgraded to an afternoon, no sleepover. No problem...A floaty for five was perfect for creating more great memories." (STEPHANIE WATSON)

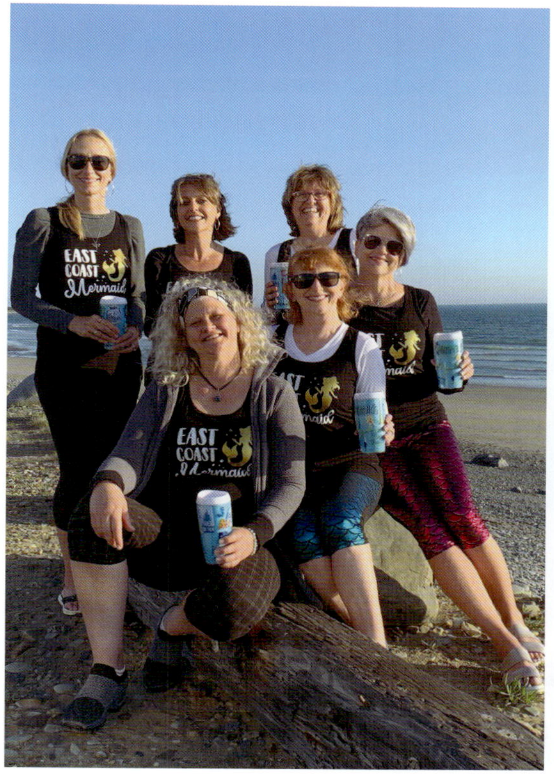

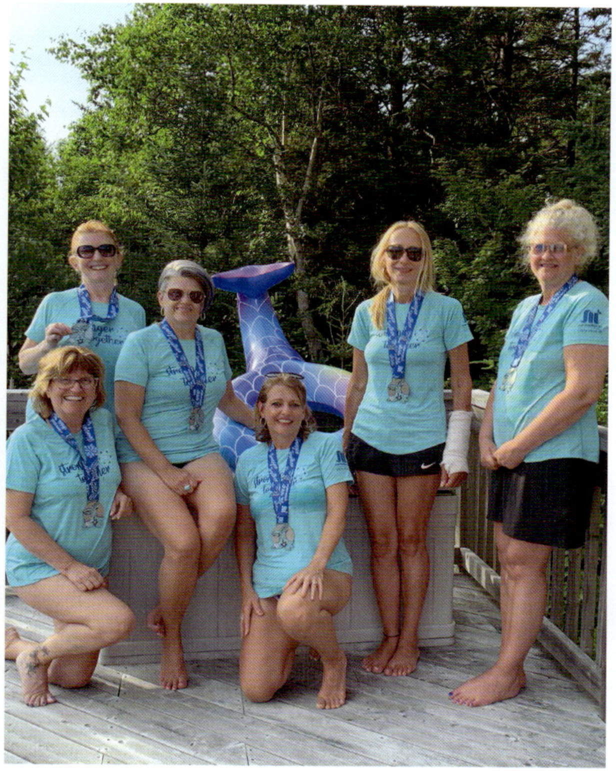

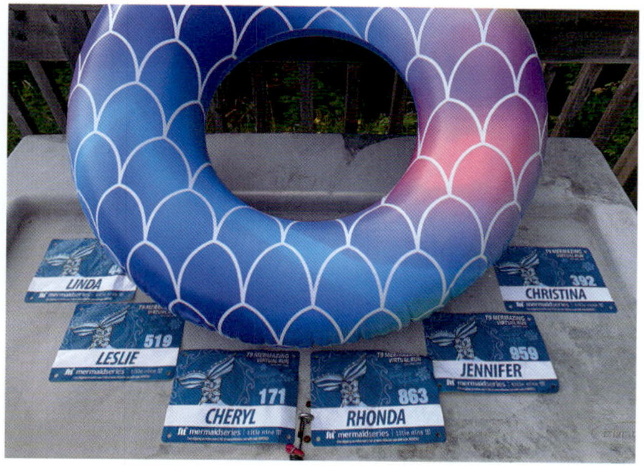

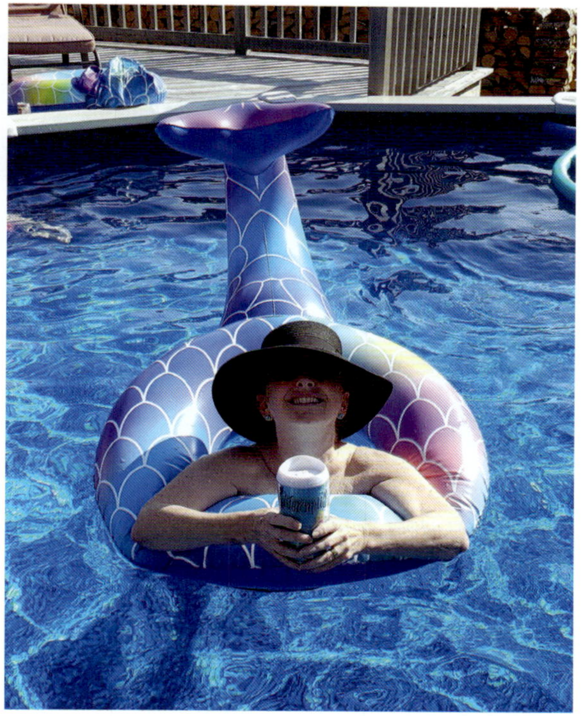

THIS PAGE: *Linda B. Deveau of Salmon River, Digby County, sent us some shots of her seasonal activities as she "pivoted, adapted, and discovered though out the year." She writes, "We have been vaccinated and some have undergone tests. Jobs have been affected and salaries reduced, however the smiles are genuine and the friendships are real—and after a year, there is still laughter. One way of coping right now on this extended lockdown was looking back on the past year of photos and realizing how blessed and lucky we are.... There is so much here in Nova Scotia to do when we think outside the box and have the support of family, friends and work colleagues. Nova Scotia and Nova Scotians are creative, adaptable, and have become extremely aware of the many hidden treasures of the province we call home."*

Of her photos, she writes, "A group trip to the Mermaid Parade on Coney Island in New York State had to be cancelled, so we decided to have our own Mermaid Weekend with a 5-K run on the Salmon River Beach instead of a 5-K run on the Coney Island Boardwalk, a pool instead of a parade, a sunset and bonfire instead of a theme park. But we were together, we were safe and healthy, and we had a mer-mazing time!" (**LINDA B. DEVEAU**)

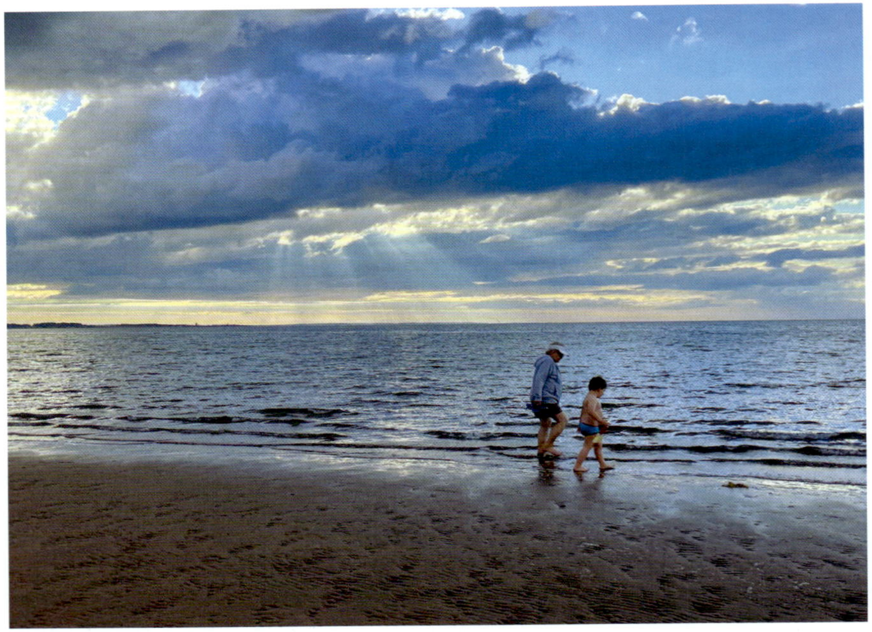

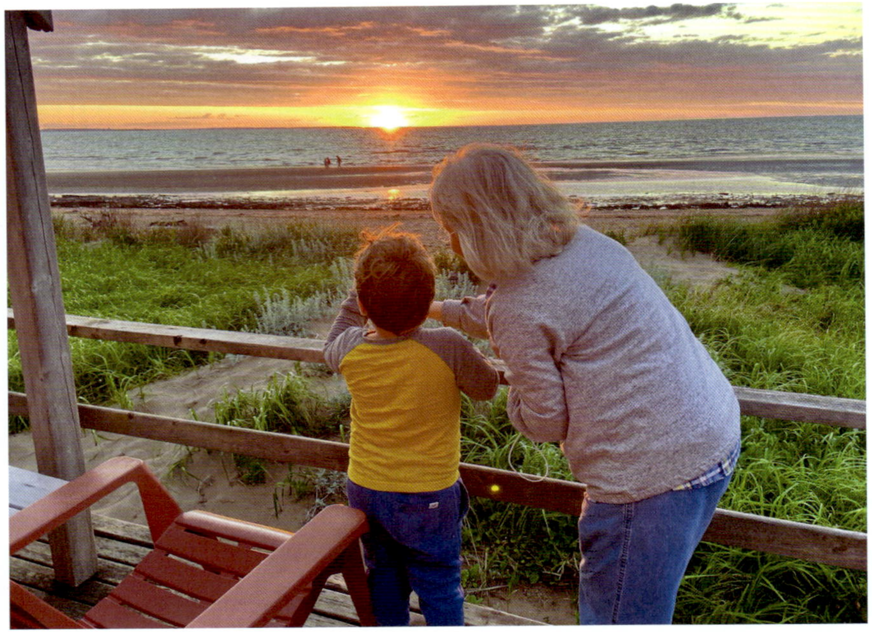

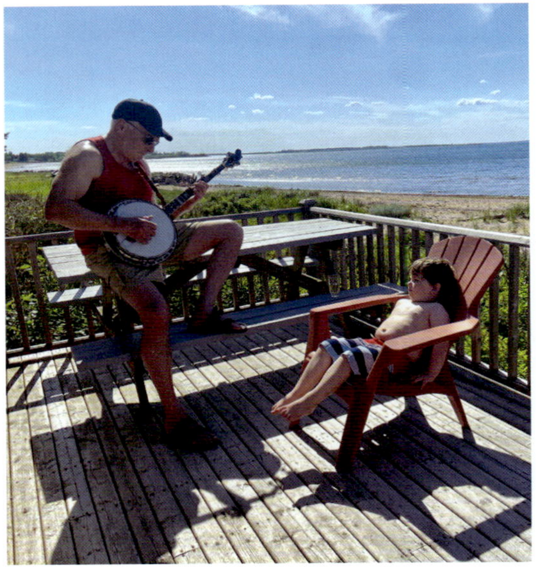

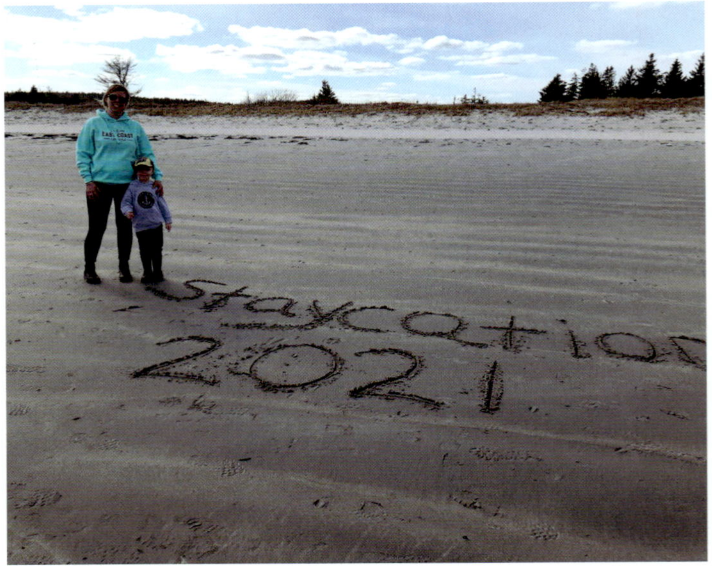

TOP LEFT AND RIGHT, BOTTOM LEFT: *Sarah Curry of Halifax sent these images of her family relaxing in Marshville in June 2021. Her nephew Emmett Curry Frizzell and his "Grammie" Janet Curry walk on the beach; Emmett and "Auntie" Dawn Mumford watch the sun set over the Northumberland Strait; Emmett enjoys some banjo music played by "Granddad" Jon Curry.* (**SARAH CURRY**)

BOTTOM RIGHT: *Tara Munroe of Elmsdale writes, "This is me and my son during our family's COVID East Coast Staycation 2021. This photo was taken at beautiful Summerville Beach in April 2021. We are sporting our East Coast attire and supporting local!"* (**TARA MUNROE**)

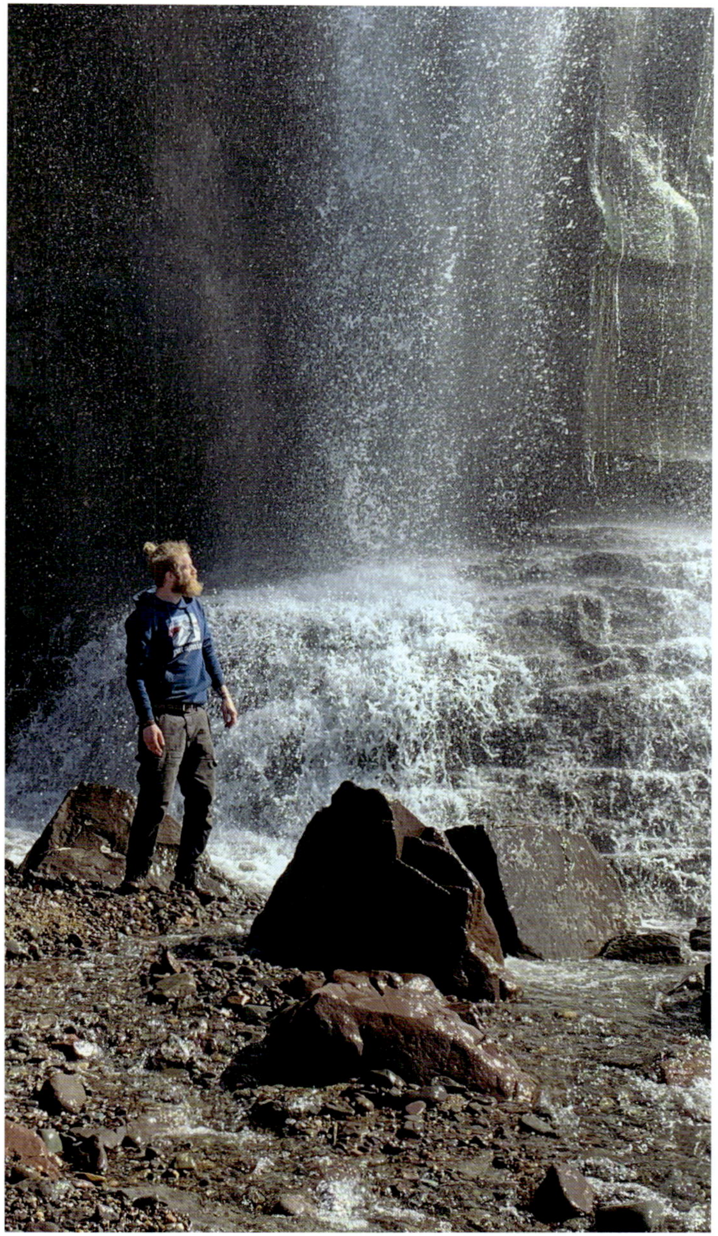

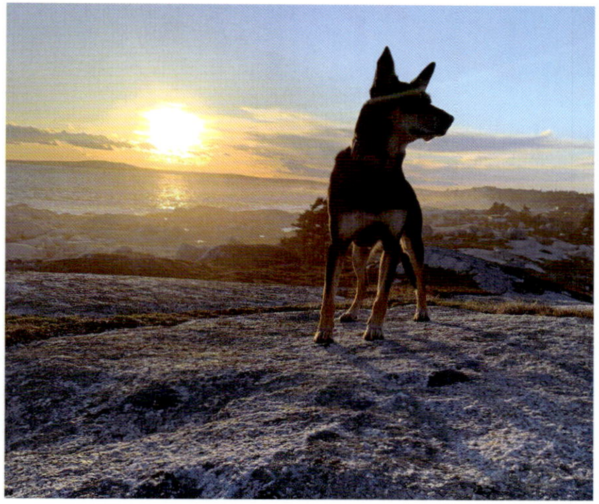

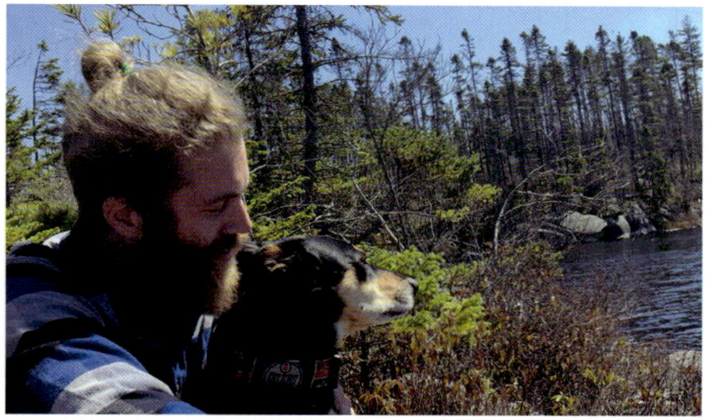

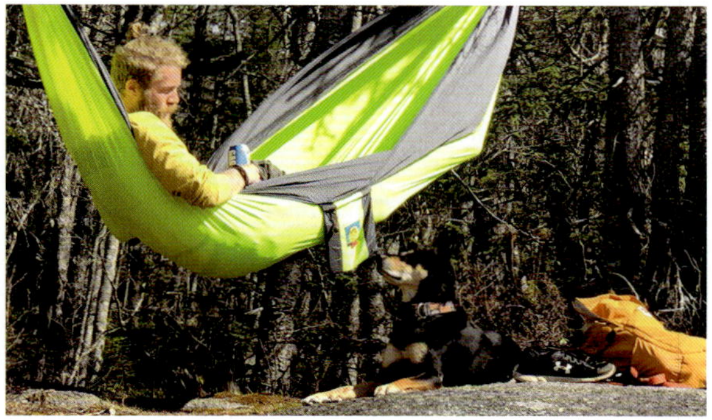

THIS PAGE: *"My name is Matthew Bowen and I'm a bartender in Halifax. I've lost my job three times in a year and had my savings decimated, but fret not, sympathetic reader, as this past year has unlocked a dormant side of myself I've sorely missed. With nothing but free time and no vehicle, I've clocked miles on the bike. The dog and I have explored endless bends of trail, star-gazed until the wee hours on a Friday (rare for a bartender), and spent nights sipping wine fireside on the beach or in the woods without once checking the clock. I've had hours rocking in the hammock, chilly early spring swims up at Long Lake, golden-hour rides through the beautiful neighbourhoods of North End Halifax and down to the waterfront—all of this in solitude. On me own.*

*"Bartending is a social existence. It's relentless people and I absolutely love it, but the pandemic has offered a reprieve I never thought I'd need to reaffirm my comfort with myself. I've realized I'm more at home on a trail, beside the water, under a canopy of trees than anywhere else. I've got my vaccine scheduled and am looking forward to picking up the pieces of my financial life. I fantasize about music festivals and packed arenas and busy vineyards and bonfires with the crew. Yet I don't feel an urgency toward everything I had before the pandemic —anxious eagerness to get there, wherever it is I'm going. I have nothing but gratitude for this universal pumping of the brakes. It's given perspective. It's been humbling. It's been pretty f*ckin' rad."* (**MATTHEW BOWEN**)

TOWARD THE FINISH LINE:
Wheelchair Racer Ben Brown

Ben Brown knows all too well the challenges of being an elite athlete in the time of COVID-19.

He has endured disruptions to his training routines, cancelled competitions, and uncertainty around whether his summer 2021 goal—the Tokyo 2020 Paralympics (delayed by coronoavirus concerns until August 2021)—would even take place as planned.

Brown had been training in March 2020 with an eye to qualifying for the Paralympics when he'd learned the games had been postponed for a year. Brown and his head coach, Ueli Albert, decided to make the best of the postponement.

"We focused on my overall fitness and endurance and technique, and I definitely got more fit," says Brown. "I put in another two thousand kilometres more than I normally do in training, and I did some virtual racing." Brown's focus is on the in the 100-, 400-, and 800-metre events in T53 category, which is for athletes who have full use of their upper body and minimal to no use of their trunk and lower extremities.

When the second wave of the pandemic hit, and gyms and training facilities were locked down again, Brown, who normally does two or three workouts a day, six days a week, set himself up with a home gym for strength training and got a roller (a treadmill for his wheelchair) to take the place of training on a track.

Restrictions on travelling outside his home community of Cambridge—not to mention Nova Scotia's notoriously capricious spring weather—made it difficult for Brown to do his usual road training. But in March 2021 Brown and his coaches flew to Victoria, British Columbia, so he could train outdoors and compete with other athletes—the same athletes he'll be competing with for a spot on the Canadian Paralympic team.

Despite the complications of training at such an elite level during the second and third waves of the pandemic, Brown is determined to stay focussed on his goals.

"Life's about learning and growing experiences," he says. "Right now I'm just putting in the work and hoping for the best.... I'm just taking it day by day, and that's all we can really do."

POSTSCRIPT

Brown did not qualify for the Tokyo Paralympics, but, true to form, he remains driven to meet his next goals. He's now aiming to qualify for his first world championships—the World Para Athletics Championships in Kobe, Japan, to be held in August 2022.

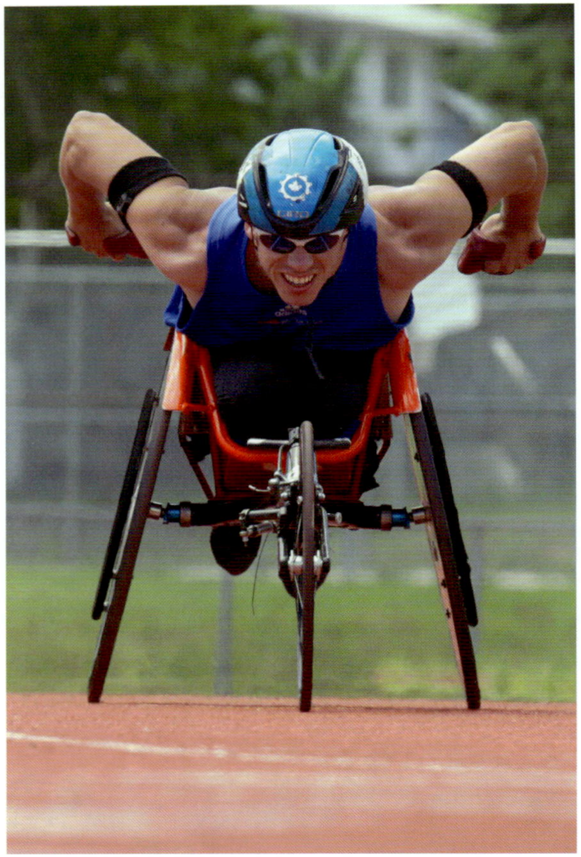

Ben Brown, Nova Scotia's top wheelchair racer, has had to adapt his training routines and adjust his goals as he's worked to stay at the top of his game through the pandemic.

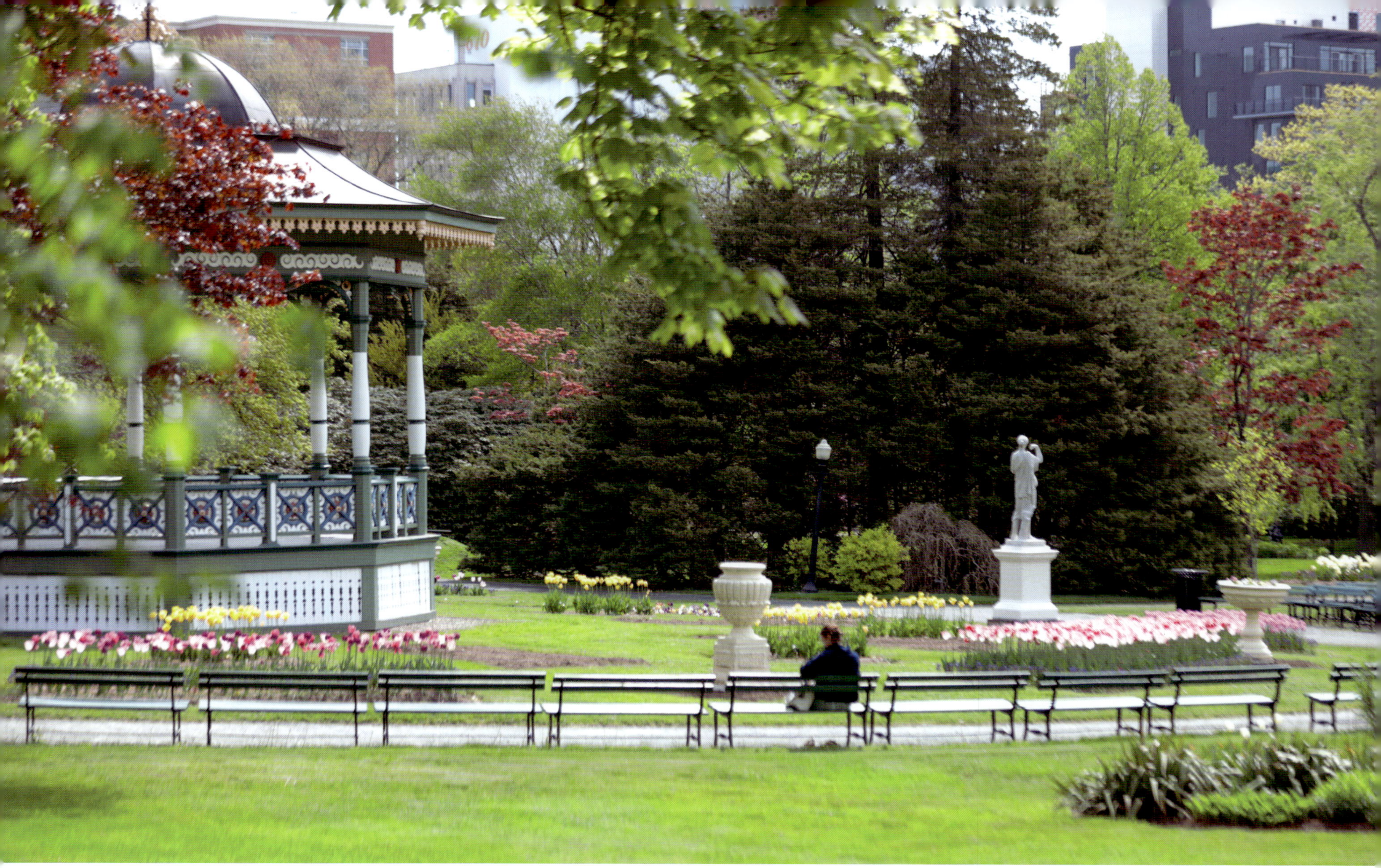

Natural social distancing was easy to achieve at the Halifax Public Gardens on this day in July 2021.

SOMETHING TO CONTRIBUTE:

Patricia Bishop, Taproot Farms

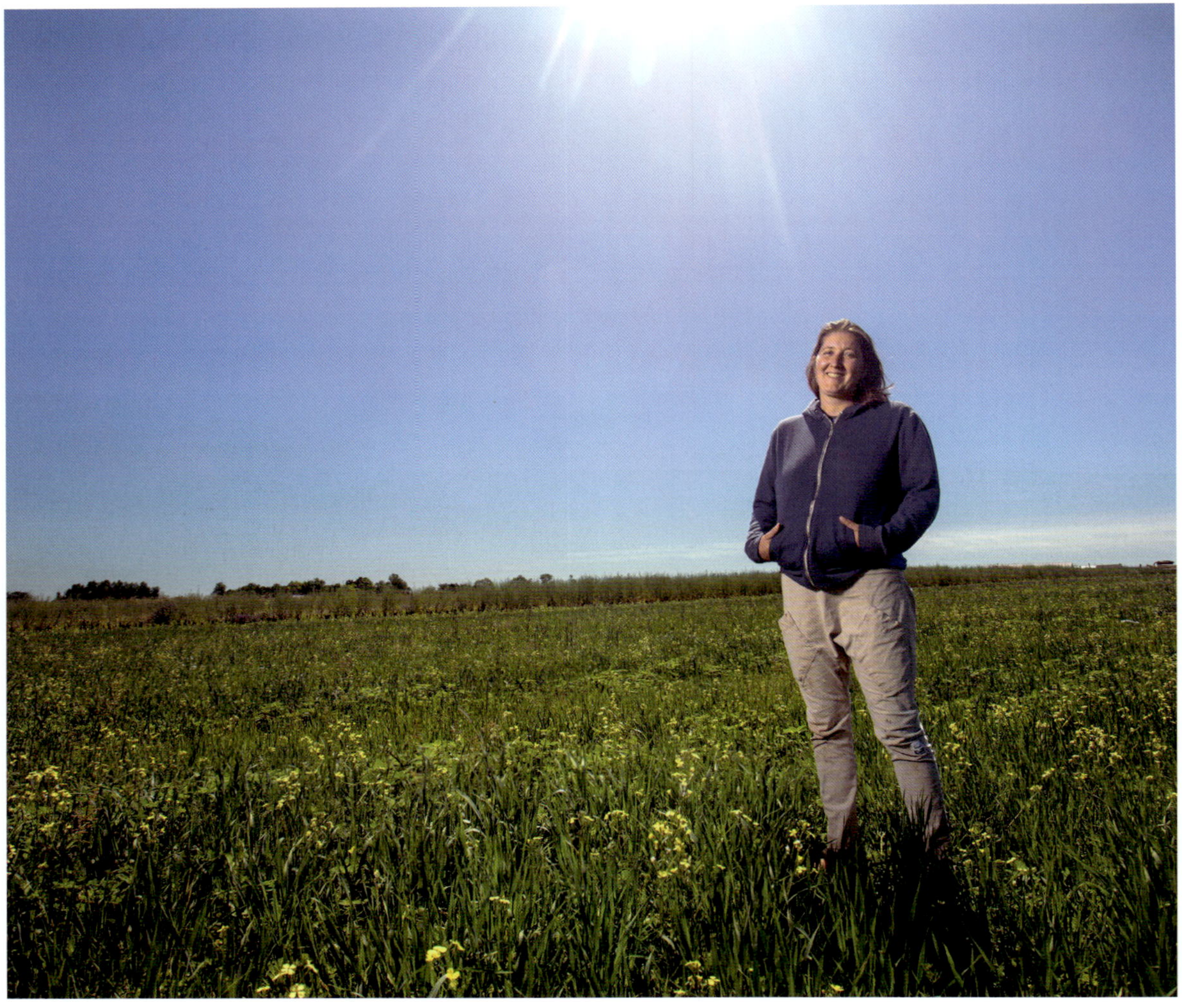

Patricia Bishop, who co-owns Taproot Farms in Port Williams, recognized early on in the pandemic that access to food could become an issue as global distribution channels were disrupted and some grocery store shelves were cleared out.

"There was certainly a lot of fear around not having food, which is, in my opinion, a good thing, because I think that typically people just get so used to having everything available to them all the time that they forget it's a fragile system," she says.

But as food supplies levelled out and the pandemic continued, she realized there was a bigger problem around food insecurity.

"People were losing their jobs and children were home, and I just started thinking about the implications if there's no money coming in and the children are home all day. I have three children and I know that kids eat a lot of snacks... and I just thought, 'Wow, there's probably a lot of hungry kids at home right now.'"

Her solution was to post on social media that if anyone who lived in her area or their kids were hungry, they could send her their civic address and

In June 2021 Patricia Bishop, who co-owns Taproot Farms in Port Williams, was one of twenty Nova Scotians to receive the Dr. Strang Community Hero Award. She was recognized for helping to feed people in need during the pandemic.

on Sunday she'd deliver a box of food. "I just needed to do something," she says. She organized a group of volunteers and started making deliveries. At its peak, they were delivering 150 boxes a week, but the demand later levelled off to about 35.

"It's not going to feed your whole family for an entire week, but it is like a snack or a part of a meal. So it's something to contribute. It's some way to get fruits and vegetables... that I know are expensive."

In June 2021 Patricia was one of twenty Nova Scotians to receive the Dr. Strang Community Hero Award. The award, named for Nova Scotia's chief medical officer of health, was given to Nova Scotians who had worked during the pandemic to keep people happy and healthy.

"I really appreciate being acknowledged and getting the award, but it was actually uncomfortable because it's taken a community of people to do this. I can appreciate that I initiated it so others could join in, so that is what's being recognized and acknowledged," she says.

"I just want to find some way to rise above to do what needs doing.... Sometimes we get paralyzed by the magnitude of problems and then it's just like—wait a minute. There is something really small we can do that can actually impact someone else."

TEMPORARY FOREIGN WORKERS AND THE PANDEMIC

International travel restrictions in 2021 brought into question whether Patricia Bishop and her husband, Josh Oulton, would be able to bring in the temporary foreign workers they need to operate Taproot Farms.

Bishop says few people understand how critical these workers are. "If we want to have these industries," she says, referring in particular to farming and fish processing, "we need to have seasonal agricultural workers." She notes few local people are interested in taking on the challenging physical labour required to work on the farm, but seasonal agricultural workers aren't averse, and they benefit from the higher salaries than what they can earn at home.

Fortunately, the federal government made allowances for temporary foreign workers to enter the country, and Nova Scotia set up education, testing, quarantine, and workplace protocols for foreign workers.

For Martel Wilson from Jamaica, that was good news. "It is very important because I come here to support my family," he says, noting he has come back to Taproot for the past seven years to support his wife and four children. He says he enjoys the work—right now he's harvesting the first crop of peas—and looks forward to heading back home in December.

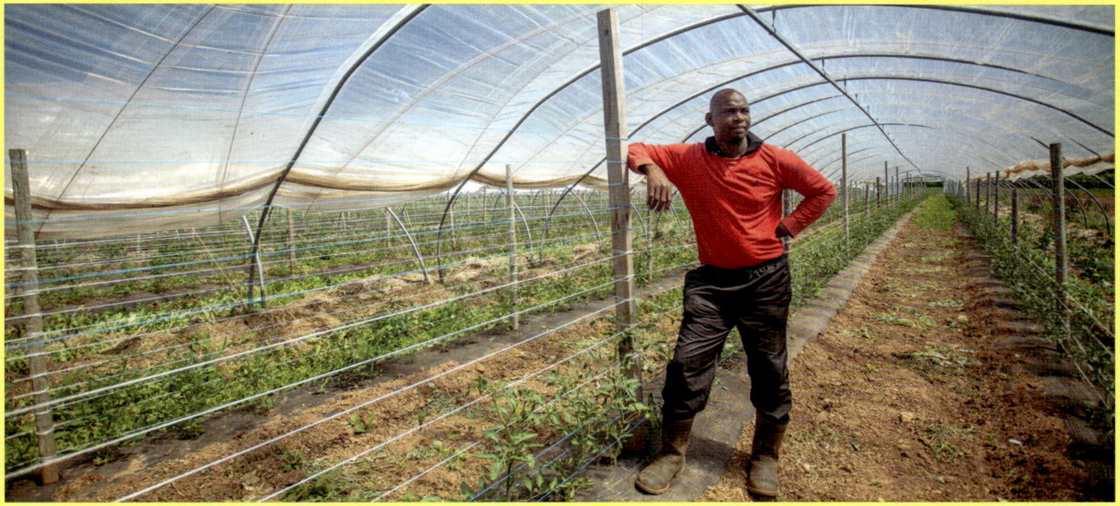

Martel Wilson is one of the essential temporary foreign workers who came from Jamaica to work at Taproot Farms in Port Williams.

HOW WE USED OUR FREE TIME

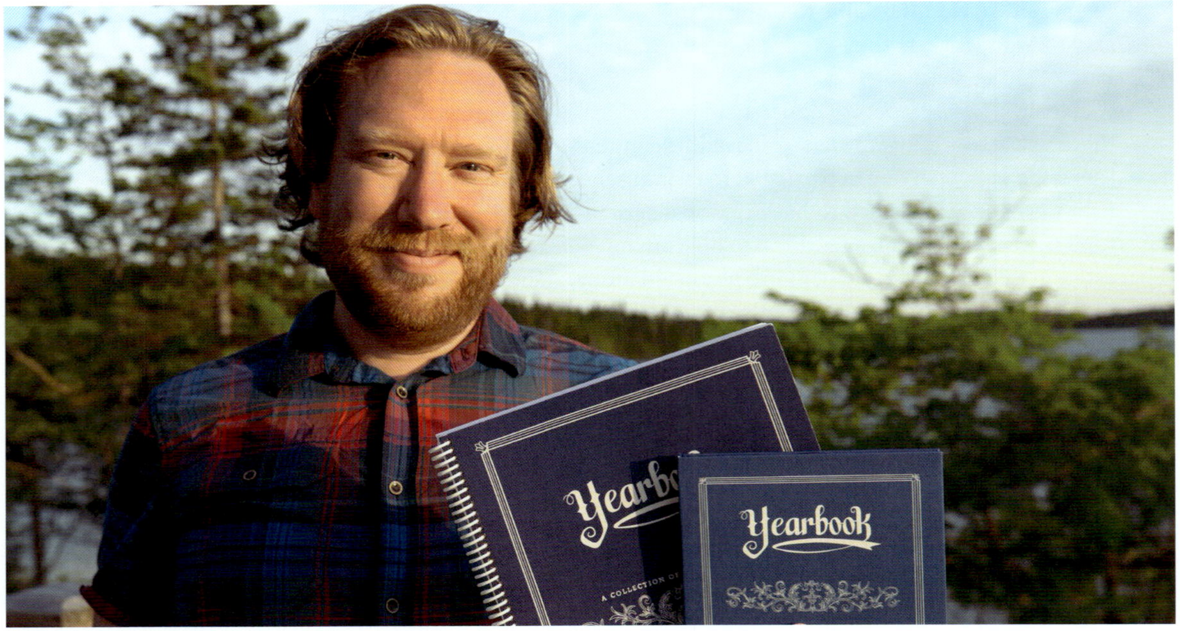

THIS PAGE: *"My name is Adam Young, and I'm writing from the community of French Road (between Marion Bridge and Gabarus on Cape Breton Island). The pandemic really put a damper on most people's plans, and it was no different for me. When it began in March 2020, I was on tour with Còig in Australia. Our gigs got cancelled, and we found ourselves scrambling to get back home to Canada. I had put a recording project on hold while joining the band for the UK/Australia tour (the UK part went off without a hitch!), and was looking forward to getting back at it.*

"Backing up a little bit, back on New Year's Day 2018 I decided on a whim to write a tune every day for one year. Once the year came to its end, I had 365 tunes and nothing to do with them, so I decided to publish a fair number of them, and to record a double album of some of my favourites with some of my favourite musicians. The layout of the book hadn't really started by the time I left for the UK, but two days before our flight to London, the orchestra I hired from Prague recorded their two pieces.

"When I got home, studios were closed, musicians couldn't gather to rehearse or perform, and everything got put on an indefinite hold. I took the time to do the layout for the book, and wrote short little snippets to accompany those tunes I could remember the stories behind. Last fall, as restrictions started to lift, I was able to make it back into the studio to finish up the recording: 22 tracks over two CDs. The first disc is a presentation of the tunes in a non-traditional way (influenced by everything from New Orleans jazz to Arcade Fire to ABBA to old doo-wop songs from the sixties to bluegrass to 8-bit video games from the eighties).

The second disc is basically an apology to the traditionalists, where those same eelven tracks are presented in a much more traditional way, with fiddles, piano, guitar, and one track with bagpipes. There are also a couple more tunes thrown in (thirty-nine, as opposed to seventeen on the first disc). It was an immense project that ended up lasting three and a half years, with fifty-eight musicians participating, and even more photographers, artists, recording engineers, editors. It's definitely the biggest project I've ever taken on, and I think in a weird way, the pandemic may have helped. Because I didn't have any gigs on the go (I was—and still am!—working my day job with Parks Canada), I had a whole lot more time than usual to think about arrangements, to sit and write descriptions, to plan how the CD packaging was going to look.

"There are so few people still buying physical copies of music, I wanted to both make this worthwhile, and to reward/thank people who still buy albums. I really think it was worth it in the end—I love how the album package turned out!

"Long story short, my tunebook was released in December 2020, and the double CD just came out on June 4, 2021. Both are available on my website, adamcdyoung.com (because I just have to make a shameless plug...)." (**ADAM YOUNG**)

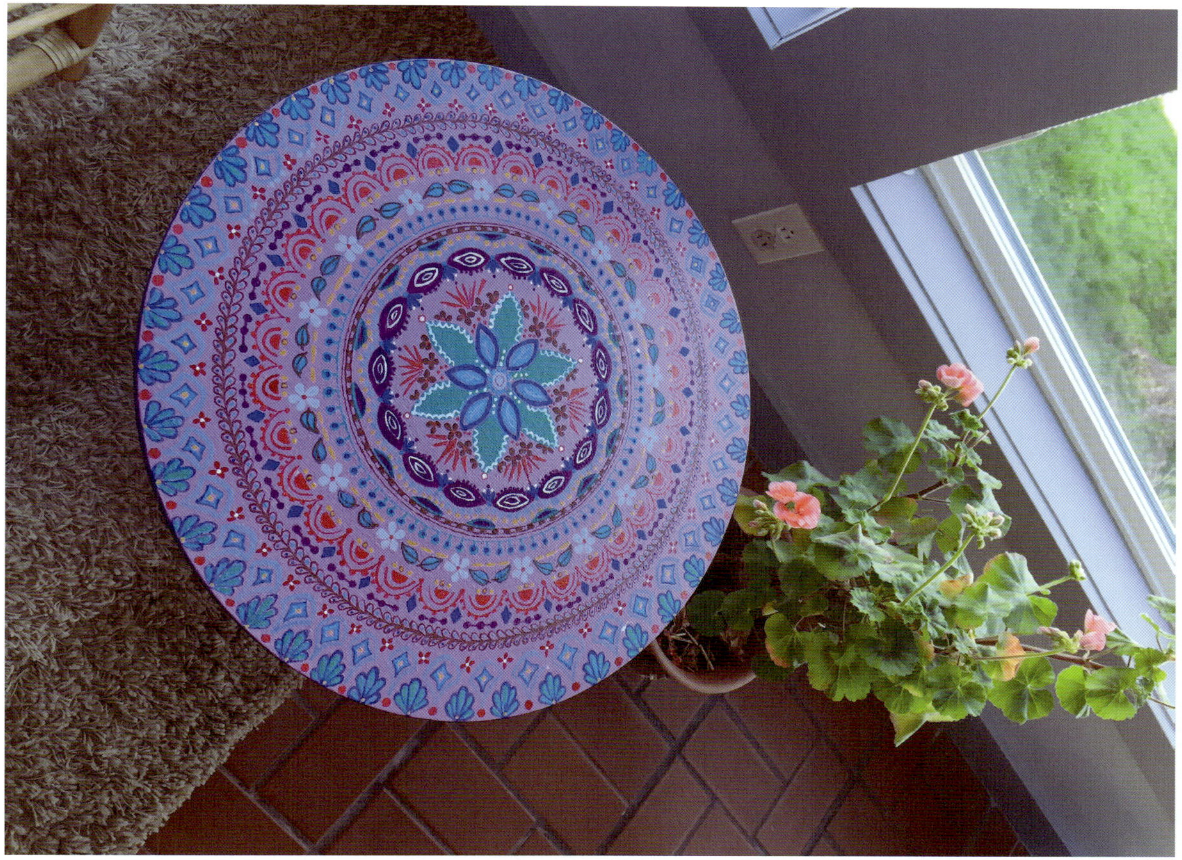

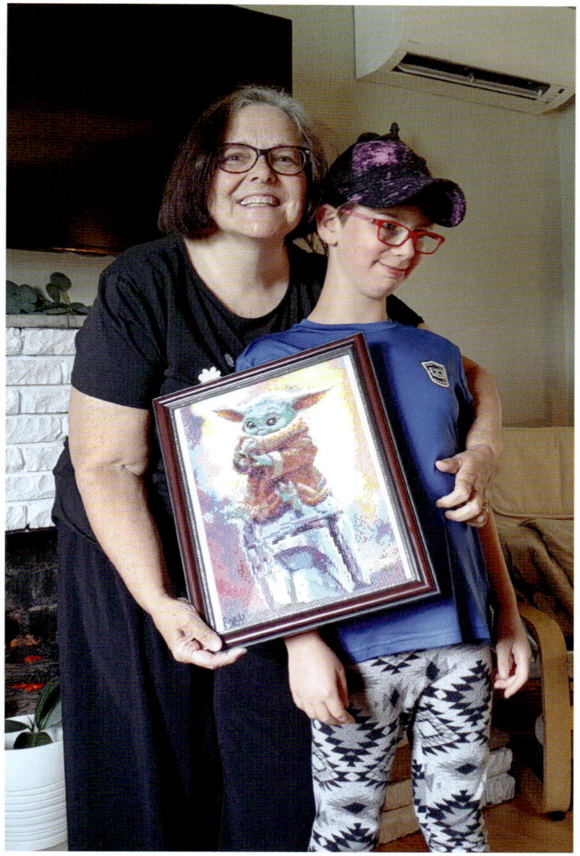

Jacqueline Halsey of Dartmouth writes, "I'd like to share something I created during the third wave lockdown. Like a lot of people, COVID-time at home meant cleaning out drawers and closets and going where no one had been for many years. That's how I came across an old kids' geometry set. With it I created what I call my Third Wave Pandemic Mandala. Finding the centre of the beat-up side table was the challenging part, as my 'πr^2' days were a distant, fuzzy memory. But I figured it out, and after giving the table a fresh coat of leftover paint from the basement, I began.

"I started in the middle with a flower, then every day I drew a wider pencil circle and painted a new pattern. The design slowly spread to the edge of the table. It was not pre-planned at all and I never knew what the next day's ring of patterns would look like—just as in life you never know what patterns a new day will bring." (**JAQUELINE HALSEY**)

Darlene Metzler of Dartmouth writes, "I lost my father to COVID during wave one at Northwood. During wave three, I was able to be a caregiver to my grandchildren when their mom was working, and I assisted with their online learning.

Here is my granddaughter Hayley MacNeil, who I gifted this craft to today. I made it during lockdown; she is Baby Yoda–obsessed. She was very pleased and I am elated to have a fun, light-hearted memory this time around." (**DARLENE METZLER**)

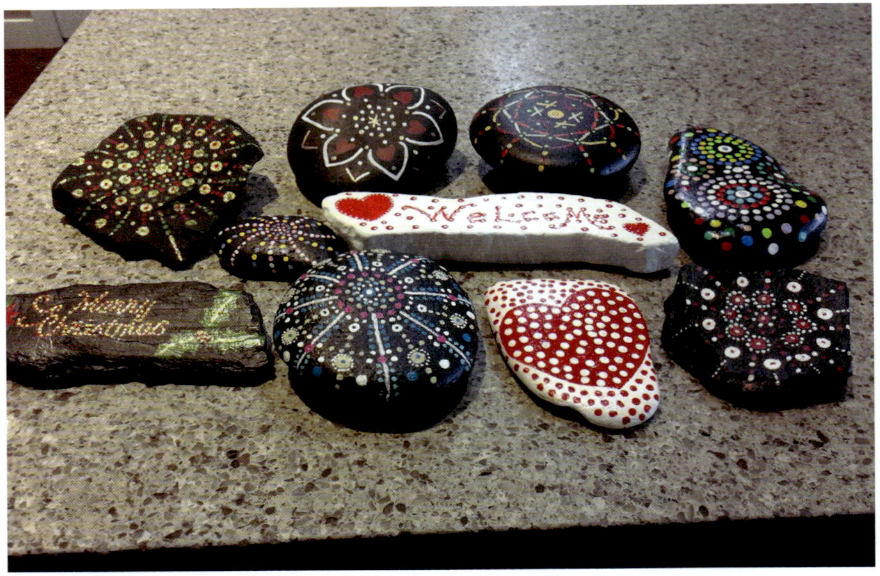

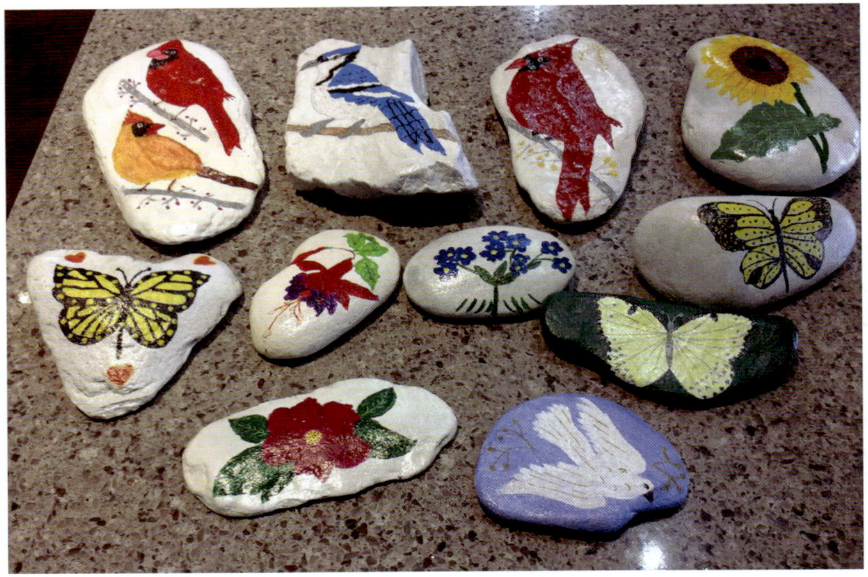

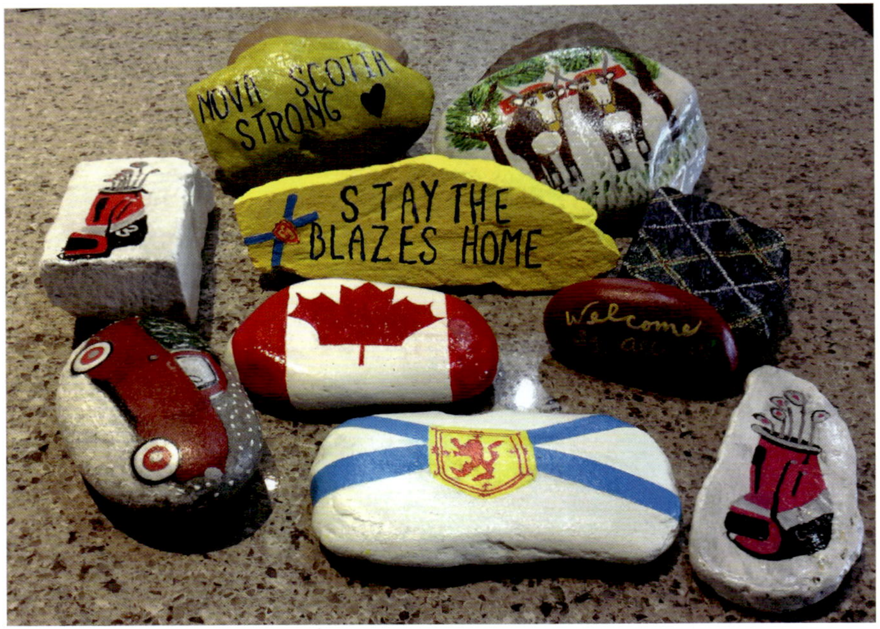

THIS PAGE: *Pamela Crowell of Halifax writes, "During the pandemic, my Mom, Elaine Jones (seventy-seven years old), began painting rocks to keep busy and to give to friends and family.*

"…During the last lockdown, my Mom painted a few large rocks that I placed in our garden, which is close to the curb of our street in Clayton Park. I thought it would be fun if my Mom made more rocks that I could place in the garden for neighbours to enjoy when they are out walking, as so many of us are during the pandemic.

"…Originally, I wanted to put out a sign that said 'Please take a rock,' but with our COVID numbers going up, I didn't think it was a good idea for various hands to be touching the stones. Instead, we are enjoying the many young families that stop to check out the rocks. There is one little guy, in particular, who stops every day with his mom or dad to inspect the rocks. He never seems to tire of seeing them, and we absolutely love knowing it gives him a little joy in his day. Just this week, my husband was in the driveway as the little fellow stopped to view them with his dad. My husband told him he could take one and he did! It has been such a treat to know that these little ones and their families are enjoying these rocks during their walks!" (**PAMELA CROWELL**)

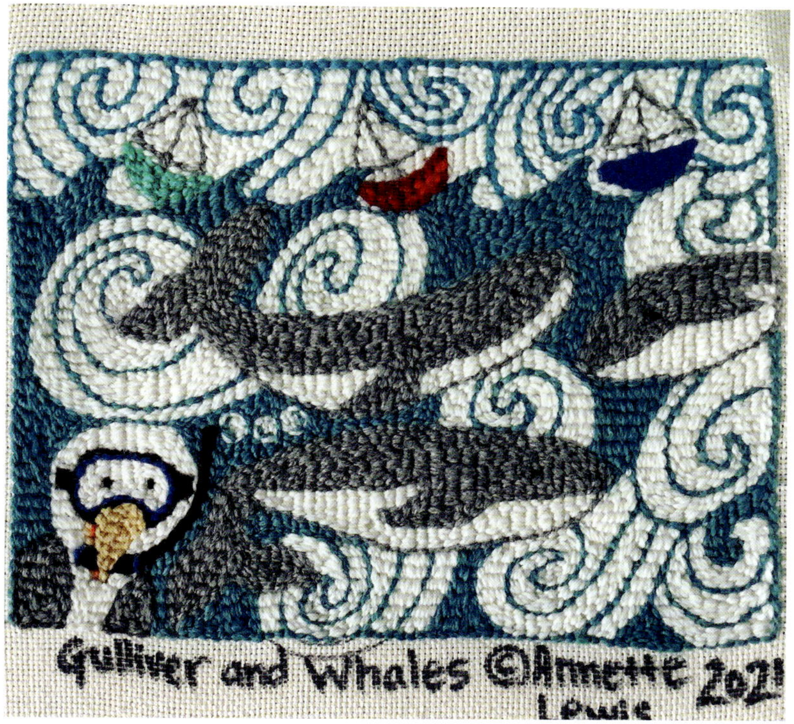

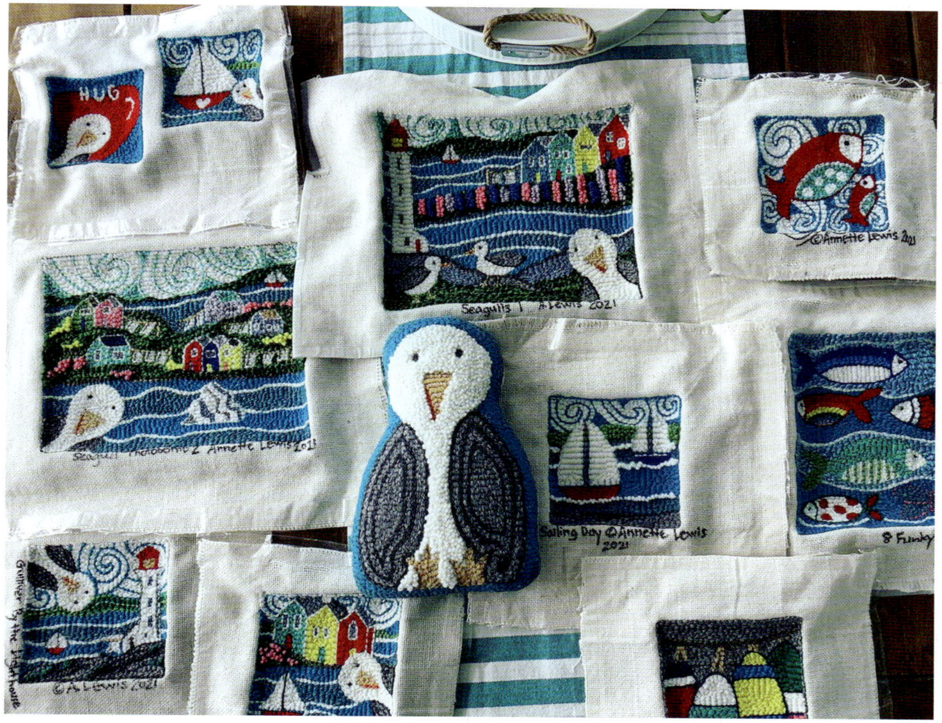

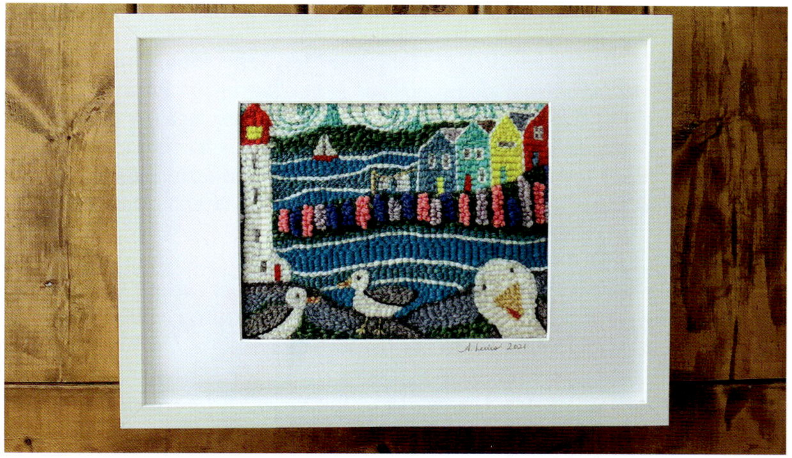

THIS PAGE: *"My name is Annette Lewis and I live in Hantsport. I am an autism teacher specialist in the Annapolis Valley. During the pandemic last year, and even more so this year, I have delved into fibre arts, more specifically, punch needle. It's a cousin to traditional rug hooking and I officially started two years ago. With the COVID-19 restrictions in place and limited options to go anywhere, my character Gulliver the Seagull was born. He has become quite popular in my online hooking community groups where we all share our projects.*

I was also off on sick leave since November 2020 due to back pain and waiting for spinal fusion surgery, which I finally had in March of this year. This craft has helped me through some challenging and painful times, so I kept on making a variety of east coast–themed artwork with clotheslines, boats, lighthouses, and now Gulliver the Travelling Seagull. It got to the point where people asked me if I sold my work and patterns. So, my husband, who just happens to be a web designer, designed my website and things are growing!" (**ANNETTE LEWIS**)

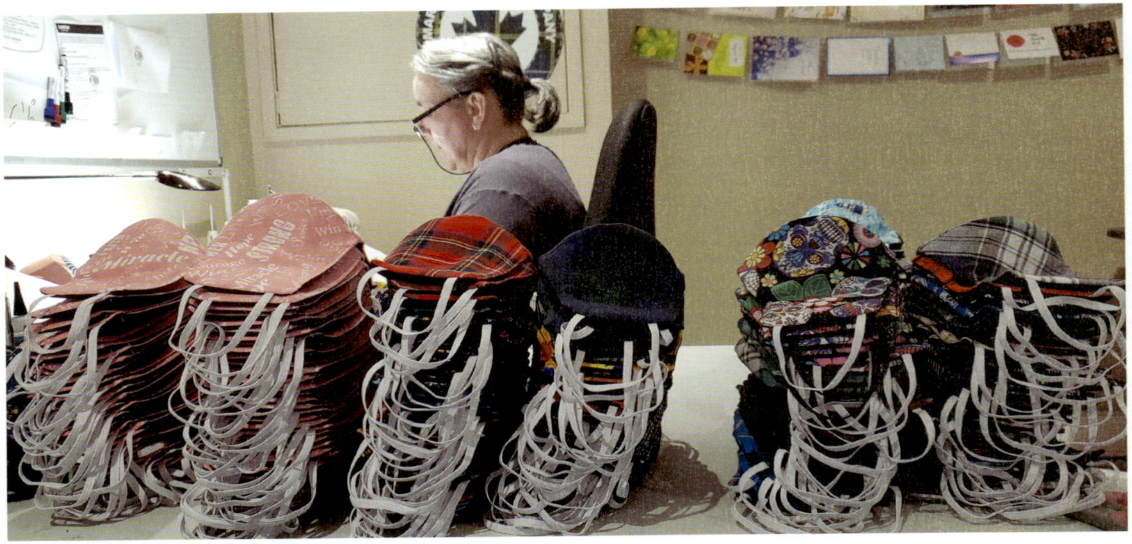

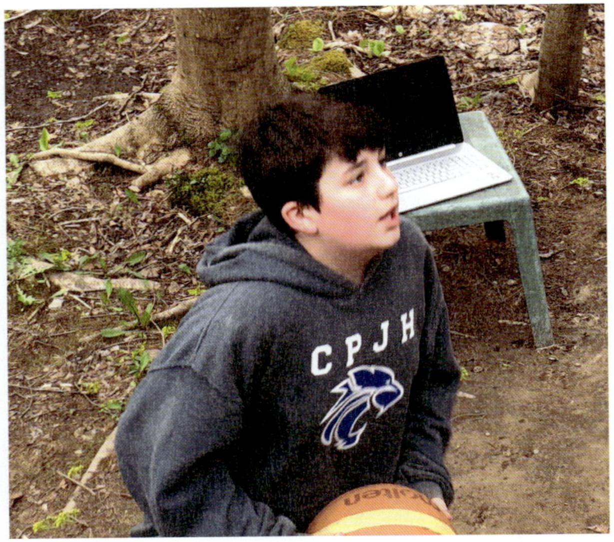

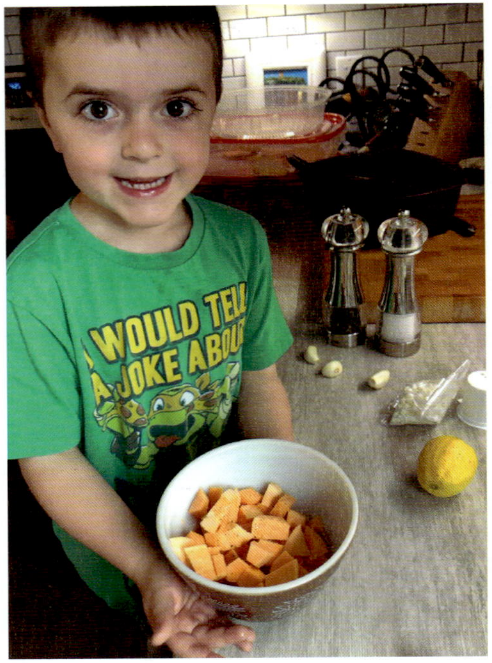

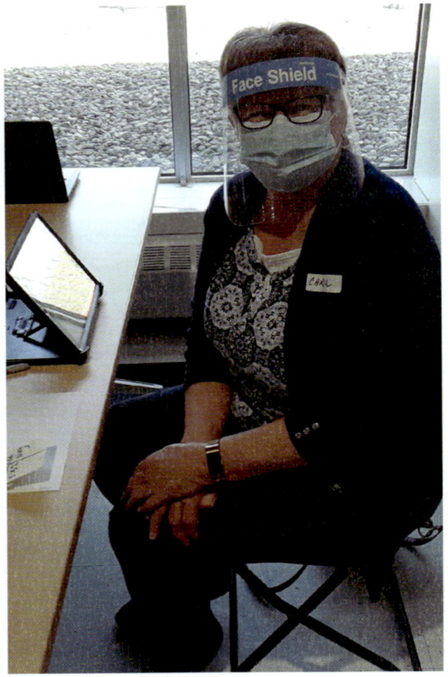

TOP LEFT: *Dale Kearney of Halifax sent this photo of his wife, Sherrie Kearney. "She has made 23,000 face masks and has donated back to local charities just under $30,000," he writes. "She has been doing this since March 2020 when the pandemic started. Sherrie had two heart attacks and a stroke nine years ago, and it has not slowed her down. She pivoted her entire tartan business when the pandemic started to just make masks to help keep people in Nova Scotia and all over Canada stay safe."* (**DALE KEARNEY**)

TOP RIGHT: *Patti Bannister of Halifax writes, "This is our thirteen-year-old son, Ryan Bannister, doing virtual gym class in the backyard. He is in grade eight at Clayton Park Jr. High and their gym teacher encourages them to get outside if they can for each class. Ryan is a bit of a basketball 'fanatic' (plays for the Bedford Eagles in non-pandemic times), so his backyard net is his usual destination for gym class."* (**PATTI BANNISTER**)

BOTTOM LEFT: *Angela Roach Fraser of Whites Lake writes, "Hazel and John Fraser have been helping out with making suppers at our house! They are learning great skills and they are so proud! They are even more inclined to try new foods."* (**ANGELA ROACH FRASER**)

BOTTOM RIGHT: *Carol Longue MacDonald of Middle Sackville volunteered at the COVID-19 pop-up testing site at Sackville Sports Stadium four weekends in a row.* (**CAROL LONGUE MACDONALD**)

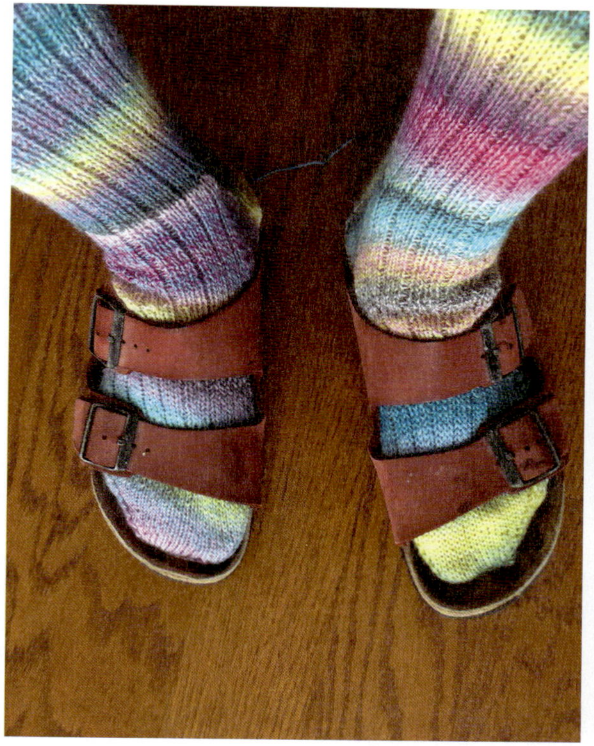

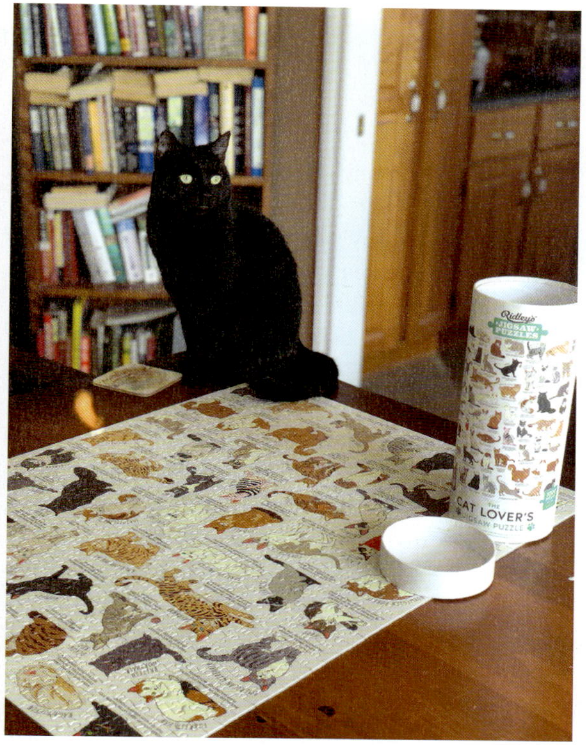

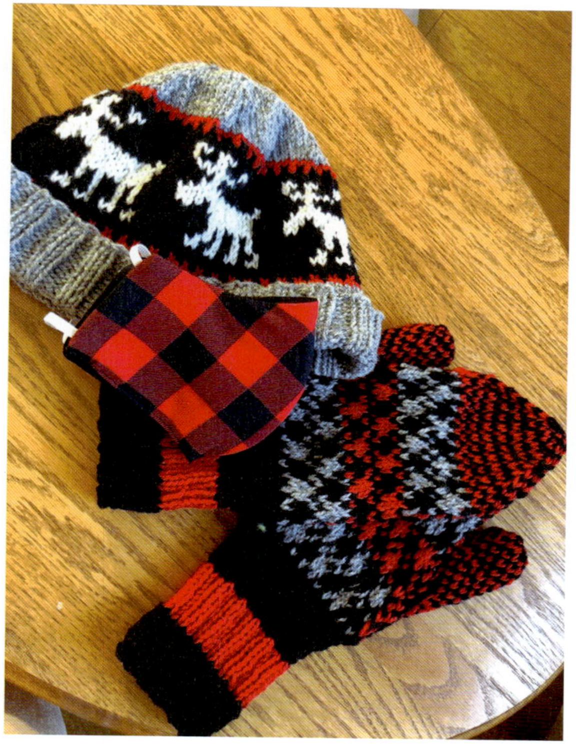

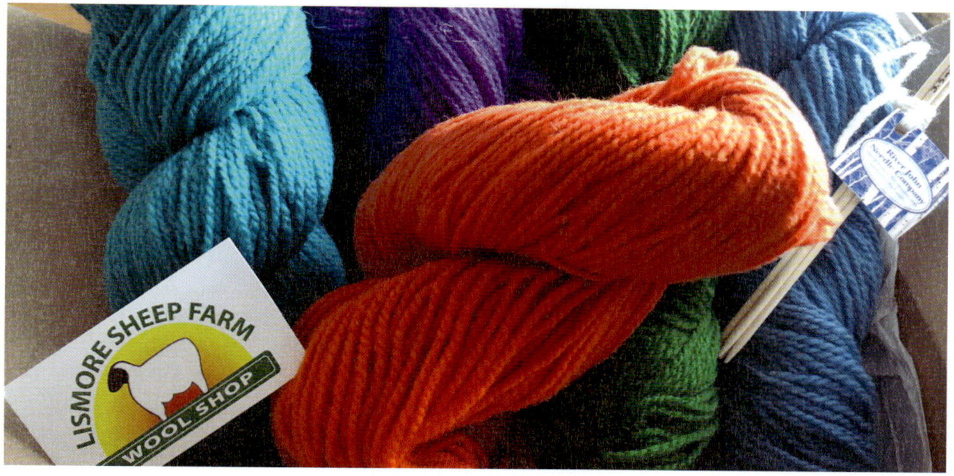

THIS PAGE: *Pam Johnson of Cole Harbour writes, "We supported local more than ever. Beautiful wool from a Nova Scotia sheep farm! Did lots of knitting....Jigsaw puzzles are a great way to pass some time. This one is Zoe-approved. The socks I recently finished knitting go nicely with Birkenstock sandals (a nod to Dr. Strang's comment about how [lockdown was] not the time to be shopping for sandals)."* **(PAM JOHNSON)**

HOME IN A PANDEMIC: *Melissa Geddes*

It's mid-July 2021 and realtor Melissa Geddes is getting ready to do something she has not done for over fifteen months: show a house. In person. To a couple from out-of-province.

The realtor and managing associate broker in Bedford had been doing most of her showings online through the third wave of the pandemic, and today, with restrictions easing, she was finally about to do business the way she used to.

Through the lockdowns in 2020 and 2021, real estate agents were considered an essential service, but the way they do business changed dramatically. Gone are the days of families roaming freely through houses and bringing parents or friends along.

"Everyone has to hand-sanitize before [entering], and we set limits on the number of people in a house, so it's just the agent and the buyers," she says. Buyers are discouraged from touching anything in the houses, and everything from door handles to light switches is wiped down after a visit.

During the first lockdown in 2020, the housing market, at that time a buyer's market, fell off due to uncertainty around the pandemic. "Realtors are self-employed; they're all independent contractors," says Geddes. "So if you're not out showing property and writing offers and making sales, then you're not putting food on the table for your own family. That started to get very stressful for many agents."

But that changed pretty quickly.

People across the country took note of Atlantic Canada's relatively low COVID-19 numbers, and the transition to working remotely had made it possible for many to conceive of living in beautiful Nova Scotia and working elsewhere. Geddes says a lot of people in other provinces had started to re-evaluate their lives during the pandemic and decided a slower, less frenetic way of life was for them.

That forced the industry to shift to a new way of selling. Using FaceTime or other online platforms, Geddes says agents could walk through house while, thousands of kilometres away, interested buyers could view the property virtually and ask questions.

"We've had a huge influx of people coming from other provinces," she says, adding that a lot of Maritimers who had moved away for work were also moving back. With that increased interest came a seller's market and another unfamiliar phenomenon in Nova Scotia: the bidding war.

"Our inventory was low before we went into lockdown," she says, referring to the 2021 lockdown during the third wave. "The inventory dropped even further and the demand went up for buyers wanting to come in."

Geddes says the team she works with has sold properties to people across Canada sight unseen—to the point where it's become routine. But that increased interest from outside buyers has made the market almost inaccessible to first-time home-buyers who are actually from Nova Scotia. Houses are selling for thousands of dollars above asking—in some cases, hundreds of thousands more.

"It's a very stressful thing from the buyer's perspective," she says. "You start to feel really, really badly because they're bidding on house after house and just not winning—and you want them to win because a lot of the time your clients become your friends."

She says the upside is for older sellers who were looking to retire, and who have seen larger than expected appreciation on their properties. "We've had some really great stories where they were retiring and downsizing and were planning to sell anyway, and they were able to take advantage of this market and retire with a considerable nest egg that they weren't going to have."

Geddes says with the ongoing low house inventory and the draw of the East Coast lifestyle, she doesn't see the market cooling down any time soon. She also thinks the way real estate is bought and sold has changed forever. "I've had clients move into their houses and I haven't been able to meet them yet," she says.

On this day, though, she's keen to meet her new prospective buyer. "I'm looking forward to actually being able to physically see people again."

FACING PAGE: *Real estate agent Melissa Geddes is looking forward to getting back to showing homes to potential buyers in person, rather than virtually, as she has had to do throughout the pandemic. The market in Nova Scotia took off on 2021, with selling prices hitting record highs and bidding wars becoming the norm.*

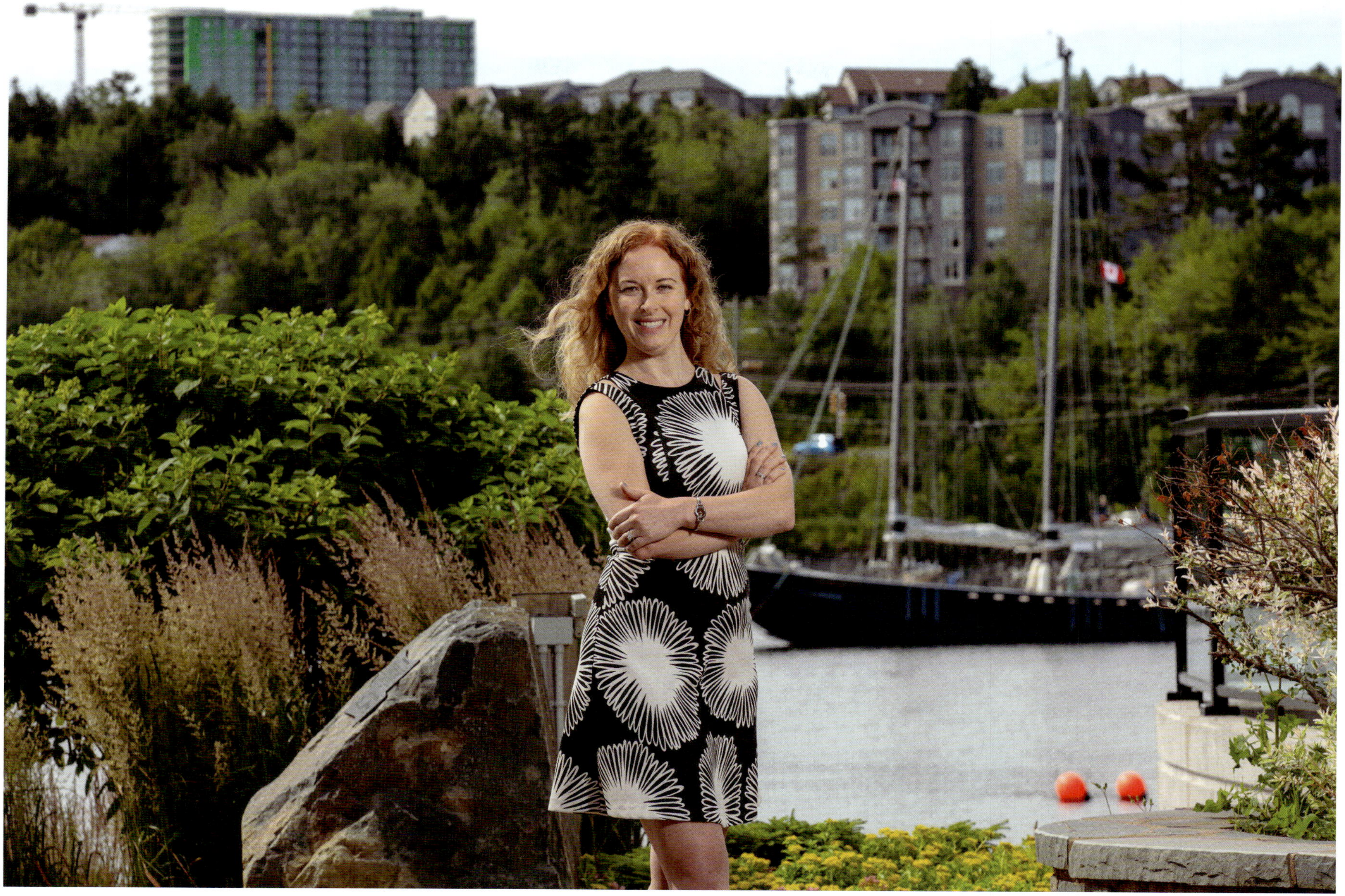

ALWAYS HAVE A PLAN C:
Davison's Pancake House

It's spring 2021, and Christine Davison sits down at an empty table at Davison's Pancake House, part of Newville Lakeview Farm in Parrsboro, with two steaming cups of coffee. Her husband, Bill, takes a seat next to her and checks his watch. A few hours earlier, the room had been bustling with families enjoying pancakes and maple syrup from a menu that features specials like the Lumberjack: pancakes (with our without blueberries), bacon, sausage, ham, beans, and homemade brown bread—all made with ingredients sourced either directly from the farm or from nearby businesses.

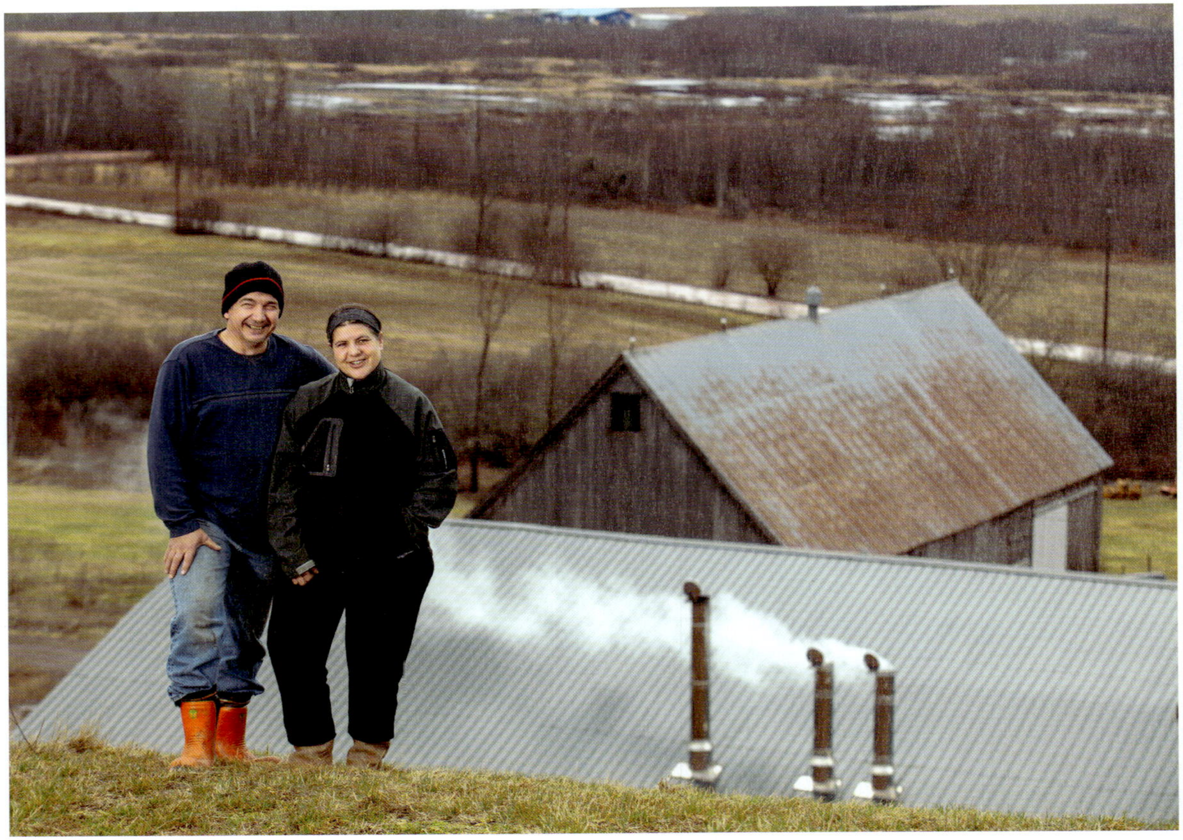

Christine and Bill Davison run Davison's Pancake House, part of Newville Lakeview Farm in Parrsboro. They've had to adapt and pivot as the provincial guidance on gathering limits has changed.

The farm has been in Bill's family for over a hundred years, but he and his family moved back and took over the operation just ten years ago. It produces wild blueberries, pumpkins, and squash in the summer, and maple syrup and maple products in the winter.

"Maple producing, years ago, used to be in the woods, and they used to do it with a horse and wooden buckets," says Bill. "There would be a shelter in the woods with a wooden floor over the evaporator." Now, thanks to Bill's engineering background, the farm has a gravity-fed system in which the sap runs downhill through tubes fed by their nearly ten thousand trees in the Cobequid Mountains. In February, when the days turn sunny and the nights are cold, the sap starts to run.

For the Newville Lakeview Farm, 2020 had started out to be a banner year.

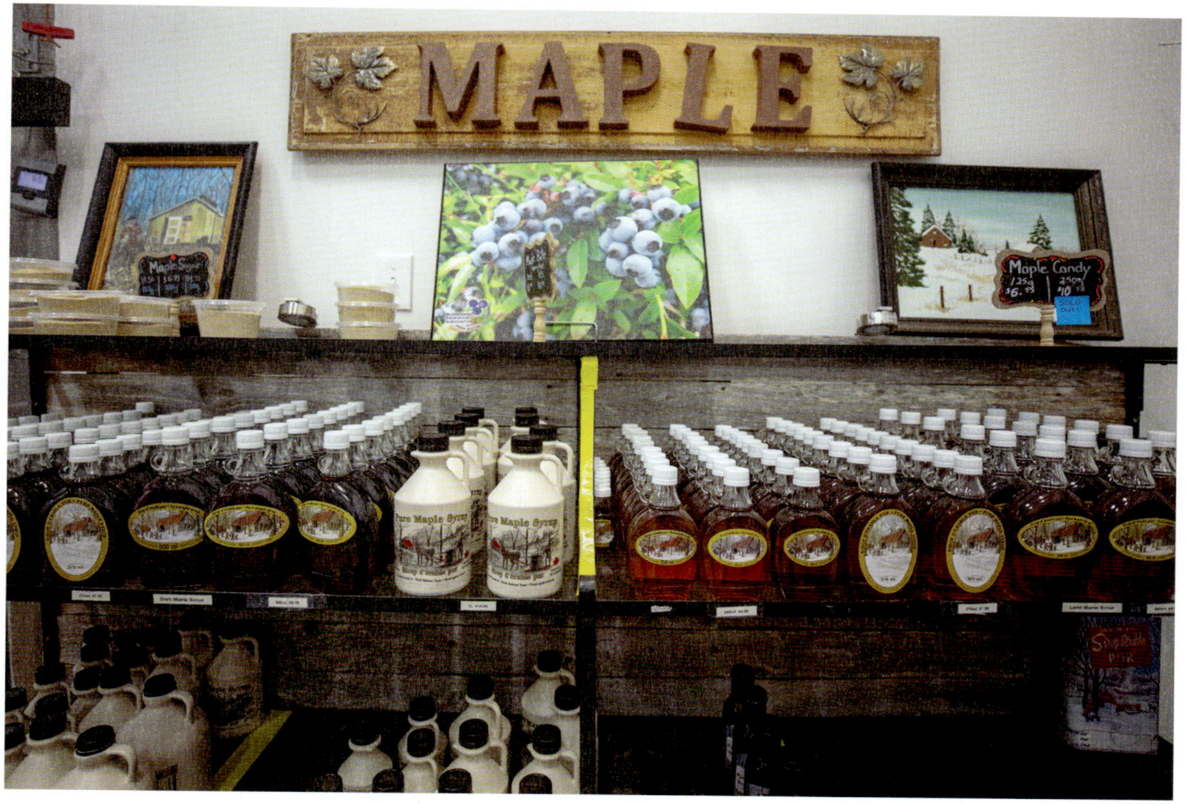

The family farm now operated by Christine and Bill Davison has been producing maple syrup for more than a hundred years.

"We opened on the fifteenth of February—the earliest we've ever opened," says Christine. "Maple syrup is affiliated with [the idea that] the winter is over. The excitement, the smell of the harvest was in everybody's heart. They were coming in with grandma, grandpa—the family unit, you know—and it was beautiful."

Families coming in for lunch also meant revenue coming through the door. Ten years ago blueberries had generated 90 percent of the farm's revenue; more recently, maple syrup and maple products and the pancake house have become the main income generators.

But after being open for only five weekends in 2020, the Davisons were forced to close when the pandemic came to the forests of Cumberland County. The farm's bulk sales to Quebec distributors also came to a halt as the first-wave lockdown took hold.

"I wasn't disappointed. We had to close," says Bill. "We have a lot of elderly people that come here, a lot of loyal customers from the community... and I don't think they should be in crowded areas."

Christine agrees. "I'm quite proud of what we did in Nova Scotia, and even though it was a big hit for us it was more important to keep our clients really safe at the time."

By February 2021, the second wave of the pandemic in Nova Scotia was behind them and restrictions were easing up. The sap started to run once again and the team went to work harvesting. Christine started to consider what the pancake house would have to look like to comply with the requirement that restaurants operate at 50 percent capacity and with social distancing.

"We contemplated this year—how much work will it be to open? Will it be worth it? But fortunately, it turned out not too bad. We did reservations and spaced people out," says Christine, adding that it was a big change from the days of bumper-to-bumper traffic on the road leading to the farm. They hired extra staff to ensure that all the regulations were followed and that their customers would be safe.

But cross-border travel restrictions had meant the loss of their New Brunswick customers, so the couple had sought out new markets around the province—and they were soon surprised to see that they were selling 30 percent more blueberries than usual. Suddenly it hit them: people were baking more. They realized their customers were becoming more aware that the food supply chain

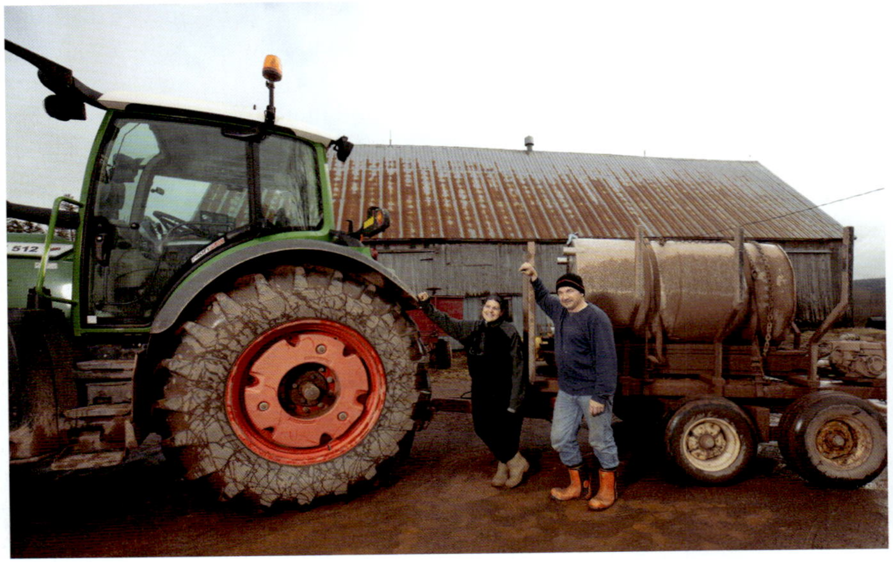

Christine and Bill Davison prepare to fire up the tractor to collect maple syrup at Newville Lakeview Farm.

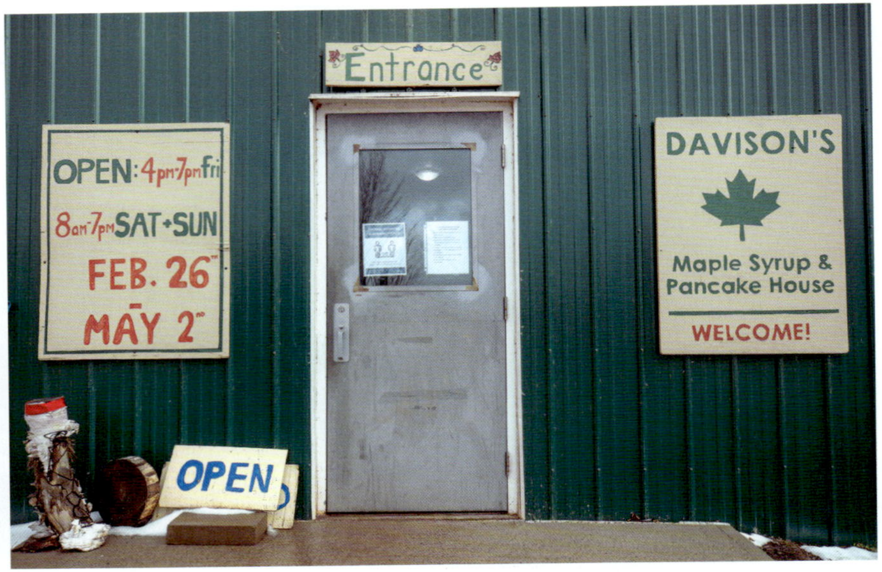

Davison's Pancake House.

begins at home and that buying local was now more important than ever. They sold their entire crop of blueberries.

They had also learned to sell themselves—to sell the farm as an experience. Christine says she loves the social aspect of watching families run around the pumpkin patch picking out the best one. But more than anything else, the pandemic has taught the Davisons the value of flexibility. "When you're in farming, you always need to have Plan A, B, and C," says Bill. "Things are not going to go with the way you think they're going to go, so you've gotta be ready."

And with that, Bill looks at his watch again and gets up from the table. "The sap is going to start overflowing," he says with a grin.

In other words, he's ready. Life goes on. It's time to get busy with Plan C.

And as Bill drives off, Christine disappears back into the barn to finish cleaning and to prepare for tomorrow—hopefully another big day.

APPROACHING NORMAL

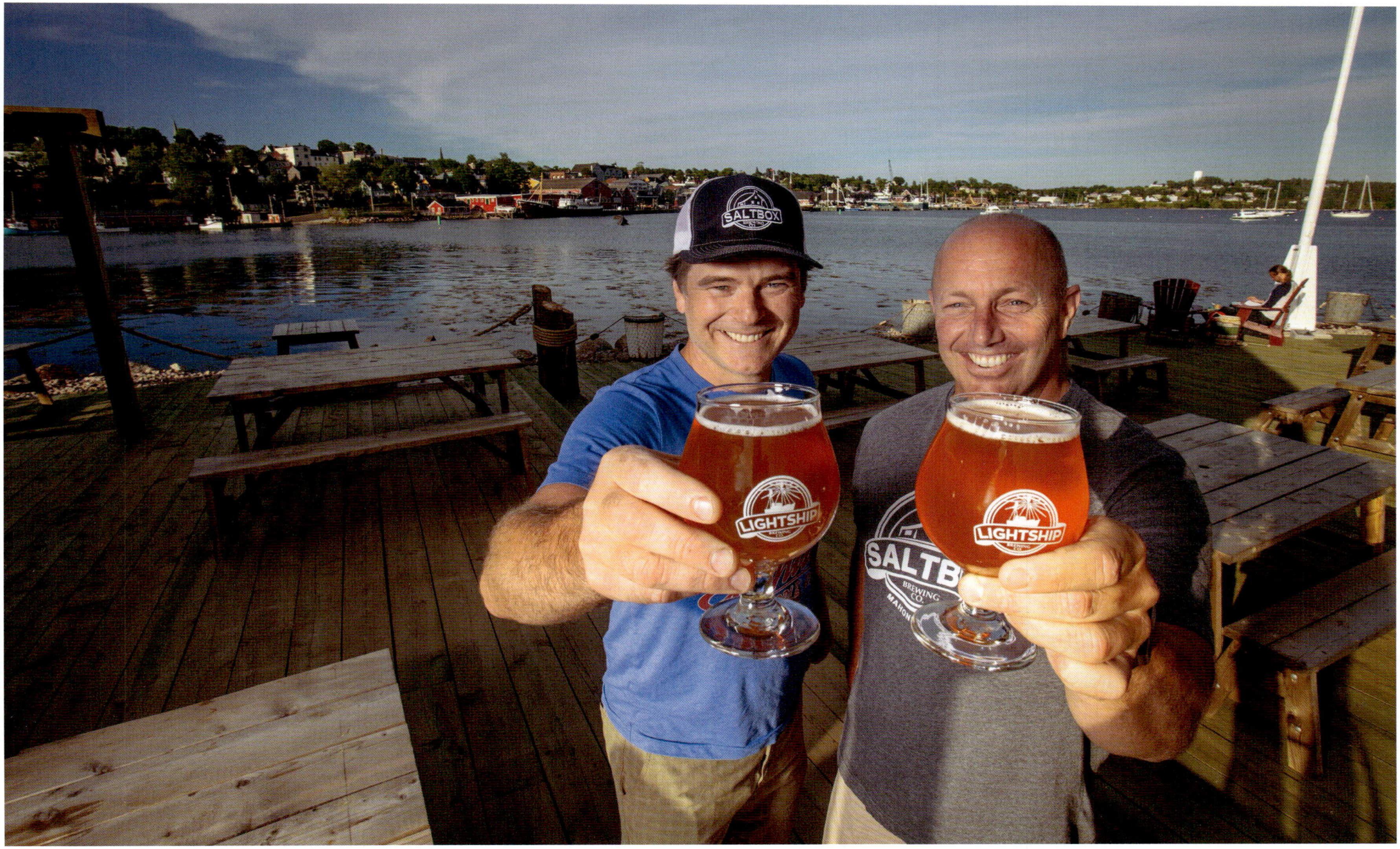

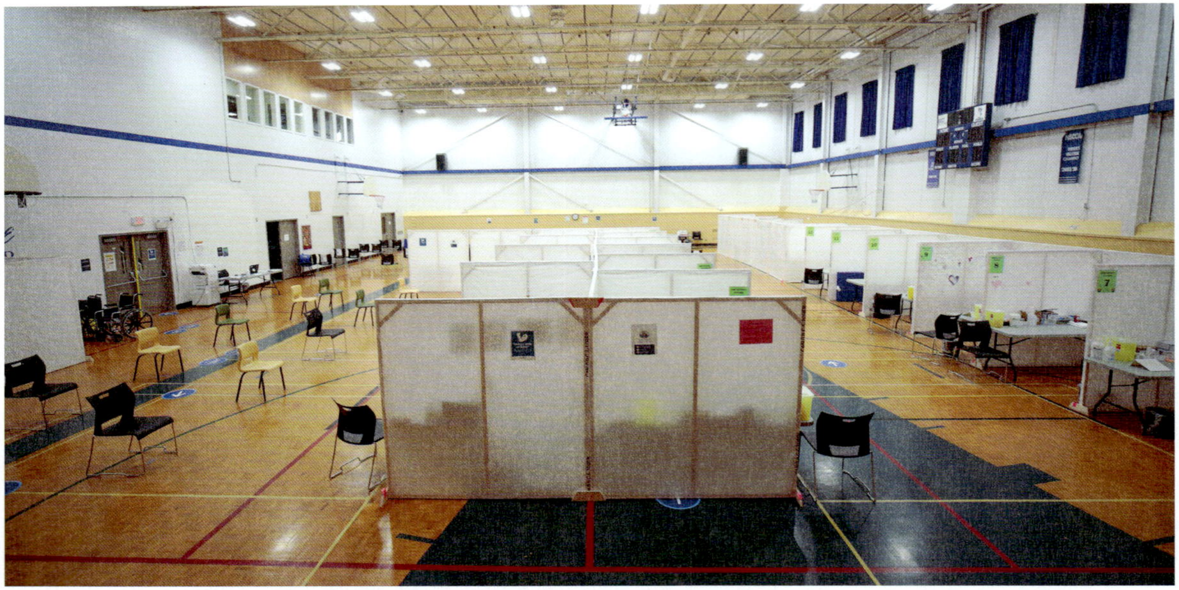

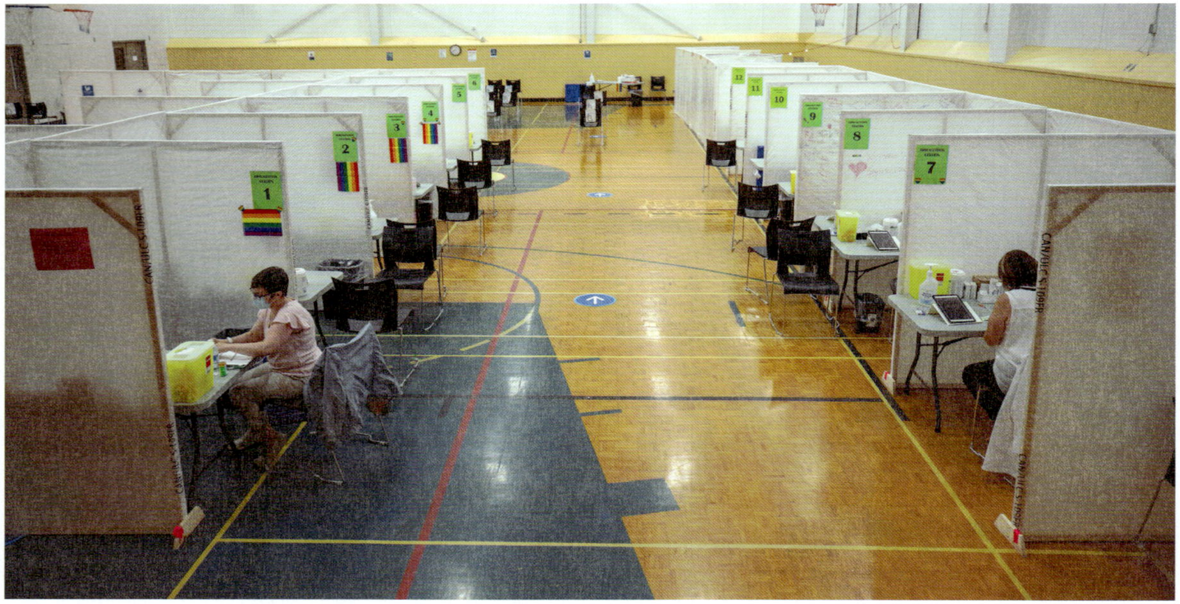

PREVIOUS PAGE: *Patrick Jardine (left) and Andrew Tanner (right), the owner/operators of Saltbox Brewing in Mahone Bay and Lightship Brewing Company in Lunenburg, raise a glass to celebrate the re-opening of their Lunenburg patio. The pair made the risky move of opening the new location in May, but their optimism proved founded by late June, as the province moved into phase two of the re-opening. "We're certainly happy we did it—and it's extremely busy now," Tanner says. "By phase three, we should be almost back to normal."*

THIS PAGE TOP AND BOTTOM: *The community vaccination clinic in Yarmouth is nearly empty as workers arrive early to prepare vaccines and get ready for their day. In mid-August 2021 many community vaccination clinics like this one were closed because a large proportion of the population had received both of their vaccines.*

NOVA SCOTIA KITCHEN PARTY

THIS AND NEXT PAGE: *Heather Cameron Thomson* hosts a live online concert in March 2021 at the deCoste Performing Arts Centre in Pictou. Thomson started the Facebook group "Ultimate Online Nova Scotia Kitchen Party (COVID-19 Edition)," in March 2020; the group has since gained more than a quarter of a million followers. Many of the performers from that group travelled to Pictou to perform at an anniversary concert in support of the Mental Health Foundation of Nova Scotia.

"We're celebrating everything that we have seen come through the Kitchen Party," says Thomson. "The copious amount of support and love that people have poured into the Kitchen Party… is absolutely incredible. So we're going to celebrate that here tonight, and we're also going to make the connection between music and mental health maybe a little bit more visible for people."

LEFT: *Katey and Pierre Aucoin of New Glasgow perform during the live show celebrating the anniversary of the Ultimate Online Nova Scotia Kitchen Party in March at the deCoste Performing Arts Centre in Pictou.* **RIGHT:** *Liam and Jack Thomson from Rocklin took part in the benefit performance.*

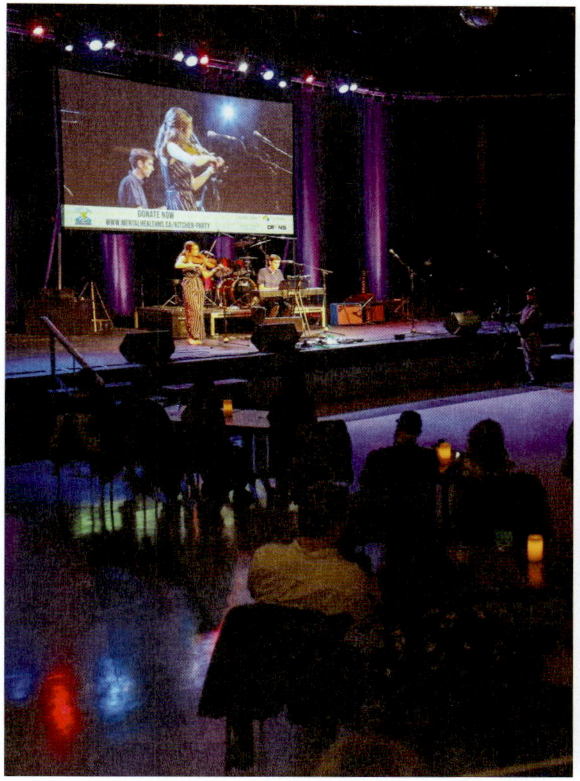

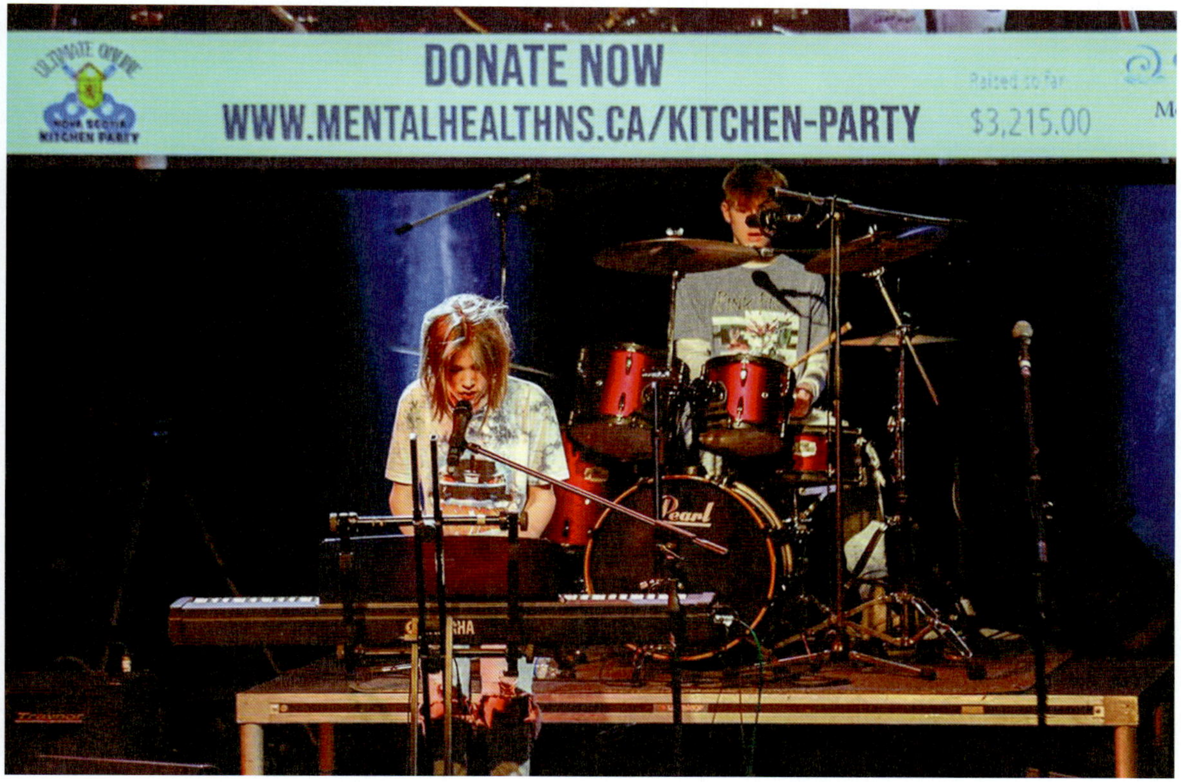

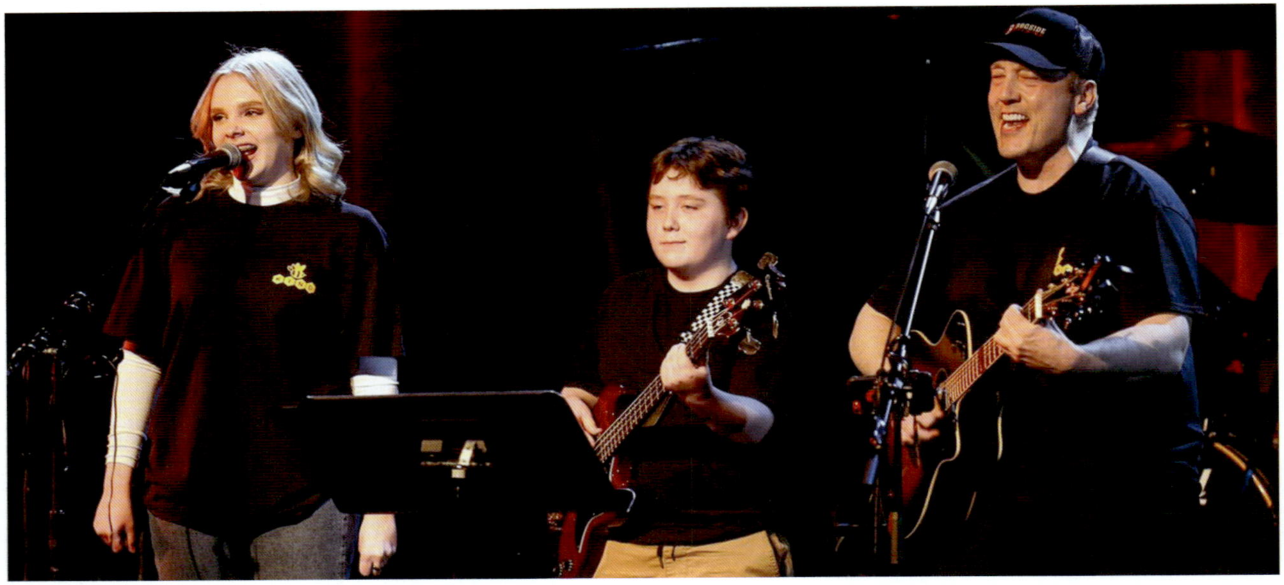

TOP: *From left, Glace Bay residents Breagh and Bryden Kelly perform alongside their dad, Jerome Kelly.*

BOTTOM: *The Dad Bod Divas from Trenton perform at the socially distanced concert at the deCoste Performing Arts Centre in Pictou.*

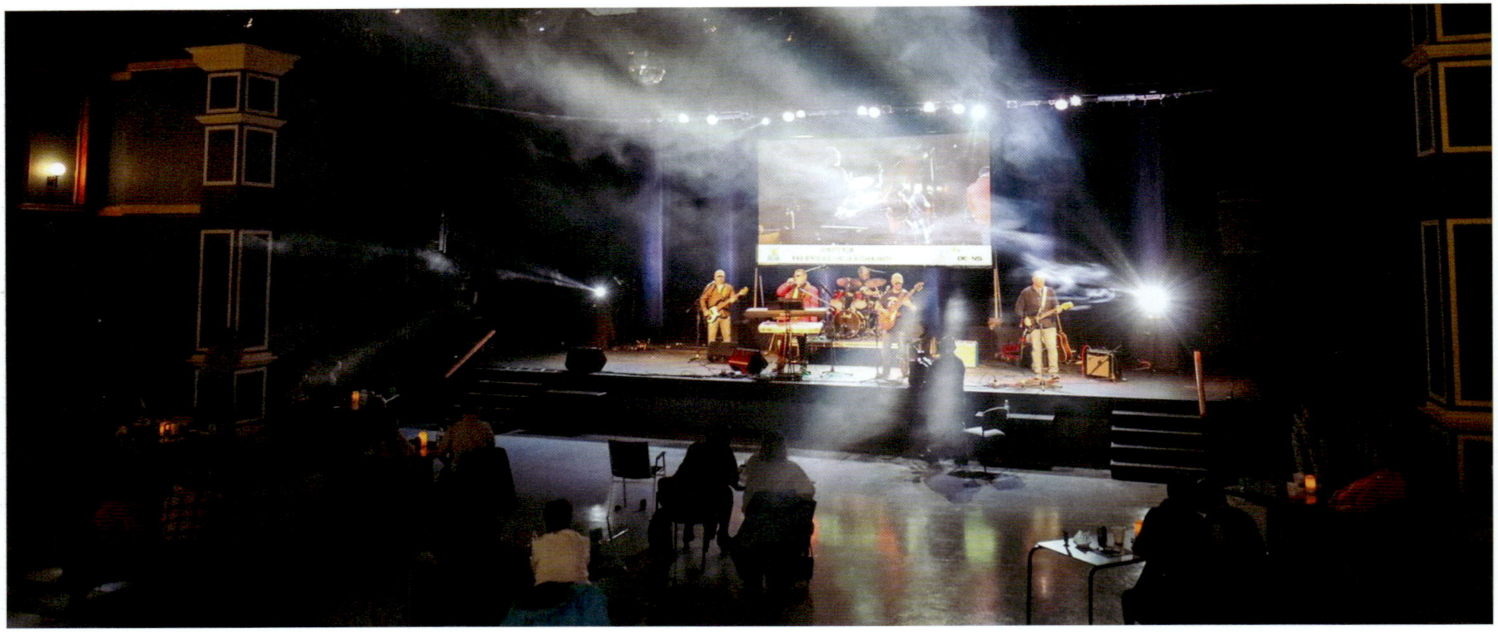

BORDER CROSSINGS

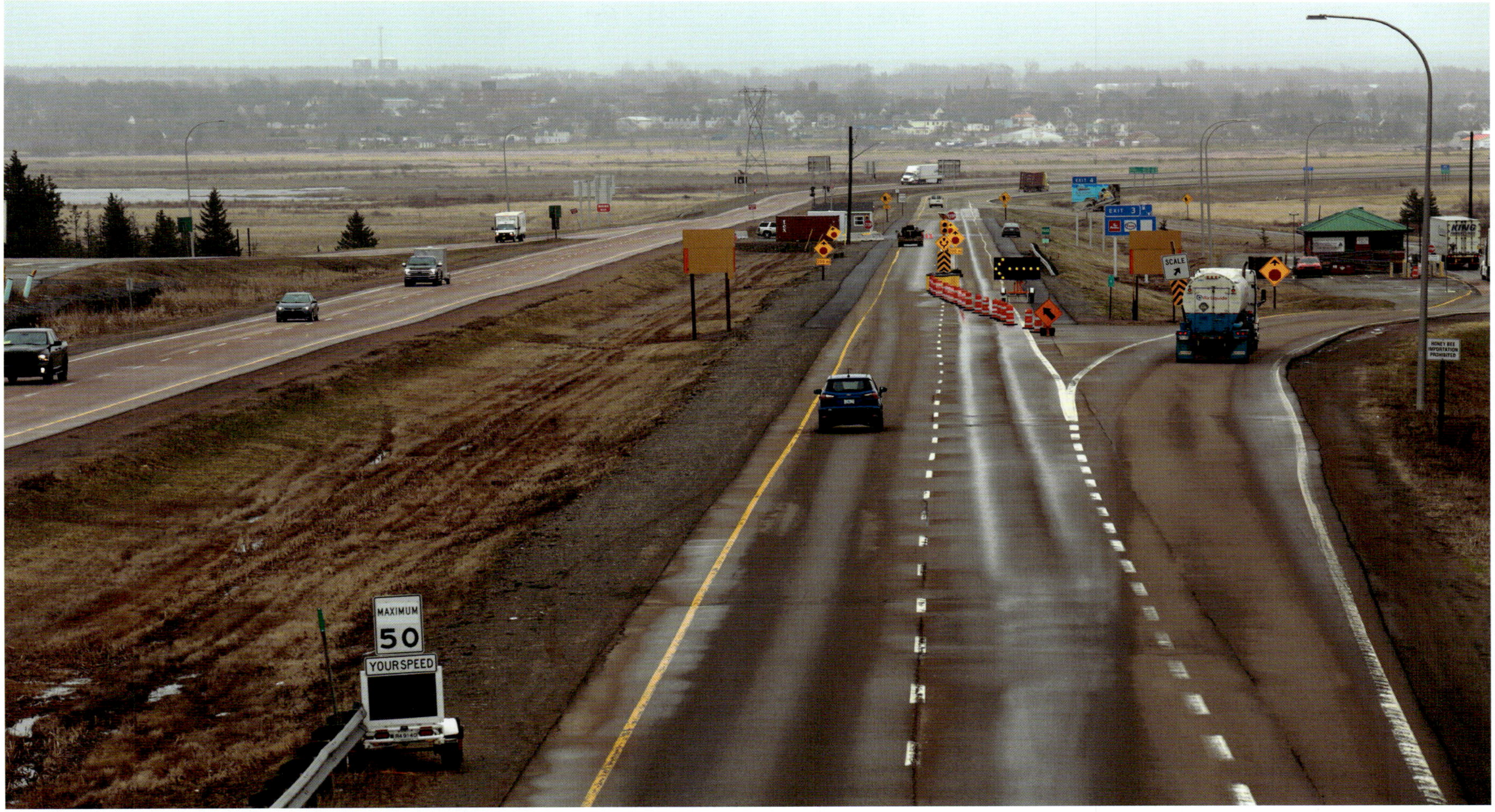

In April 2021, and again in August 2021, restrictions on the New Brunswick border were imposed due to increasing concerns about rising numbers of COVID infections in that province.

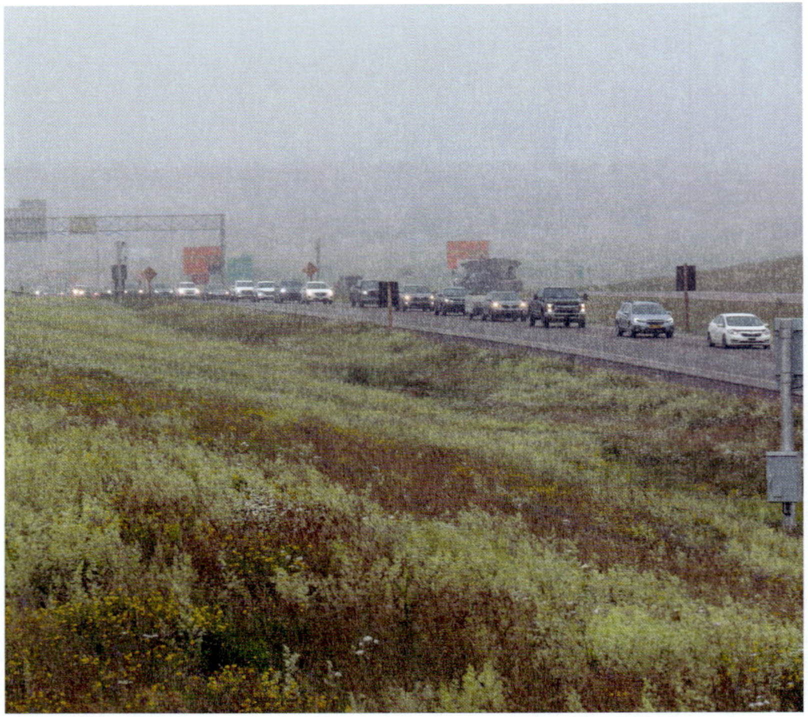

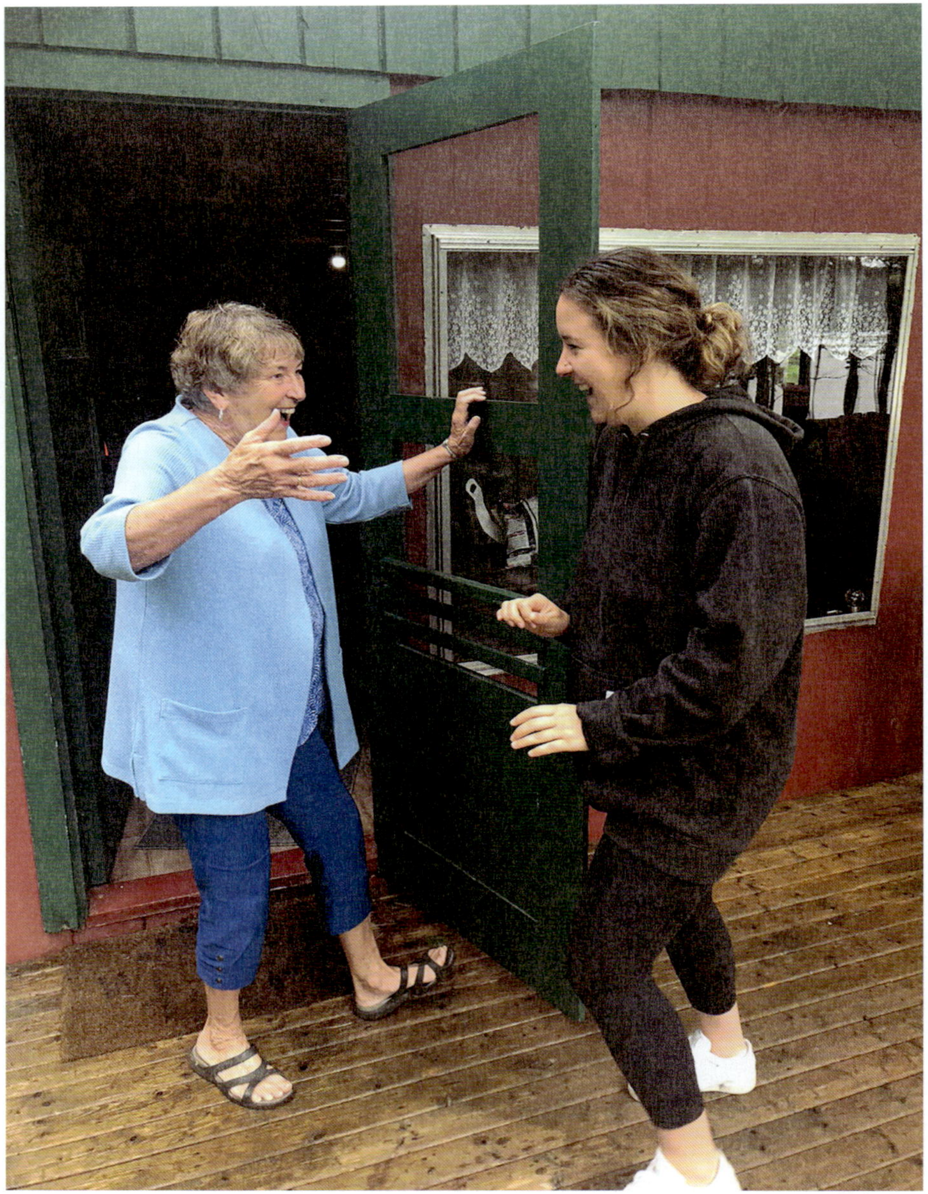

ABOVE: *In June 2021, people travelling from New Brunswick, Prince Edward Island, or Newfoundland and Labrador were allowed to enter Nova Scotia without having to self-isolate. In August 2021, fully vaccinated citizens and permanent residents of the United States (US) were permitted to enter Canada for non-essential travel.*

RIGHT: *Patricia Bill is a grandmother from Kentville. "I have nine wonderful grandchildren who are scattered from sea to sea to sea and in the US," she says, "and, of course, the pandemic made it impossible for us to visit. The closest was my granddaughter [Rachael Burton] in [Fredericton,] New Brunswick. Just a tiny border separated us—so near, and yet so far. Just imagine the sheer joy for both of us when I opened the door at my cottage to see her standing there. It was the first of many joyful reunions for us all."*

ACKNOWLEDGEMENTS

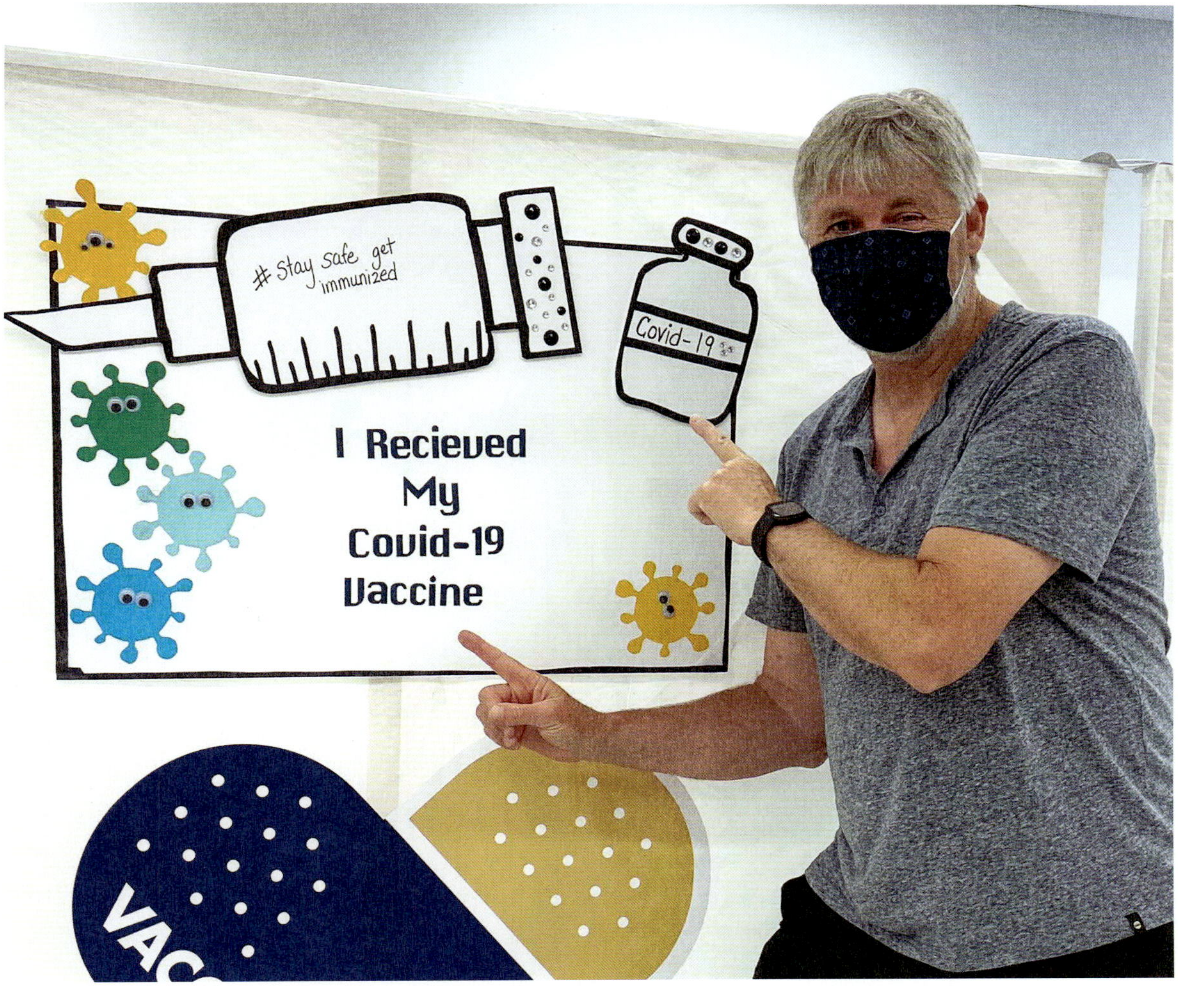

Thumbs (well, index fingers) up at the community clinic in Amherst where Len Wagg received his second vaccination dose on July 2, 2021.

Even after Stay the Blazes Home: Dispatches from Nova Scotia During the COVID-19 Pandemic was published in November 2020, dozens of stories of dedicated Nova Scotians doing incredible pandemic-related things remained untold. It was at the launch of that first book that Dr. Strang asked, "What's next?" Little did we know back then that we would still be in the grips of the pandemic a year later.

Dr. Strang's question planted the seed for a follow-up. To Nimbus general manager Terrilee Bulger and managing editor Whitney Moran—thanks for listening to the idea and finding a way to fit this book into an already-full roster for Fall 2021.

This book could not have been done without the assistance of the folks at the Nova Scotia Health Authority (NSHA). To all of those who agreed to be interviewed and photographed, and who took time out of their busy schedules—thank you. To John Gillis, director of online engagement and media relations at NSHA, and to NSHA team members from one end of the province to the other, including Megan Tonet,

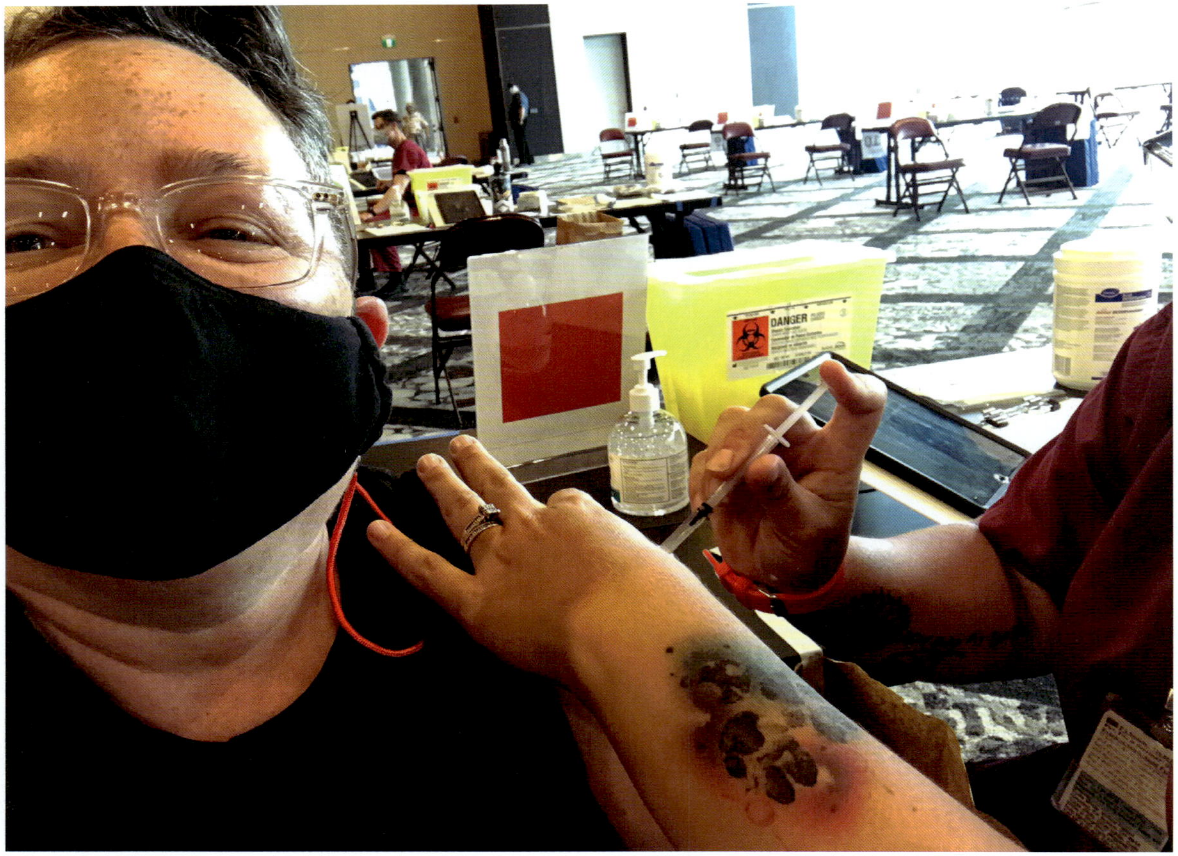

Angela Mombourquette was relieved to receive her second jab at the Halifax Convention Centre in July 2021.

Brendan Elliott, Jaimee Dobson, Margaret Angus, and Kristen Rector—thank you. This book could not have been done without your assistance. And thank you for helping Nova Scotians through the pandemic over the last two years.

Thanks to all the Nova Scotians who so generously shared their vaccination selfies and their staycation photos. Thanks to every Nova Scotian who wore their mask, kept their distance, endured many uncomfortable nose-swabs, and got double-vaxxed. You've made the world a safer place.

Finally, thanks to our families. From Len: to Sandy, Brett, Kiya, and Jodi—thanks for all the help and encouragement on this project as well as many others. From Angela: Wendy, Joc, and Uncle Jack—thanks for always being proud of what I do.